Contents

Section Four

Statements of Standard Accounting Practice

Accounting Standards 1980

Prepared by members of the staff
of the Technical Directorate

The Institute of Chartered Accountants
in England and Wales
P.O. Box 433
Chartered Accountants' Hall
Moorgate Place
London EC2P 2BJ.

No responsibility for loss occasioned to any person acting or refraining from action as a result of any material in this publication can be accepted by the authors or publisher.

ISBN 0 85291 2714

Preface

This book presents in one convenient volume all UK Exposure Drafts and Statements of Standard Accounting Practice extant at 1st June 1980, together with an index to SSAPs for ease of reference.

The Accounting Standards Committee is now in its eleventh year and significant progress has been made in the development of standards of financial reporting in the UK. Statements of Standard Accounting Practice and Exposure Drafts are frequently referred to by producers and users of financial statements in the course of their work. It is hoped that this book will prove a useful reference work.

The opportunity has been taken to include a summary of the history, constitution and operation of the Accounting Standards Committee.

Section One

History of the Accounting Standards Committee

Accounting standards in the United Kingdom and Ireland are established by the Councils of the six major accountancy bodies acting on the proposals of the Accounting Standards Committee ('ASC').

ASC (originally known as the Accounting Standards Steering Committee) was set up in January 1970 by the Council of the Institute of Chartered Accountants in England and Wales with the object of developing definitive standards for financial reporting. *The Statement of Intent on Accounting Standards in |the |1970's* is reproduced as Appendix One to this section.

The Institute of Chartered Accountants of Scotland and the Institute of Chartered Accountants in Ireland became members of the Committee in 1970, the Association of Certified Accountants and the Institute of Cost and Management Accountants joined in 1971 and the Chartered Institute of Public Finance and Accountancy in 1976.

From 1st February 1976 ASC was reconstituted as a joint committee of the six member bodies who act collectively through the Consultative Committeee of Accountancy Bodies ('CCAB').

Objects and Constitution of ASC

The Committee's objects are to propose for the approval of the Councils of the governing bodies definitive standards of financial accounting and reporting. Its objects encompass (a) fundamentals of financial accounting, (b) definition of terms used, (c) application of fundamentals to specific classes of business and (d) the form and content of financial statements, including presentation and disclosure.

The Committee's constitution including the terms of reference is given in Appendix Two to this section.

Membership of ASC

ASC has twenty-three members who are appointed as nominees of the six member bodies as follows:

Institute of Chartered Accountants in England and Wales	12
Institute of Chartered Accountants of Scotland	3
Institute of Chartered Accountants in Ireland	2
Association of Certified Accountants	2
Institute of Cost and Management Accountants	2
Chartered Institute of Public Finance and Accountancy	2
	23

The chairman and vice-chairman of ASC are appointed by the chairman of the Consultative Committee of Accountancy Bodies on the recommendation of ASC and subject to the approval of CCAB. Sir Ronald Leach was the chairman of the committee from its formation in 1970 until 30th June 1976. Sir William Slimmings, who became chairman of the committee on 1st July 1976, was succeeded by Mr. T. R. Watts on 1st June 1978.

Members of the ASC as at 1st June 1980

T. R. Watts C.B.E. (Chairman)	Price Waterhouse & Co.
D. S. Morpeth (Vice-Chairman)	Touche Ross & Co.
N. Berman	National Westminster Bank Ltd.
K. G. Bishop	Debenhams Ltd.
D. A. Boothman	Binder Hamlyn
A. K. Burns	Stokes Kennedy Crowley & Co.
Professor H. C. Edey	London School of Economics and Political Science
H. J. Gardner	Reckitt and Coleman Ltd.
P. M. D. Gibbs	Phillips & Drew
J. P. Grenside	Peat, Marwick, Mitchell & Co.
D. C. Hobson	Coopers & Lybrand
B. H. F. Johnson	The Electricity Council
J. McKinnon	Imperial Group Ltd.
L. T. Miller	Ernst & Whinney
A. Morrison C.B.E.	Anglian Water Board
A. W. Nelson	Opass Billings Wilson & Honey
B. D. G. Ogle	Formerly ICI Ltd.
E. J. Patrick	Oxford City Council

J. Pearcy	ICI Ltd.
K. J. Sharp	Head of the Government
	Accountancy Service
D. G. Sherriff	Ernst & Whinney
S. P. Wilkins	Deloitte Haskins & Sells
1 vacancy	

The Consultative Group of ASC

ASC's terms of reference require it to 'consult as appropriate with representatives of finance, commerce, industry and government and other persons concerned with financial reporting'.

To this end, ASC has formed a Consultative Group, with the following constitution and terms of reference:

1. The Accounting Standards Committee will establish a Consultative Group composed of nominees of organisations representative of those concerned with financial reporting as producers or users of financial statements.
2. The number of members of the Consultative group and the organisations invited to nominate representatives to it shall be determined from time to time at the sole discretion of the Accounting Standards Committee.
3. The Consultative Group will be convened by the Chairman of the Accounting Standards Committee at least three times each year.
4. The Consultative Group will be consulted by the Accounting Standards Committee on matters relating to the programme, proposals and work of the Accounting Standards Committee.
5. The views of the Consultative Group will be reported to the Accounting Standards Committee.

Bodies represented on the Consultative Group are as follows:
Association of Investment Trust Companies
Association of Unit Trust Managers
Bank of England
British Bankers Association
British Insurance Association
British Institute of Management
Building Societies Association
Confederation of British Industry
Confederation of Irish Industry
Department of Trade

Government Statistical Service
Inland Revenue
Institute of Chartered Secretaries and Administrators
Institute of Directors
International Accounting Standards Committee
Issuing Houses Association
National Association of Pension Funds
National Economic Development Council
Panel on Takeovers and Mergers
Royal Institution of Chartered Surveyors
Smaller Firms Council of the Confederation of British Industry
Society of Investment Analysts
The Law Society
The Stock Exchange
Trades Union Congress.

The procedure by which accounting standards are developed

Accounting standards

Statements of Standard Accounting Practice ('accounting standards') describe methods of accounting approved by the Councils of the governing bodies for application to all financial accounts intended to give a true and fair view of financial position and profit or loss.

The accountancy bodies expect their members who assume responsibilities in the respect of financial statements to observe accounting standards. Where this responsibility is evidenced by the association of members' names with such financial statements in the capacity of directors or other officers the onus is on them to ensure that the existence and purpose of standards are fully understood by non-member directors and other officers, and to use their best endeavours to ensure that standards are observed or, if they are not observed, that significant departures from them are disclosed and explained in the financial statements and their effect, if material, disclosed.

Where members act as auditors or reporting accountants the onus is on them not only to ensure disclosure of significant departures but also, to the extent that their concurrence is stated or implied, to justify them.

The accountancy bodies have power to inquire into apparent failure by their members to observe accounting standards or to disclose departures therefrom.

Accounting standards are formally supported by The Stock Exchange. As a condition of quotation, companies must undertake to circulate with the annual report of the directors a statement by the directors as to the reasons for adopting an alternative basis of accounting in any case where the auditors have stated that the financial statements are not drawn up in accordance with the standard accounting practices approved by the accountancy bodies.

Working arrangements
ASC approves in advance a long range programme of work and indicates the priority which should be given to subjects in the programme. The stages in the development of an accounting standard may be summarised under the following headings:
(a) research;
(b) drafting sub-committee;
(c) internal exposure;
(d) meetings with interested parties;
(e) publication of Exposure Draft for general comment;
(f) evaluation of comments;
(g) publication of Statement of Standard Accounting Practice
Each of these stages is outlined in the following paragraphs.

(a) Research
Before any work is undertaken on a proposed accounting standard it is usual for one or more research studies to be commissioned. The researchers may be professional firms of accountants, industrial and commercial firms or academics. The aim of a research study, which may take several months to prepare, is to review theory and current practice, examine authoritative pronouncements in the UK and overseas, summarise bibliography and suggest possible lines for development.

Copies of the research studies are placed in the libraries of the governing bodies of ASC and are available for loan to members. The research studies which have been published in book form are listed in Appendix Four to this section.

(b) Drafting sub-committee
When the research studies are completed, a sub-committee is formed to prepare a draft accounting standard. The sub-committee consists of about six to nine members nominated by ASC. Every effort is made to ensure that the sub-committee is representative of practice, industry, commerce and the academic world and is fairly balanced between specialist and non-specialist interests. The time taken for a sub-

committee to complete its work depends on many factors including the complexity of the subject and liaison with similar bodies outside the UK and Ireland.

(c) Internal exposure
The draft accounting standard is subjected to detailed scrutiny within the governing bodies to remove, as far as possible, any inconsistencies before it is considered by ASC. The draft is sent to the Technical Committees (or equivalent) of the governing bodies and to regional groups. In total about 1,000 copies of a document are printed at this stage and are scrutinised in detail by committees whose membership is widely representative both geographically and in employment terms. The committees prepare written comments on the draft accounting standard which are submitted to the drafting sub-committee which revises the paper in the light of comments received. The revised draft, together with the comments from the Technical Committees, is then forwarded to ASC.

(d) Meetings with interested parties
As well as consulting the Technical Committees of the governing bodies, the members of ASC normally discuss the contents of a draft accounting standard at a series of meetings with financial directors and senior officials of companies whose financial statements will be affected in a significant way by the proposals under review.

(e) Publication of Exposure Draft for general comment
ASC considers the draft accounting standard, which has gone through a lengthy process of internal consultation before coming to the committee, and may amend it as appropriate before authorising its publication as an exposure draft. Exposure drafts are distributed in booklet form by the governing bodies of ASC and are re-printed in the leading accounting journals. In total more than 100,000 copies of exposure drafts are published for comment in the UK, Ireland and overseas.

(f) Evaluation of comments
The comments received on exposure drafts are collated by the ASC secretariat and copies are sent to each member of ASC. ASC sets up a panel to reconsider the exposure draft in the light of the comments received from the public and from regional Committees of the governing bodies.

Copies of all comments made on exposure drafts, unless the writer has asked for them to be regarded as confidential, are available for inspection by interested parties in the libraries of the CCAB bodies, and are sent to all commentators where practicable.

(g)   Publication of Statement of Standard Accounting Practice (SSAP)
The time lag between the publication of an exposure draft and the publication of an accounting standard allows adequate time to be given to assess all views which are expressed on an exposure draft. In addition, where there are major legal or taxation implications in an exposure draft, legal and other consultations may be held as necessary.

ASC prepares the SSAPs and recommends them to the Councils of the six governing bodies. Each Council discusses the proposed standard and if thought fit approves it for issue to its own members. It is usual for each Council to approve a standard subject to it being approved by the other five Councils.

Other consultative processes
All representations on the problems of implementing accounting standards which are made to ASC are examined in detail. When necessary a panel of ASC members is set up to review points of difficulty and revisions to SSAPs are made as the occasion demands.

The programme of ASC

Accounting Standards published to date
Sixteen Statements of Standard Accounting Practice have been published up to 1st June 1980. SSAP7 (Provisional) *'Accounting for changes in the purchasing power of money'* was withdrawn in January 1978 and SSAP11 *'Accounting for deferred taxation'* in October 1978. The other statements are reproduced in full in Section Four.

Exposure drafts which have been issued but have not yet been converted to SSAPs are also reproduced in full in Section Two.

Review of the year 1979/80

MATERIAL PUBLISHED:
Accounting Standards published
One Statement of Standard Accounting Practice was published during the year:

		Issued
SSAP16	*Current cost accounting*	March 1980

Exposure drafts published
One exposure draft was published during the year: *Issued*
ED25   *Accounting for the results of associated*
                companies   October 1979

Research studies published
Three research studies prepared for the committee were
published during the year:
The employment statement in company reports by
E R Thompson and Anne Knell
Simplified financial statements by A E Hammill
Added value in external financial reporting by
M Renshall, R Allan and K Nicholson

Submissions published
Two collections of submissions received were themselves
considered to be of sufficient general interest to justify
separate publication during the year: *Issued*
Submissions on the Accounting Standards Committee's
consultative document *Setting accounting standards*   May 1979
Submissions on the Accounting Standards Committee's
exposure draft 24 *Current cost accounting*   January 1980

WORK IN HAND
ED25 *Accounting for the results of associated companies*
The requirements of SSAP1 *Accounting for the results of associated
companies,* originally published in 1971, were reviewed by ASC during the
year. 72 letters of comment were received in response to the committee's
request for views on the operation in practice of the standard and 172
companies co-operated by providing information on the manner in which
they had accounted for 650 companies in which they held more than 20%
of the share capital. From the comments received, it is evident that SSAP1
Accounting for the results of associated companies has stood the test of
time well. The results of the review were published as ED25 *Accounting
for the results of associated companies* in October 1979. The proposed
amendments seek to clarify the issues in the original standard rather than
to alter the main principles.

SSAP16 *Current cost accounting*
At the same time that SSAP16 *Current cost accounting* was published,
ASC announced that a sub-committee was being established to monitor
the effectiveness of the standard and to continue the development of the
subject as necessary. This will form a permanent feature of ASC's work
for the foreseeable future.

Public hearings

ASC extended its consultative procedures in 1979/89 by holding public hearings to enable interested persons to present a case in open session, and to be questioned on their views by members of the committee. Three series of public hearings were held in Dublin, Glasgow and London. In July 1979, responses to the consultative document *Setting accounting standards* were heard; in October/November 1979 submissions on ED24 *Current cost accounting* were heard and in April 1980 submissions on ED25 *Accounting for the results of associated companies* were heard. In total more than 80 people appeared at the hearings.

Consultative Group

Two meetings of the Consultative Group of ASC were held during the year. At the first meeting, members of the Group debated the proposals in *Setting accounting standards*. The second meeting was taken up with a discussion on the proposals in ED24 *Current cost accounting* and the proposals in a preliminary paper on *Simplified financial reports*.

Other consultative procedures

The Committee continued its practice of holding meetings with financial directors and senior officials of companies which may be affected in a significant way by proposed exposure drafts. In November 1979, members of the Committee met with finance directors of 40 companies with major overseas interests to discuss the latest developments in the area of accounting for foreign operations, and to seek their views on possible lines of development on this subject.

Meetings with representative bodies

Members of the Committee are always willing to meet delegations from representative bodies to discuss matters which have arisen in the implementation of accounting standards. Meetings were held during the year with The Association of Investment Trust Companies, the Brewers' Society, the Building Societies Association, The Royal Institution of Chartered Surveyors, The Accepting Houses Committee and the Equipment Leasing Association.

Industry sector committees

To enable the views of specialised sectors of industry and commerce to be more fully understood by ASC, sub-committees exist to consider the impact on these industry sectors of proposed and existing accounting standards. An oil and gas sub-committee was formed during the year to join the existing sub-committees on banking and insurance.

Liaison with other standard setting bodies
During the year the Committee expanded its policy of establishing closer links with other major standard setting bodies. Several visits were paid to the US Financial Accounting Standards Board by members of the Committee. Subjects discussed during the visits were inflation accounting , foreign currency transactions and the conceptual framework project. Visits were received from members of the Australian Accounting Research Foundation, the Canadian Institute of Chartered Accountants, the Belgian Commission Bancaire, the FASB, the South African Accounting Practices Board and the Counseil National de la Comptabilite (Paris).

REVIEW OF FUTURE WORK
Investment properties
The Committee has studied the problems of accounting for investment properties and will make recommendations to the CCAB Councils on appropriate action to be taken on SSAP12 *Accounting for depreciation.* This contains an exemption for investment properties in respect of accounting periods starting before 1 January 1980. The study of the accounting practices adopted by property investment companies will continue in 1980.

Setting accounting standards
The Committee will complete in 1980 a report on the changes which it considers should be made to its constitution, composition, consultative processes and working procedures in the light of the submissions it has received on its consultative document. The implications of the conclusions will be discussed with its parent bodies.

Exposure Drafts in issue
Six exposure drafts have been issued which have not yet been converted to accounting standards. Work is in progress on these exposure drafts as follows:

(a) ED25 *Accounting for the results of associated companies*—the period for comment on this exposure draft remained open until 31 March 1980.

(b) ED23 *Accounting for contingencies*—a proposed accounting standard together with a technical release explaining the changes which have been made to the proposals in the exposure draft have been agreed by the Committee and final approval of the Standard by the Councils of the governing bodies is expected during 1980.

(c) ED22 *Post balance sheet events* — a proposed accounting standard together with a technical release explaining the changes which have been made to the proposals in the exposure draft have been agreed by the Committee and final approval of the standard by the Councils of the governing bodies is expected during 1980.

(d) ED21 *Accounting for foreign currency transactions* — 116 commentators submitted 354 pages of comment on this exposure draft. A revised text has been prepared by a sub-committee and discussed in outline at a meeting with finance directors of companies with major interests overseas. The Committee is participating in the review of the standards which have been issued by the FASB and the CICA in an endeavour to achieve as far as possible a degree of international harmonisation in this area. A further exposure draft is expected to be published during 1980.

(e) ED16 *Supplement to 'Extraordinary items and prior year adjustments' (SSAP6)* — this exposure draft dealt with two subjects, foreign currencies which is now being progressed as part of the review of ED21 *Accounting for foreign currency transactions,* and fixed assets which is now being progressed as part of the work on SSAP12 *Accounting for depreciation.*

(f) ED3 *Accounting for acquisitions and mergers* — this exposure draft was put in abeyance following conflicting views on the legality of the proposals on merger accounting. The law in this area is now being reviewed by the Department of Trade in the light of EEC directives and proposed EEC directives. ASC is in close contact with the Department of Trade on this subject and progress on a standard is likely to resume in 1980 now that the Department's consultative paper *Accounting for acquisitions and mergers* has been published.

Discussion papers and exposure drafts in preparation
Discussion papers and exposure drafts on the subjects of *Accounting for pension funds, Accounting for pension costs in company accounts* and *Accounting for leases* are at various stages of preparation. These subjects are complex and extensive consultations have been entered into during the preparatory stage with preparers and users of financial statements. The documents may be published during 1980. A paper on the problems of accounting for goodwill arising from the impact of the EEC 4th Directive may be published during 1980 to seek the views of the public on possible lines of development.

Subjects under study

The following subjects are being studied by members of the Committee:

Simplified financial statements
Valued added statements
Analysed reporting
Employment report
Accounting for charities
Petroleum Revenue Tax
The conceptual framework of accounting

LIAISON WITH OTHER STANDARD SETTING BODIES

It is intended that liaison with other standard setting bodies will become a regular and important feature in forthcoming years. Liaison will be continued and improved with those bodies with whom ASC is already in contact and further contacts with national bodies are in the preliminary stage. Liaison is also being improved or established, through appropriate channels, with international bodies who are becoming concerned with accounting standards, such as OECD, UN, and EEC.

Appendix One · Statement of Intent on Accounting Standards in the 1970's

At the outset of the 1970's, the Council of the Institute of Chartered Accountants in England and Wales reaffirms its continuing determination to advance accounting standards. The Council issues the following statement for the information of directors, accountants, auditors, and users of company accounts to make clear the steps the Council intends to take in pursuit of its aims in the field of accounting standards and as a reminder of some of the basic problems in the preparation of financial statements.

ACCOUNTING STANDARDS

It is the Council's intention to advance accounting standards along the following lines:

1. Narrowing the Areas of Difference and Variety in Accounting Practice

The complexity and diversity of business activities gives rise to a variety of accounting practices justifiably designed for and acceptable in particular circumstances. While recognising the impracticability of rigid uniformity, the Council will intensify its efforts to narrow the areas of difference and variety in accounting practice by publishing authoritative statements on best accounting practice which will, wherever possible, be definitive.

2. Disclosure of Accounting Bases

The Council intends to recommend that when accounts include significant items which depend substantially on judgements of value, or on the estimated outcome of future events or uncompleted transactions, rather than on ascertained amounts, the accounting bases adopted in arriving at their amounts should be disclosed.

3. Disclosures of Departures from Established Definitive Accounting Standards

The Council intends to recommend that departures from definitive standards should be disclosed in company accounts or in the notes thereto.

4. Wider Exposure for Major Proposals on Accounting Standards

In establishing major new accounting standards the Council will provide an opportunity for appropriate bodies to express their views by giving wide exposure to its draft proposals.

5. Continuing programme for encouraging improved Accounting Standards in Legal and Regulatory measures

The Council will continue its programme of suggesting appropriate improvements in accounting standards established by legislation, of which the proposals on "Companies Legislation in the 1970's" submitted to the President of the Board of Trade in March this year are an example. The Council will also continue to support and encourage the improvement of accounting standards in relevant regulatory measures such as the City Code on Take-Overs and Mergers and Stock Exchange Requirements.

AUDITING

In support of the proposals on accounting standards outlined, the Council will, after appropriate notice, recommend that if disclosures of accounting bases or of departures from definitive accounting standards is not made in the accounts or in the notes thereto, appropriate reference should be made in auditors' reports.

SUPPORT AND MAINTENANCE OF STANDARDS

The Council will do all in its power to assist and support members in the observance of established standards. To this end, it intends to strengthen its machinery for investigating and pointing the lessons of lapses from standards.

RESTATEMENT OF THE UNDERLYING NATURE OF COMPANY ACCOUNTS

Those who prepare, audit and use company accounts should keep in mind the following essential points, against the background of which this statement of intent is issued.

—Company accounts are presented by directors, not by auditors. The auditor's function is to express an independent opinion on the truth and fairness of the view presented by the accounts.

—The activities of a company are continuous, whereas the period covered by the accounts is no more than an arbitary segment of time out of a company's continuing existence. The determination of amounts of income and expenditure properly attributable to an accounting period, particularly in respect of uncompleted transactions, and of amounts at which related items are shown in the balance sheet, can be arrived at only by informed judgement exercised in accordance with accounting conventions.

IMPLEMENTATION

The Council will forthwith establish machinery for furthering these proposals and to this end will seek the advice and assistance of representatives of industry, finance and commerce.

Appendix Two · Accounting Standards Committee Constitution

(As amended with effect from 1st February 1976)

Governing bodies

1. The governing bodies shall be the Institute of Chartered Accountants in England and Wales, the Institute of Chartered Accountants of Scotland, the Institute of Chartered Accountants in Ireland, the Association of Certified Accountants, the Institute of Cost and Management Accountants and the Chartered Institute of Public Finance and Accountancy. A governing body may withdraw from participation by written notice from its Council to the Councils of the other governing bodies.

Objects

2. The Committee's objects shall be to propose for the approval of the Councils of the governing bodies definitive standards of financial accounting and reporting. Its objects encompass (a) fundamentals of financial accounting, (b) definition of terms used, (c) application of fundamentals to specific classes of business, and (d) the form and content of financial statements, including presentation and disclosure.

Terms of reference

3. The Committee's terms of reference are:
   'Bearing in mind the intention of the governing bodies to advance accounting standards and to narrow the areas of difference and variety in accounting practice by publishing authoritative statements on best accounting practice which will wherever possible be definitive—
   (a) To keep under review standards of financial accounting and reporting.
   (b) To publish consultative documents with the object of maintaining and advancing accounting standards.
   (c) To propose to the Councils of the governing bodies statements of standard accounting practice.
   (d) To consult as appropriate with representatives of finance, commerce, industry and government and other persons concerned with financial reporting.'

Powers

4. The Committee shall have authority to issue proposals (including amendments of existing statements) on financial accounting and reporting

15

standards in its own name in the form of exposure drafts or other types of consultative document for comment. It must be made clear in any drafts so issued that they do not have the authority of the Councils of the governing bodies.

5. After a suitable period has been allowed for comment, the Committee shall lay its proposals before the Councils of the governing bodies in final form of approval.

6. When the Committee's proposals are presented to the Council of the English Institute in the final form they shall be accompanied by formal statements reporting whether the Councils of the other bodies have given the proposals their approval or whether they dissent, giving reasons in the latter case. The decisions of the Council of one body shall not be binding on the other bodies.

Membership
7. The Committee shall consist of not more than 23 members appointed annually from 1st July. Of these, three places shall be reserved for nominees of the Council of the Institute of Chartered Accountants of Scotland, two places for nominees of the Council of the Institute of Chartered Accountants in Ireland, two places for nominees of the Council of the Association of Certified Accountants, two places for nominees of the Council of the Institute of Cost and Management Accountants and two places for nominees of the Council of the Chartered Institute of Public Finance and Accountancy. The remaining places shall be occupied by members of the Institute of Chartered Accountants in England and Wales appointed by the Council of that body.

8. Members may not appoint substitutes to attend meetings in their absence, nor may they be accompanied by aides or advisers.

9. The members shall not regard themselves as representing sectional interests but shall be guided by the need to act in the general interest of the community and of the accountancy profession as a whole.

Officers
10. The chairman and vice-chairman shall be appointed by the chairman of the Consultative Committee of Accountancy Bodies on the recommendation of the Accounting Standards Committee and subject to the approval of CCAB. Their term of office shall be two years. They shall be eligible for reappointment.

11. The vice-chairman is empowered to act in the absence of the chairman. In the absence of both, the chairman of CCAB may appoint a temporary chairman.

Quorum
12. A majority of the membership shall constitute a quorum.

Voting
13. Each member shall have one vote.

14. A majority of those present and voting shall settle all matters other than approval of an exposure draft for release and the submission for approval by the Councils of the governing bodies of proposed accounting standards.

15. The approval of a two-thirds majority of the whole membership of the Committee shall be required for the release of an exposure draft and the submission for approval by the Councils of the governing bodies of proposed accounting standards.

16. Votes may be taken by show of hands or by postal ballot.

17. The chairman shall have a casting vote where a simple majority is required.

Operating policy
18. In carrying out its work the Committee may obtain such assistance from such other organisations and persons as it sees fit and shall be free to settle its day-to-day operating procedures so long as they are consistent with this constitution.

Staff
19. The Committee shall be assisted by the staff of the Technical Directorate of the Institute of Chartered Accountants in England and Wales.

Amendment of constitution
20. This constitution may be amended by authority of the Councils of the governing bodies.

Appendix Three • Documents published by or for ASC since 1970

*(Note: Statements of Standard Accounting Practice, which
are prepared by ASC but published by the Councils
of the governing bodies, are listed in full
in Section Four from page 000)*

Title	Date
ED1 *Accounting for the Results of Associated Companies*	June 1970
ED2 *Disclosure of Accounting Policies*	January 1971
ED3 *Accounting for Acquisitions and Mergers*	January 1971
ED4 *Earnings per Share*	March 1971
Inflation and Accounts (discussion paper and fact sheet)	September 1971
ED5 *Extraordinary Items and Prior Year Adjustments*	August 1971
ED6 *Stocks and Work in Progress*	May 1972
ED7 *Accounting for Extraordinary Items* (replaced ED5)	July 1972
Notes on Accounting for Corporation Tax under the Imputation System (Discussion Paper)	September 1972
ED8 *Accounting for Changes in the Purchasing Power of Money*	January 1973
ED9 *The Accounting Treatment of Grants under The Industry Act 1972*	March 1973
ED10 *Accounting for Value Added Tax*	May 1973
ED11 *Accounting for Deferred Taxation*	May 1973
ED12 *The Treatment of Taxation under the Imputation System in the Accounts of Companies*	May 1973
ED13 *Statements of Source and Application of Funds*	April 1974
Evidence to the Inflation Accounting Committee (Sandilands Committee)	April 1974
A review of the Relationship between Historical Cost Accounting, Current Purchasing Power Statements, and Replacement Cost Accounting (Evidence to the Sandilands Committee)	October 1974
A Note on Last in First Out (LIFO), First in First Out (FIFO), Base Stock and CPP Supplementary Statements (Evidence to the Sandilands Committee)	October 1974

ED14 *Accounting for Research and Development*	January 1975
ED15 *Accounting for Depreciation*	January 1975
The Corporate Report (Discussion Paper)	August 1975
ED16 *Supplement to 'Extraordinary Items and Prior Year Adjustments'*	September 1975
Initial Reactions to the Report of the Inflation Accounting Committee	October 1975
Inflation Accounting—The Interim Period	December 1975
ED17 *Accounting for Research and Development— revised* (replaced ED14)	April 1976
The Corporate Report and the Future Programme of ASC	July 1976
ED18 *Current Cost Accounting*	November 1976
ED19 *Accounting for Deferred Taxation*	May 1977
ED20 *Group Accounts*	July 1977
ED21 *Accounting for foreign currency transactions*	September 1977
Inflation Accounting—an Interim Recommendation	November 1977
ED22 *Accounting for post balance sheet events*	February 1978
Price Level Accounting—Statement of Intent	July 1978
Setting Accounting Standards: a consultative document	September 1978
ED23 *Accounting for contingencies*	November 1978
ED24 *Current Cost Accounting*	April 1978
Guidance Notes on ED24	April 1979
ED25 *Accounting for the results of associated companies*	October 1979
Guidance Notes on SSAP 16	March 1980

Most of the above publications have been reprinted in the professional journals; those which have not may be consulted in the libraries of the accountancy bodies.

Appendix Four • Published research and other studies associated with the work of ASC

Annual Surveys of Published Accounts:

1968/69	£1.95
1969/70	£2.75
1970/71	£3.00
1971/72	£3.25
1972/73	£4.95
1973/74	£5.75
1975	£7.25
1976	£7.95
1977	£9.95
1978	£10.95
1979	£12.95

Guidance Manual on Current Cost Accounting prepared by the
Inflation Accounting Steering Group (1976) £6.25
Brief Guide to the Exposure Draft on Current Cost Accounting
prepared by the Inflation Accounting Steering Group £0.75
Background papers on ED24 Current Cost Accounting
prepared by the Inflation Accounting Steering Group £1.95
Group Accounts: The fundamental principals, form and content
by R. M. Wilkins £8.95
Accounting Values and Inflation by W. T. Baxter £5.95
Depreciation by W. T. Baxter £5.85
The Corporate Report—a discussion paper £2.00
*Practical Aspects of Deferred Tax Accounting—a working guide
to SSAP8 and SSAP11* by I. P. A. Stit £7.75
The Private Shareholder and the Corporate Report by
T. A. Lee and D. P. Tweedie £7.95
Statements of Source and Application of Funds by
R. W. Knox £6.25
Analysed Reporting: a background study by A. F. Lamb £8.95
*Value Added Statement: a review of its use in corporate reports
by M. F. Morley £4.50
Simplified Financial Statements by A. E. Hammill £4.95
The Employment Statement in Company Reports
by E. R. Thompson and Anne Knell £4.95
Added Value in External Financial Reporting by M. Renshall,
R. Allan and K. Nicholson £5.95

Research Committee Occasional Papers:—

No. 1	*The Treatment of inflation in the published accounts of companies in overseas countries* by R. W. Scapens	£3.50
No. 4	*Accounting for price changes—a practical survey of 6 methods* by A. Hope	£3.50
No. 8	*The Corporate Report: an academic view*	£3.50
No. 9	*Post Balance Sheet Events* by R. L. Dunlop and N. C. E. Land	£3.50
No. 10	*Accounting for pensions in company accounts* by a working party from Unilever Limited	£3.50
No. 11	*Disclosure of Overseas Operations of United Kingdom Companies* by K. J. Tuckwell and A. G. Piper	£3.50
No. 12	*The Reporting of Company Financial Results to Employees* by L. D. Parker	£3.50
No. 13	*A Study of the Relative Usefulness of Six Accounting Measures of Income* by J. Arnold and M. El-Azma	£3.50
No. 14	*An International Comparison of Group Accounting* by M. W. Pendlebury	£3.50
No. 16	*An International Comparison of Group Accounting* by M. W. Pendlebury	£3.50

Accountants Digest series:—

AD38 *Valuation of stock and work in progress* by C. L. Nunn	£1.50
AD69 *Group Accounts* by R. M. Wilkins	£3.25
AD70 *Deferred Tax* by D. C. Hobson and R. J. Munson	£3.25
AD74 *Accounting for Research and Development* by G. W. Eccles and W. L. Lifford	£2.50

*Not available from ICAEW.

The above publications are obtainable, post free, from:—
> The Publications Department
> The Institute of Chartered Accountants
> in England and Wales
> P.O. Box 433
> Chartered Accountants' Hall,
> Moorgate Place,
> London, EC2P 2BJ.

Appendix Five • U.K. and International Standards

The Councils of the CCAB bodies made significant changes in June 1977 to the way in which international standards should be dealt with in the UK and Ireland as a result of amendments to the IASC's Agreement and Constituion, ratified in October 1977. As a consequence: —
(a) The Councils of the CCAB bodies will determine the date from which an International Standard is applicable in the UK and Ireland;
(b) As far as possible the requirements of the International Standards will be incorporated into UK and Irish Standards so that only one set of documents needs to be consulted;
(c) In the event that certain provisions of an International Standard are not accepted for incorporation into UK and Irish Standards, that fact will be published by the Councils of the CCAB bodies. This may lead to noncompliance with an International Standard even though UK and Irish Standards have been followed. Such noncompliance should be disclosed by the directors in a note to the financial statements (but its effect need not be quantified).

The International Standards adopted to date are listed below, indicating where appropriate, which UK and Irish Standards incorporate them.

International Standard		*UK & Irish Standard*	
IAS1	Disclosure of accounting policies	SSAP2	Disclosure of accounting policies
IAS2	Valuation and presentation of inventories in the context of the historical cost sytem	SSAP9	Stocks and work in progress
IAS3	Consolidated financial statements	SSAP1	Accounting for the results of associated companies
		SSAP14	Group accounts
IAS4	Depreciation accounting	SSAP12	Accounting for depreciation
IAS5	Information to be disclosed in Financial Statements		*
IAS6	Accounting Treatment of Changing Prices		*
IAS7	Statement of changes in Financial Position	SSAP10	Statements of source and application of funds
IAS8	Unusual and Prior Period Items and Changes in Accounting Policies	SSAP6	Extraordinary items and prior year adjustments

IAS9	Accounting for Research and Development Activities		*
IAS10	Contingencies and Events Occuring After the Balance Sheet Date		*
IAS11	Accounting for Construction Contracts	SSAP9	Stocks and work in progress
IAS12	Accounting for Taxes on Income		*
IAS13	Presentation of Current Assets and Current Liabilities		*

*Not yet applicable in UK and Ireland

Section Two

The texts of Exposure Drafts extant at 1st June 1980
are reproduced in full in this Section.

20 January 1971 ED3

Accounting for acquisitions and mergers

Contents

Part	Paragraph numbers

Accounting for acquisitions and mergers

For many years all amalgamations of businesses, whether by way of an exchange of shares or for cash or some other consideration, were regarded as the acquisition of one company by another and were therefore accounted for in accordance with the traditional accounting methods relating to the issue of shares and to the acquisition of assets. In more recent years, however, the practice has developed of distinguishing between amalgamations which represent substantial changes in the ownership and business of at least one of the companies and those which represent a continuation of the former ownership and businesses of the amalgamating companies. The emergence of this distinction has to be recognised and accounting standards must therefore be introduced to deal with the changed circumstances.

Part 1 Explanatory note

1 The practice of distinguishing between company amalgamations which represent substantial changes in the ownership of the combining businesses and those which represent the continuance of the former ownership and businesses has led to the development of a different method of accounting for the latter type of amalgamation. A transfer to new ownership is accounted for as an acquisition, that is as a purchase of assets in accordance with traditional accounting methods, but continuing ownership in a continuing business is accounted for as a merger which in practice means that there is no change in the amounts at which assets, liabilities, reserves and undistributed profits of the amalgamating companies are recorded.

2 The main differences between the two methods of accounting are in the treatment of pre-acquisition profits, goodwill and share premium. There are legal bars to the distribution of pre-acquisition profits and share premium to shareholders. Under the merger method the accumulated profits at the date of the merger are not regarded as pre-acquisition profits and they are therefore treated as remaining available for distribution. Similarly, no goodwill or share premium arises because the shares issued in exchange are recorded at their nominal value for the reasons explained below.

3 In theory, the parties to a merger may agree amongst themselves the accounting basis on which they will pool their interests, in the same way as when unincorporated businesses combine. Practical considerations and the requirements of company law have brought about a treatment under which, where there is a merger, no change is recognised in the amounts at which the assets, liabilities, reserves and undistributed profits of the amalgamating companies are recorded, except to achieve uniformity of accounting practices between the businesses. On this basis the shares transferred to the holding company would be recorded in the books of the holding company at the book amount of the net assets underlying the shares transferred. However, if this amount exceeds the nominal value of the shares issued in exchange, the Companies Act 1948 requires the excess to be treated as a share premium with restrictions on its distribution. This defeats the merger concept that existing reserves and undistributed profits remain available for distribution, and has led to adoption of the practice of recording the shares transferred to the holding company in the books of that company at the nominal value of the shares issued in exchange. (A note on the legal aspects appears in paragraph 25 below).

4 In the case of an acquisition, on the other hand, because the concept underlying it is that of a purchase, the acquiring company will record the shares acquired at cost. Cost will be the value of the consideration given. (This is considered further in paragraphs 9 and 10 below).

5 The main concept underlying a merger is one of continuity of the amalgamating businesses. No assets have been distributed to shareholders and no new capital has been subscribed. The only change that has taken place is in the separate ownerships which are considered to have been pooled into one common ownership and reallocated among the individual owners. If the concept of continuity of ownership of the amalgamated businesses is to have any validity, it is essential that there should be no gross disparity in size between the amalgamating businesses, otherwise the owners of the smaller business would not have a sufficiently material voice in the affairs of the amalgamated business. For this reason the relative sizes of the amalgamating companies are an important factor in distinguishing a merger from an acquisition ; the definition adopted in this Statement deems gross disparity of size to exist if the shareholders of any one company to be party to an amalgamation will have more than three times the equity voting rights of the shareholders of any other company party to the amalgamation (see paragraph 7 below).

Part 2 Definition of terms

Acquisitions

6 All business amalgamations are acquisitions except those which comply with the conditions characterising a merger stated in paragraph 7 below.

Mergers

7 A merger as defined in this Statement occurs on the amalgamation of two or more companies if all the following conditions are met :

(a) the substance of the main businesses of the constituent companies continues in the amalgamated undertaking ; and
(b) the equity voting rights of the amalgamated undertaking to be held by the shareholders of any one of the constituent companies is not more than three times the equity voting rights to be held by the shareholders of any of the other constituent companies ; and
(c) the amalgamation results from an offer to equity voting shareholders and not less than 90% in value of the offer is in the form of equity voting capital with rights identical with

29

the equity voting capital rights of the offeree company or companies already in issue ; for this purpose convertible loan stock or equity voting capital which can be converted into cash through an underwriting agreement is not to be regarded as equity voting capital ; and

(d) the offer is approved by the voting shareholders of the company making the offer and it is accepted by shareholders representing at least 90% of the total equity capital (voting and non-voting) of the company or companies receiving the offer.

In an amalgamation of three or more companies, some may satisfy the conditions here stated and others may not ; the amalgamation would then be treated as part merger, part acquisition (see paragraph 13 below).

Part 3 Proposed standard accounting practice

Acquisitions

8 Where one company acquires the shares of another they should be recorded in the books of the acquiring company at cost, which will be the value of the consideration given. If the consideration is cash or loan stock cost will be the amount of cash paid or the present value of loan stock issued. If the consideration takes the form of an issue of shares by the acquiring company, cost will be the fair value of the shares issued. The fair value should be determined by reference to the market value or, where this is not ascertainable, by reference to the value of the underlying net tangible and intangible assets acquired. Market value of the consideration given for this purpose does not necessarily mean the quoted market price, which normally relates to small blocks of shares and is subject to a number of outside influences. Regard should be had to all the relevant factors including any underwriting of the price of the shares involved. Where the value ascribed to shares issued exceeds their nominal value, the excess will be recorded as a share premium.

9 The total purchase consideration should be allocated between the underlying net tangible and intangible assets on the basis of a fair value of the acquired net assets to the acquiring company. If this is not done by means of adjusting the values in the books of the acquired company, it should be done on consolidation. Any excess of the total consideration over the value ascribed to net tangible assets and identifiable intangible assets such as trade marks, patents or development expenditure, will represent goodwill.

10 The terms of the agreement may state that the date of acquisition shall be taken as a date earlier than that on which consideration actually passes. For the purpose of the holding company's accounts, however, the date of acquisition should not be taken as earlier than the date when substantial agreement was reached on the terms of the acquisition or the date as from which the income of the subsidiary accrued to the holding company ; in no circumstances should it be earlier than the date of the last audited balance sheet of the subsidiary. Where part of the consideration consists of cash or loan stock, an interest adjustment is necessary if profits of the subsidiary are introduced prior to the date of payment of cash or issue of loan stock.

11 Pre-acquisition profits or losses of the acquired company are reflected in the value of its net assets at the date of acquisition. Distributions to the acquiring company from pre-acquisition profits should be applied accordingly as a reduction of the cost of the shares.

12 The extent to which the results of the group are affected by profits or losses of subsidiaries brought in for the first time should be disclosed. Moreover, in any period in which a material change in the composition of the group has taken place, the consolidated accounts should contain sufficient information to enable shareholders to appreciate the effect on the results.

Mergers

13 Any amalgamation of companies which meets all the conditions set out in paragraph 7 above should be dealt with as a merger for the purpose of financial accounts. Where three or more companies are parties to a single amalgamation the conditions may be satisfied as regards some of the companies concerned but not as regards others. In these circumstances the amalgamation should be treated as a merger in respect of the qualifying companies and as an acquisition in respect of the remainder.

14 The shares transferred to the holding company as part of a merger should be recorded in the books of that company at the nominal value of the shares it issues in exchange.

15 As a result of using the nominal value, the only difference to be dealt with on consolidation will be the difference between the nominal value of the shares issued as consideration and the nominal value of the shares transferred to the holding company. Where the nominal value of the shares issued is less than that of the shares transferred the difference should be treated as an undistributable reserve arising on consolidation. Where the nominal value of the shares issued is greater than that of the shares received in exchange the difference is the extent to which the reserves of the subsidiary have been in effect capitalised as a result of the merger and it should therefore be treated on consolidation primarily as a reduction of reserves ; it should be applied firstly against any unrealised surplus and secondly against revenue profits or realised surpluses.

16 For the purpose of this Statement, reserves derived from revenue profits or realised surpluses are regarded as distributable reserves. Undistributable reserves will include unrealised surpluses on the revaluation of fixed assets.

17 Where there is additional consideration in some form other than equity shares (within the limitations of paragraph 7 (c) above), the value of such additional consideration should be added to the nominal value of the shares issued by the holding company in exchange in order to arrive at the amount at which the shares of the subsidiary should be recorded for the purpose of calculating the difference referred to in paragraph 15 above.

18 As a result of adopting these procedures, the reserves in the consolidated accounts will be the total of the reserves of the constituent companies increased by any reserve arising on consolidation or reduced by any part of the reserves of subsidiaries which have been in effect capitalised as a result of the merger.

19 The net amount of the distributable reserves of a subsidiary as at the date upon which the merger takes place, that is, after deducting those reserves which have been in effect capitalised as a result of the merger, should be treated by the holding company as being available for distribution to its members. If a subsidiary declares dividends out of profits earned prior to the date of the merger in excess of such net amount, the excess should be applied by the holding company in reduction of the cost of the investment.

20 Any debit balance on profit and loss account in a subsidiary at the date of the merger should be set off first against the aggregate distributable reserves.

21 In the consolidated accounts for the period in which the merger took place the profits or losses of subsidiaries brought in for the first time should be included for the entire period without any adjustment in respect of that part of the period prior to the merger. The extent to which the results of the group are affected by the profits or losses so brought in should however be disclosed. Corresponding amounts should be restated as if the merger had been in force throughout the previous period and at the previous balance sheet date, and the financial accounts of the amalgamated undertaking should disclose that an amalgamation accounted for as a merger has taken place during the period under review.

22 The financial accounts for the period in which a merger took place should also disclose particulars of the companies party to the merger, giving
(a) the names of the constituent companies;
(b) particulars of securities issued in respect of the merger;
(c) details of significant accounting adjustments amongst the constituent companies to achieve consistency of accounting bases, and of the financial effects of such changes.

Two methods not alternatives

23 An amalgamation which meets all the conditions set out in paragraph 7 must be accounted for as a merger; it is not acceptable to account for it as an acquisition. Conversely, an amalgamation which does not meet all the merger conditions must be accounted for as an acquisition.

Date from which effective

24 The methods of accounting for amalgamations set out in this Statement should be adopted as soon as possible and regarded as standard for amalgamations initiated after 31 December 1970.

Part 4 Note on legal requirements

25 There is legal opinion to support the propriety in law of the practice of recording in the books of a holding company, at the nominal value of the shares issued, shares received by the holding company in exchange for shares issued.

26 However, in order to comply with the requirements of paragraph 4(3) of Schedule 2 to the Companies Act 1967, the accounts of the holding company must include a statement that the shares of the subsidiary company are recorded at an amount equivalent to the nominal value of the shares issued in exchange. If additional consideration in some form other than equity shares is added to the nominal value of the shares issued in exchange (as stated in paragraph 17 above) the statement required by paragraph 4(3) of Schedule 2 to the Companies Act 1967 must be amended accordingly.

Supplement to "Extraordinary Items and Prior Year Adjustments"

Contents

Supplement to "Extraordinary Items and Prior Year Adjustments"

This proposed statement forms an addition to the Statement of Standard Accounting Practice No. 6 "Extraordinary Items and Prior Year Adjustments" and should be read in conjunction therewith.

Part 1 Explanatory Note

1   The purpose of Statement of Standard Accounting Practice No. 6 "Extraordinary Items and Prior Year Adjustments" (SSAP 6) is to require all profits and losses recognised in the accounts of the year (other than prior year adjustments and unrealised surpluses on revaluation of fixed assets) to be recognised in the profit and loss account for the year. Need for clarification of the Standard has arisen in respect of :

  (a) accounting for deficits on the revaluation of fixed assets ;
  (b) accounting for surpluses and deficits arising on the realisation of revalued fixed assets ;
  (c) accounting for the revenue effects of translating foreign currencies.

2   These topics may later form the subject of separate accounting standards but there is a present need for guidance pending the issue of those standards.

Revaluation of Fixed Assets

3   The revaluation of fixed assets is a departure from the concept of historical cost accounting on which accounts have been traditionally based. Paragraph 13 of SSAP 6 states that unrealised surpluses on revaluation of fixed assets should be credited direct to reserves. Questions have arisen as to the treatment of revaluation deficits. It has been concluded that deficits arising on such revaluations should be charged to the profit and loss account for the year to the extent that they exceed any surplus held in reserves and identified as relating to previous revaluations of the same assets.

Realisation of Fixed Assets

4 When fixed assets are disposed of the difference between the written down amount and the sale proceeds should be included in the profit and loss account for the year. Whether this difference constitutes an extraordinary item will depend on whether it has the characteristics discussed in paragraph 3 of SSAP 6. An amount held in reserves in respect of previous revaluations of those assets should be regarded as having become a realised surplus. It should not, however, be reported as part of the profit for the year.

Foreign Currency Translation

5 The policy or policies to be adopted for the translation of amounts denominated in foreign currency is a subject currently under study with a view to the issue of a separate accounting standard. Two methods are commonly used : the temporal (or historical rate) method and the closing rate method. The subject is one in which conflicting opinions are strongly held and it must be expected that some time will elapse before a standard is issued which will describe the method or methods of accounting to be applied.

6 Meanwhile it has been concluded that, subject to paragraph 7 below, exchange differences should be dealt with through the profit and loss account. They should be regarded as 'extraordinary items' only if they arise from transactions which are themselves regarded as coming within that definition.

7 Exchange differences on translation of fixed asset amounts (arising from the use of the closing rate method) should be treated as if they were unrealised surpluses or deficits on revaluation of fixed assets. Accordingly, such differences relating to fixed assets should be dealt with direct through reserves except insofar as they represent :
    (a) deficits not covered by amounts held in reserves, or
    (b) the recovery of deficits previously charged to the profit and loss account ;
in both cases in respect of previous translations of those assets.

8 Exchange differences arising on translations of borrowings in a foreign currency may also call for special treatment.

9 Whichever translation policy is adopted for other items, borrowings denominated in a foreign currency should be translated at closing rate and, as a general rule, exchange differences arising on such translation should be dealt with through profit and loss account as they arise.

10 However, where such exchange differences are losses, to pass them through the profit and loss account without any corresponding offset in respect of gains arising on the translation of overseas assets would not make commercial sense because the processes of borrowing overseas and acquiring fixed assets overseas are usually parts of a single commercial policy and in practical terms are usually unaffected by the changing value of sterling.

11 It is therefore desirable that a "cover" method should be permitted in the circumstances described. As a matter of practice, it is considered that it should be permissible for exchange losses arising on the translation of foreign currency net borrowings to be wholly or partly offset for profit and loss account purposes against an equal or smaller gain arising on translating overseas fixed assets (less depreciation) at the closing rate. The use of the term "net" borrowings is designed to include the situation in which foreign currency borrowings are wholly or partly matched by foreign currency cash or similar balances so that the "net" borrowings in that case would be the foreign currency borrowings less the foreign currency cash or similar balances.

12 It may be noted that the accounting problem which it is proposed to meet in this way does not arise from the inadequacy of the translation method employed but from the inadequacy of preparing group financial statements without restatement for the changes in purchasing power of currencies which result in changes to their related strengths.

Part 2 Proposed Standard Accounting Practice

Revaluations and realisations of fixed assets

13 Unrealised surpluses on revaluations of fixed assets should be credited direct to reserves. Unrealised deficits on revaluations of fixed assets should be debited to the profit and loss account of the year to the extent that they exceed any surplus held in the reserves and identified as relating to previous revaluations of the same assets. They should be classified as ordinary or extraordinary according to their nature.

14 When fixed assets are realised, the surpluses or deficits compared with the book value should be recognised in the profit and loss account for the year and classified as extraordinary items or otherwise according to their nature. Any reserve identified as being in respect of previously unrealised surpluses on the revaluation of those assets thereby becomes a realised surplus but should not be reported as part of the profit for the year.

Foreign Currency Translation

15 Exchange differences arising from conversion of foreign currencies and from translation of amounts denominated in a foreign currency should, unless advantage is taken of the alternative treatment set out in paragraph 16, be dealt with in the profit and loss account as part of the ordinary activities of the business, except that:

(a) differences arising from extraordinary items should themselves be treated as extraordinary items, and

(b) differences arising on translation of fixed asset amounts should be treated as if they were unrealised surpluses or deficits on revaluation of fixed assets.

16 Exchange losses arising on the translation of foreign currency net borrowings may be wholly or partly offset for profit and loss account purposes against an equal or smaller gain arising on translating overseas fixed assets (less depreciation) at the closing rate.

17 Whether or not advantage is taken of the alternative treatment in paragraph 16, foreign currency borrowings should be translated at closing rate.

Accounting for foreign currency transactions

Contents

Accounting for foreign currency transactions

This statement considers and deals with the accounting treatment of the conversion and translation of amounts stated in foreign currencies in the context of the historical cost basis of accounting including the circumstances where under that system certain assets have been revalued in the financial statements: it does not deal with foreign currency conversions and translations in the context of current cost accounting.

Part 1 Explanatory note

Background

1 Foreign operations may be carried out through a branch, subsidiary or associated company which maintains accounting records in terms of the foreign currency. For accounting purposes it is necessary to translate the complete financial statements of the separate entity for incorporation into the reporting company's financial statements. A company may also enter into transactions denominated in a foreign currency which need to be translated for recording in its own financial statements.

2 Companies engaged in foreign operations pay and receive amounts in foreign currencies which are converted from or to other currencies. Differences on exchange may arise because the amounts which are paid or received when currencies are converted may differ from the amounts at which a transaction was originally recorded.

3 Translation of foreign currencies presents problems because exchange rates are subject to continuous change as a result of market forces. There are two rates of exchange that can reasonably be used to translate the amount of an asset or liability : the exchange rate ruling at the date of the balance sheet that is being prepared ; or the exchange rate ruling at the date when the asset or liability was acquired or the book value established. These rates are known as the 'closing rate' and the 'historical rate' respectively.

Alternative methods of translation

4 A number of methods of translation have been used for accounting purposes in the past. The different methods essentially consist of using various combinations of the closing rate and the historical rate in the translation process. In this standard two methods of translation are recognised ; the 'closing rate method' and the 'temporal method'.

The closing rate method

5 Under the closing rate method all items in balance sheets are translated at the rate of exchange ruling on the balance sheet date. Where this method is used an exchange difference will result if the rate of exchange at the balance sheet date is different from the rate of exchange at the previous balance sheet date or at the date when the transaction was recorded.

6 When using the closing rate method amounts in the profit and loss account are translated at the closing rate of exchange or at the average rate for the accounting period.

The temporal method

7 Under the temporal method assets, liabilities, revenues and expenses are translated at the rate of exchange ruling at the date on which the amount recorded in the accounts was established (i.e., the historical rate). Any assets or liabilities which are carried at current values at the balance sheet date in the financial statements of an overseas subsidiary or branch are translated at the rate of exchange ruling at the balance sheet date (i.e., the closing rate).

8 Under the temporal method differences on exchange will arise because differing rates are used to translate the different elements in financial statements. Surpluses or deficits will also arise when assets and liabilities are revalued.

Choice of method

9 The closing rate method is based on the concept that a reporting company has a net investment in a foreign operation and what is at risk from currency fluctuations is the net investment. The results of the foreign

42

operations are considered to be best reflected in financial statements by translating them as well as the foreign assets and liabilities at the closing rate. It is important to realize that the closing rate method restates historical cost amounts at current rates of exchange ; it does not produce a statement of the current values of net assets denominated in foreign currencies.

10 The closing rate method possesses the following advantages :–

(a) It deals effectively with the situation where fixed assets located overseas have been financed by foreign currency borrowings and a change in the exchange rate results in offsetting gains and losses.

(b) The relationship existing between balances in accounts as originally prepared in a foreign currency is preserved in the translated accounts whereas this is not the case where historical rates are used for translating certain assets.

(c) It is not necessary to maintain sterling records of fixed assets and inventories located overseas which would be required if historical rates were to be used.

(d) It is simple to operate and the results are easily understood by users of accounts.

11 The temporal method is based on the concept that a single enterprise is reporting and foreign operations are an extension of the activities of the parent body. The historical cost basis of accounting requires that assets should normally be stated at cost, less depreciation and provisions for any permanent diminution in value. Consistency in applying accounting principles to the financial statements prepared by both local and foreign operations is achieved by translating at historical rates foreign transactions stated at historical cost.

12 The closing rate method and the temporal method are both considered acceptable methods.

Treatment of exchange differences under the Closing Rate method of translation.

13 The results of foreign based operations to be included as profit from ordinary operations should normally be the profit before taxation and extraordinary items shown in the financial statements of the foreign subsidiary or branch, translated at the closing or average rate. Extraordinary items should similarly be translated at the closing or average rate and shown as extraordinary items in the financial statements of the reporting company.

14 Gains and losses resulting from fluctuations in exchange rates are a normal incident of trading for a company which engages in foreign operations. However as translation differences may distort the results derived from ordinary activities of the business it is desirable to report them either as a separate item after the profit for the year from ordinary operations or, where appropriate as movements on reserves on the basis set out in paragraphs 15 to 19.

15 Exchange differences on translation of fixed asset amounts should be treated as if they were unrealised surpluses or deficits on revaluation of fixed assets. Such differences should be reported as movements on reserves except insofar as they represent:

(a) deficits not covered by amounts held in reserves in respect of previous translations of those assets, or

(b) the recovery of deficits previously charged to the profit and loss account in respect of previous translations of those assets, in which cases they should be dealt with through the profit and loss account.

16 Borrowings denominated in a foreign currency should be translated at closing rates and, as a general rule, exchange differences arising on such translations should be dealt with as they arise and reported as part of the exchange differences as a separate item after the profit for the year from ordinary operations.

17 However, where such exchange differences are deficits it would not make commercial sense to report these as losses without allowing for any corresponding offset in respect of gains arising on the translation of overseas fixed assets, because the processes of borrowing overseas and acquiring fixed assets overseas are usually parts of a single financial policy and in practical terms are usually unaffected by the changing value of sterling.

18 It is therefore desirable that a 'cover' method should be permitted in the circumstances described. As a matter of practice, it should be permissible for exchange deficits arising on the translation of foreign currency net borrowings to be wholly or partly offset for profit and loss account purposes against an equal or smaller surplus arising on translating the net book amount of overseas fixed assets at the closing rate. The use of the term 'net' borrowings is designed to include the situation in which foreign currency borrowings are partly matched by foreign currency cash or similar balances.

19 Translation differences which are not reported as movements on reserves should be reported as a separate item after the profit for the year from ordinary operations. Such differences will include gains or losses on current assets and current liabilities.

20 Differences which arise from the conversion, as opposed to the translation, of one currency to another should be taken into account in the profit and loss account as part of the profit for the year from ordinary operations.

Treatment of exchange differences under the Temporal method of translation.
21 All translation and conversion differences which arise under the temporal method should form part of the profit for the year classified appropriately as profit for the year from ordinary operations or extraordinary items. Under the temporal method fixed assets are translated at historical rates and therefore it is not possible to offset deficits on borrowings denominated in foreign currencies against surpluses arising on fixed assets.

Part 2 Definition of Terms

22 *Translation* is the process whereby financial data denominated or measured in one currency are expressed in terms of another currency. It includes both the expression of individual transactions in terms of another currency and the expression of a complete set of financial statements prepared in one currency in terms of another currency.

23 *Conversion* is the process of exchanging ownership of a sum of money in one currency, or the right thereto, for a sum of money in another currency, or the right thereto.

24 *Net borrowings* are borrowings in foreign currencies less foreign currency cash or similar balances.

25 A *foreign exchange rate* is the rate at which the currencies of two countries are exchanged.

26 The *historical rate* is the foreign exchange rate that (a) was applicable at the date of the original transaction or (b) existed on a subsequent date on which the item was revalued.

45

27 The *closing rate* is the foreign exchange rate ruling at the balance sheet date.

28 Under the *closing rate method* assets and liabilities are translated into sterling using the rate of exchange at the date of the balance sheet. Where forward exchange contracts have been arranged in respect of debtors and creditors the contract rate of exchange is used instead of the closing rate. Revenue items may be translated using either the closing rate of exchange or the average rate of exchange for the period.

29 Under the *temporal method* assets, liabilities, revenues and expenses are translated at the rate of exchange ruling at the date on which the amount recorded in the accounts was established (i.e., the historical rate). Any assets or liabilities which are carried at current values at the balance sheet date in the financial statements of an overseas subsidiary or branch are translated at the rate of exchange ruling at the balance sheet date (i.e., the closing rate).

Part 3 Proposed Standard Accounting Practice

30 Assets and liabilities which are located overseas or denominated in a foreign currency should be translated by using the closing rate method or the temporal method.

Closing rate method

31 The profit for the year shown in the accounts of a foreign subsidiary or branch should be translated at the closing or average rate and reported as part of the profit for the year distinguishing between results from ordinary operations and extraordinary items.

32 Exchange differences relating to fixed assets should normally be dealt with through reserves. However such exchange differences should be dealt with in the profit and loss account insofar as they represent:
  (a) deficits not covered by amounts held in reserves in respect of previous translations of those assets, or
  (b) the recovery of deficits previously charged to the profit and loss account in respect of previous translations of those assets.

33 Exchange differences arising on the translation of foreign currency net borrowings should be dealt with in the profit and loss account except that exchange deficits on foreign currency net borrowings may be wholly

46

or partly dealt with through reserves by being offset against an equal or smaller gain arising on translating the net book amount of overseas fixed assets.

34 All exchange translation differences which are not dealt with through reserves or offset under the conditions set out in paragraph 33, should be reported in the profit and loss account as a separate item after the profit for the year from ordinary operations.

Temporal method

35 All translation differences arising from the use of the temporal method should be reported as part of the profit for the year, distinguishing between results from ordinary operations and extraordinary items.

Conversion differences

36 Exchange differences arising from the conversion of foreign currency amounts, as opposed to translation differences, should be reported as part of the profit for the year, distinguishing between results from ordinary operations and extraordinary items. This will apply whether the closing rate or the temporal method is adopted for translation purposes.

Disclosure

37 The methods used in the translation of the financial statements of foreign-based operations and the treatment accorded to foreign exchange differences should be disclosed in financial statements.

38 Any movements on a reserve account arising from translation differences should be disclosed separately in notes to the accounts.

Date from which effective

39 The accounting and disclosure requirements set out in this statement should be adopted as soon as possible and regarded as standard in respect of accounts relating to periods starting on or after (date to be inserted after exposure).

Appendix 1

The appendix is for general guidance and does not form part of the Statement of Standard Accounting Practice.

The following example illustrates the presentation of the profit and loss account in which foreign exchange transactions are translated using the closing rate method.

Statement of profit and loss for the year
ended 31 December 1977

Note:	1977 £'000	1976 £'000
Turnover	195,000	162,000
(1) Operating Profit	18,600	15,400
(2) Interest Payable	1,740	1,320
Profit before taxation, exchange gain/(loss) and extraordinary items	16,860	14,080
(2) Taxation	8,500	7,100
Profit before exchange gain/(loss) and extraordinary items	8,360	6,980
(3) Exchange gain/(loss)	1,130	(250)
(2) Extraordinary items	950	640
Profit attributable to members of the company	10,440	7,370
Ordinary Dividends	5,000	4,000
Retained Profit	5,440	3,370
	Pence	Pence
Earnings per ordinary share before exchange gain/(loss) and extraordinary items	20.9	17.5

Notes:

(1) This item will normally include the operating profit shown in the accounts of overseas subsidiaries translated at the closing or average rates of exchange together with exchange differences resulting from the conversion of foreign currency amounts during the year.
It may be necessary, before translation, to make adjustments to the profits shown in the accounts of the foreign subsidiary or branch to bring them into line with the accounting policies adopted by the group.

(2) These items will normally include the relevant amounts shown in the profit and loss account of the foreign subsidiary translated at closing or average rates.

(3) This item will include translation differences not included in (1) and (2) above and any exchange differences which cannot be dealt with through reserves under the conditions set out in paragraphs 32 and 33.

Accounting for post balance sheet events

Contents

Accounting for post balance sheet events

Part 1 Summary of proposals and explanatory note

1 Events of significance arising after the balance sheet date need to be reflected in financial statements if they provide additional evidence of conditions that existed at the balance sheet date and materially affect the estimates made in arriving at amounts included in the financial statements.

2 To prevent financial statements from being misleading, disclosure needs to be made in notes to the financial statements of other significant events arising subsequent to the balance sheet date which provide evidence of conditions not existing at the balance sheet date, but on which information is necessary for a proper understanding of the financial statements.

3 A post balance sheet event for the purpose of this standard is one which occurs between the balance sheet date and the date on which the financial statements are approved by the directors.

4 Events which occur after the date on which the financial statements are approved by the directors do not come within the scope of this standard. (If such an event has a material effect on the financial statements, the directors will have a responsibility to ensure, by publishing the relevant information, that users of the financial statements are not misled.)

Classification of post balance sheet events

5 Events occurring after the balance sheet date may be classified into two categories; 'adjusting events' and 'non-adjusting events'.

6 Adjusting events are events which provide additional evidence relating to conditions existing at the balance sheet date, requiring the revision of estimates used in the preparation of the financial statements. Examples of adjusting events include subsequent information affecting provisions for bad debts and amounts received or receivable in respect of insurance claims which were in the course of negotiation at the balance sheet date.

7 Additionally there are certain adjusting events which for statutory reasons or because of their special nature are necessarily or customarily reflected in the financial statements. These include proposed dividends, amounts appropriated to reserves, the effects of changes in taxation on profits earned up to the balance sheet date and dividends receivable from subsidiary and associated companies.

8 Non-adjusting events are events which arise subsequent to the balance sheet date and concern conditions which did not exist at that time. Therefore they do not result in changes in estimates used in preparing financial statements, and should not be provided for within the financial statements. They may, however, be of such materiality that their disclosure is required in notes to the financial statements to ensure that the financial statements do not present a misleading position. Examples of non-adjusting events include the issue of new share or loan capital, major changes in the composition of the company and the financial consequences of losses of fixed assets or stocks as a result of catastrophes such as fire or flood.

Disclosure in financial statements

9 Since adjusting events do no more than provide additional evidence in support of items in financial statements, no separate disclosure of them is normally required.

10 In determining which non-adjusting events are of sufficient materiality to require disclosure, regard should be had to all matters which are necessary to enable users of financial statements to appraise the position of the company.

Part 2 Definition of terms

11 *Financial statements* are balance sheets, income statements, profit and loss accounts and such other statements and notes which are intended to give a true and fair view of financial position and profit or loss.

12 *Company* includes a partnership, association or business enterprise which comes within the scope of statements of standard accounting practice.

13 *Directors* include the corresponding officers of organisations which do not have directors.

14 *Post balance sheet events* are those significant events, both favourable and unfavourable, which occur between the balance sheet date and the date on which financial statements are approved by the directors.

15 *Adjusting events* are post balance sheet events which provide evidence of conditions existing at the balance sheet date which need to be reflected in the financial statements.

16 *Non-adjusting events* are post balance sheet events which concern conditions which did not exist at the balance sheet date. They do not result in a revision of the amounts shown in the financial statements, but they need to be disclosed by way of notes to the financial statements.

Part 3 Proposed standard accounting practice

17 Financial statements should be prepared on the basis of conditions existing at the balance sheet date. Post balance sheet events ('adjusting events') leading to a revision of amounts to be included in the financial statements should be taken account of where:
    (a) the events provide additional evidence with respect to conditions that existed at the balance sheet date and affect the estimates used in preparing the financial statements; or
    (b) the adjustment is required because of statutory or conventional requirements.

18 Disclosure should be made in notes to the financial statements of other post balance sheet events ('non-adjusting events') which:
    (a) do not affect the condition of assets or liabilities at the balance sheet date, but do represent abnormal changes to them since that date; or
    (b) do not relate to the financial position at the balance sheet date, but are of such importance that their non-disclosure would affect the ability of the users of the financial statements to make proper evaluations.

19 In respect of events occurring after the balance sheet date which require disclosure the following information should be provided (by way of supplementary statements if appropriate) :
    (a) a description of the nature of the event;
    (b) an estimate of the financial effect, or a statement that such an estimate cannot be made.

Date from which effective

20 The accounting practices set out in this statement should be
adopted as soon as possible and regarded as standard in respect of
financial statements relating to accounting periods beginning on or after
(date to be inserted after exposure).

Accounting for contingencies

Contents

Accounting for contingencies

The provisions of this statement of standard accounting practice should be read in conjunction with the Explanatory Foreword to accounting standards and need not be applied to immaterial items.

The following subjects are excluded from the scope of this Statement:
  (a) Obligations under pension plans – a separate Standard "Accounting for Pension Costs in Company Accounts" currently under preparation will include this subject.
  (b) Commitments arising from long term hire or lease contracts – separate Standards dealing with Accounting for Leases currently under preparation will include this subject.

Part 1 Explanatory note

1 The term contingency used in this Statement is restricted to a condition or situation which exists at the balance sheet date, the ultimate outcome of which, gain or loss, will be confirmed only on the occurrence or non-occurrence of one or more substantially uncertain future events. The term does not include a condition or situation normally accounted for under the accruals and/or prudence concepts of SSAP2 'Disclosure of accounting policies'.

2 Other contingencies may arise between the balance sheet date and the date on which the financial statements are approved by the directors. Such contingencies are post balance sheet events which will be dealt with in the standard "Accounting for Post Balance Sheet Events".

3 Contingencies existing at the balance sheet date need to be taken into consideration when preparing financial statements if their outcome could affect the financial position of the company. The assessments of the outcome and of the financial effect of contingencies are determined by the judgement of the management of the company. This judgement is based on consideration of information available up to the date on which the financial statements are approved by the directors and will include a review of events occurring after the balance sheet date, supplemented by experience of similar transactions and, in appropriate cases, reports from independent experts.

Accounting treatment and disclosure

4 The treatment of a contingency existing at the balance sheet date is determined by its expected outcome.

5 Provision for losses will normally be accrued in the financial statements, under the fundamental accounting concepts of SSAP2, where it is probable that a future event will confirm a loss which can be estimated with reasonable accuracy at the date on which the financial statements are approved by the directors.

6 Gains dependent upon a future event whose occurrence is substantially uncertain will not be accrued in the financial statements but will be accounted for if and when the event occurs. The existence and nature of a contingent gain should be disclosed in the financial statements if it is appropriate to do so in order to ensure that the financial statements do not present a misleading position.

7 A contingent loss which is not dealt with under the accruals concept should be disclosed in the financial statements in order to ensure that they do not present a misleading position. Such disclosure may include :
   (a) a possible amount, in excess of that accrued in the financial statements, relating to a particular condition or situation ; or
   (b) a loss which cannot justifiably be accrued in the financial statements due to the uncertainty of a future event ; or
   (c) special circumstances which require explanation.

8 In determining which contingent losses are of sufficient materiality to require disclosure in the financial statements regard should be had to all matters which are necessary to enable users of the financial statements to appraise the position of the company. The nature of the contingency should be disclosed together with an estimate of the amount of possible loss. Where a reliable estimate of the financial effect cannot be made, this fact should be disclosed.

9 A potential loss to an enterprise may be reduced or avoided because a contingent liability is matched by a related counter-claim or claim against a third party. In such cases the amount of any accrual under the accounting concepts of SSAP2 or the amount to be disclosed in the financial statements may be determined after taking into account the probable recovery under the claim. However, the likelihood of success, and the probable amount of the claim and the counter-claim should be separately assessed, and separately disclosed where appropriate.

10 In evaluating the amount of a contingency regard should be had to the special circumstances of each situation, and, where relevant, whether the amount should be stated before or after taking account of tax relief or tax charge. As an example, in the case of a substantial legal claim against a company the factors to be considered would include the progress of the claim at the date on which the financial statements are approved by the directors, the opinions of legal experts or other advisers, the experience of the company in similar cases and the experience of other companies in similar situations.

11 Where the uncertainties which create a contingency in respect of an individual transaction are common to a large number of similar transactions, the amount of the contingency need not be individually determined but may be based on the group of similar transactions and the separate transactions which may result in a loss need not be identified.

12 This standard should be read with reference to Part 4, Note of legal requirements.

Part 2 Definition of terms

13 *Financial Statements* are balance sheets, profit and loss accounts, statements of source and application of funds, notes and other statements, which collectively are intended to give a true and fair view of financial position and profit or loss.

14 *Company* includes any enterprise which comes within the scope of statements of standard accounting practice.

15 *Directors* include the corresponding officers of organisations which do not have directors.

16 *Contingency* is a condition or situation which exists at the balance sheet date, where :

(a) the ultimate outcome, gain or loss, will be confirmed only on the occurrence or non-occurrence of one or more substantially uncertain future events ; and

(b) the gain or loss is not accounted for in accordance with the accruals and/or prudence concepts of SSAP2 'Disclosure of accounting policies'.

Part 3 Proposed standard accounting practice

17 The existence of a contingent gain or loss should be disclosed in the financial statements.

18 In respect of contingencies which require disclosure the following information should be provided :
(a) the nature of the condition or situation existing at the balance sheet date ;
(b) the uncertainties which affect the future outcome ; and
(c) an estimate of the financial effect made at the date on which the financial statements are approved by the directors ; or a statement that such an estimate cannot be made.

19 The date on which the financial statements are approved by the directors should be disclosed in the financial statements.

Date from which effective

20 The accounting practices set out in this statement should be adopted as soon as possible and regarded as standard in respect of financial statements relating to accounting periods beginning on or after (date to be inserted after exposure).

Part 4 Note of legal requirements

21 Paragraph 11 (5) of Schedule 2 to the Companies Act 1967, paragraph 11 (4) of Schedule 6 to the Companies Act 1963 (Republic of Ireland) and paragraph 11 (5) of Schedule 2 to the Companies (Northern Ireland) Order 1978 require the following to be stated by way of note, or in a statement or report annexed, if not otherwise shown :
"The general nature of any other contingent liabilities not provided for and, where practicable, the aggregate amount or estimated amount of those liabilities, if it is material".
Insurance companies may avail themselves of certain exemptions in this field (see paragraph 24 of Schedule 2 to the Companies Act 1967, paragraph 24 of Schedule 6 to the Companies Act 1963 (Republic of Ireland) and paragraph 24 of Schedule 2 to the Companies (Northern Ireland) Order 1978). However, such exemptions are modified in respect of returns prepared and filed by insurance companies in accordance with

the Insurance Companies Act 1974, the Insurance Acts 1909-1971 (Republic of Ireland) and the Insurance Companies (Northern Ireland) Order 1976.

Part 5 Compliance with International Accounting Standard no. 10 'Contingencies and events occuring after the balance sheet date'

22 Compliance with the requirements of Statement of Standard Accounting Practice No.   ACCOUNTING FOR CONTINGENCIES will automatically ensure compliance with International Accounting Standard No. 10 CONTINGENCIES AND EVENTS OCCURRING AFTER THE BALANCE SHEET DATE as far as contingencies are concerned.

Accounting for the results of associated companies

Contents

Accounting for the results of associated companies
(Issued 29 October 1979)

The provisions of this proposed statement of standard accounting practice should be read in conjunction with the Explanatory Foreword to accounting standards and need not be applied to immaterial items.

Part 1   Explanatory note

1 Statement of Standard Accounting Practice 1 'Accounting for the Results of Associated Companies' was issued in January 1971 to introduce a uniform accounting treatment for investments in companies, the policies of which, although they are not subsidiaries of the investing company, are subject to significant influence by the investing company.

2 It is accepted accounting practice for a company not to take credit in its own (i.e. non-consolidated) profit and loss account and balance sheet for its share of the profits of other companies (subsidiary or otherwise) which have not been distributed. The view is taken that the inclusion of undistributed profits would ignore the separate legal entities of the companies concerned and, as regards the investing company, be in breach of the principle that credit should not be taken for investment income until it is received or receivable.

3 However, where a company conducts an important part of its business through the medium of other companies, whether more or less than 50% owned, the mere disclosure of dividend income (or mere inclusion of dividend income alone) is unlikely to be sufficient to give shareholders adequate information regarding the sources of their income and of the manner in which their funds are being employed.

4 At one time such operations were usually carried out through the medium of subsidiary companies. It was for this reason that companies legislation required the preparation of group accounts, normally in the form of consolidated accounts. At the time of the original standard there had been two important developments. One was the growing practice of companies to conduct parts of their business through other companies

61

(frequently consortium or joint venture companies) in which they had a substantial but not a controlling interest. The other was the importance which investors have come to attach to earnings per share and the price/earnings ratio (P/E ratio). To ensure that the investing company's accounts as a whole gave adequate information, and provided a total of earnings from which the most meaningful ratios could be calculated, it was considered necessary that the coverage of consolidated accounts should be extended to include (within the framework of the existing law) the share of earnings or losses of companies which were described in the standard as associated companies.

5 This approach recognised a difference in principle between the nature of investments in associated companies (as defined in the standard) and other forms of trade investment. The essence of the distinction was that the investing company actively participates in the commercial and policy decisions of its associated companies; it thus has a measure of direct responsibility for the return on its investment, and should account for its stewardship accordingly, whereas it will not normally seek to exert direct management influence over the operating policy of other companies in which it invests, and should continue to deal with them in accordance with traditional accounting methods.

6 The broad concept underlying the accounting treatment of the results of associated companies was the adoption in modified form of the consolidation procedures used for subsidiary companies. It followed from this that the investing group's share of associated companies' profits and losses would be reflected in its consolidated profit and loss account, and its share of their post-acquisition retained profits or surplus would be reflected in its consolidated balance sheet, though not in its own balance sheet as a legal entity.

7 As part of its normal programme of reviewing standards the Accounting Standards Committee (ASC) reconsidered the principles contained in SSAP 1 during 1979, meanwhile SSAP 1 continues in force.

8 The proposed standard continues the basic principles and requirements of the original standard. However, as part of the review ASC has incorporated some changes both in the definition of an associate and the presentation of the information involved.

9 The proposed standard has been drafted to apply to companies incorporated under the Companies Acts. The principles laid down in it are, nevertheless, applicable to financial statements of any entity, whether incorporated or not, which invests in another entity or entities.

Part 2   Definition of terms

10 *A company* includes any enterprise which comes within the scope of statements of standard accounting practice.

11 *A group* is a holding company and its subsidiaries.

12 *An associated company* is a company not being a subsidiary of the investing group or company in which:
>
> (a) the investing group or company's interest is effectively that of a partner in a joint venture or consortium and the investing group or company is in a position to exercise a significant influence over the associated company; or
>
> (b) the investing group or company's interest is for the long term and is substantial, and, having regard to the disposition of the other shareholdings, the investing group or company is in a position to exercise a significant influence over the associated company.

Significant influence over a company essentially involves participation in the financial and operating policy decisions of that company (including dividend policy) but not necessarily control of those policies. Representation on the board of directors is indicative of such participation, but will neither necessarily give conclusive evidence of it nor be the only method by which the investing company may participate.

13 Where the investing group or company holds 20% or more of the equity voting rights of a company, it should be presumed that the investing group or company has the ability to exercise significant influence over that company unless it can clearly be demonstrated that the investing group or company is not in a position to exercise significant influence. For example, there may exist one or more other large shareholdings which prevent the investing company exerting such influence.

14 Where there is an investment by the investing group or company in less than 20% of the equity voting rights of a company it should be presumed that the investing group or company does not have the ability to exercise significant influence unless the investing group or company can clearly demonstrate, and the associate concurs, that it is in a position to exercise significant influence under the terms of this standard.

15 Where different companies in a group hold shares in a company, for the purposes of establishing whether or not significant influence is presumed to exist, the investment in that company should be taken as the aggregate of the holdings of the investing company together with those of its subsidiaries but not its associates.

16 Use of the term 'associated company' should be restricted to the meaning defined in this standard.

Part 3　　Proposed standard accounting practice

Bases of accounting for associated companies

17 Income from investments by a company or its subsidiaries in associated companies (as defined in Part 2 above) should be brought into account on the following bases:
  (a) In the investing company's own accounts: the dividends received or receivable by the investing company.
  (b) In the investing group's consolidated accounts (see paragraph 23): the investing group's share of profits less losses of associated companies.

Profit and loss account items*

18 *Profit before tax.* The investing group should include in its consolidated accounts the aggregate of its share of before-tax profits less losses of associated companies. The item should be shown separately and suitably described, for example as 'share of profits less losses of associated companies'.

19 *Taxation.* The tax attributed to the share of profits of associated companies should be disclosed separately within the group tax charge in the consolidated accounts.

*Examples of profit and loss accounts drawn up to give the information required are shown in Appendices 1 & 2

20 *Extraordinary items.* The investing group's share of aggregate extraordinary items dealt with in associated companies' accounts should be included with the group share of extraordinary items, unless the amount is material in the context of the group's results when it should be separately disclosed.

21 *Net profit retained by associated companies.* There should be shown separately the investing group's share of aggregate net profits less losses retained by associated companies.

22 *Other items.* The investing group should not include its attributable share of associated companies' items, such as turnover and depreciation, in the aggregate amounts of these items disclosed in its consolidated accounts. Where the results of one or more associated companies are material in the context of the investing group's accounts such additional information should be given by way of notes to the accounts. In judging materiality regard should be had not merely to the group's share of the net profit of an associated company but also to the scale of its operations in relation to those of the group.

23 An investing company (other than a wholly owned subsidiary), which does not prepare consolidated accounts, should show the above information by adapting its own profit and loss account if practicable, or by preparing a separate profit and loss account. References in this Statement to investing groups and consolidated accounts are to be taken as embracing such additional information in the case of investing companies which do not have subsidiaries or which do not otherwise prepare consolidated accounts.

Balance sheet items*

24 Unless shown at a valuation, the amount at which the investing company's interests in associated companies should be shown in the investing company's own accounts is the cost of the investment less any amounts written off.

*An example of a consolidated balance sheet drawn up to give the information required is shown in Appendix 3

25 The amount at which the investing group's interests in associated companies should be shown in the consolidated balance sheet is the total of:

- (a) the investing group's share of the net assets other than goodwill of the associated companies stated, where possible, after attributing fair values to the net assets at the time of acquisition of the interest in an associated company, and
- (b) the investing group's share of the goodwill of the associated companies together with
- (c) the premium paid (or discount) on the acquisition of the interests in the associated companies.

Item (a) should be disclosed separately but items (b) and (c) may be shown as one aggregate amount.

26 Loans between associated companies and the group should be separately disclosed in the consolidated balance sheet together with the group's interests in the associates. Amounts owed by associated companies to the investing group should not be netted against amounts owed by the investing group to other associated companies.

27 Balances representing normal trading transactions between the associated companies and the investing group should be included under current assets or liabilities as appropriate, with separate disclosure if material in the context of the investing group's accounts.

28 More detailed information about the associated companies' tangible and intangible assets and liabilities should be given if the interests in the associated companies are material in the context of the investing group's accounts. In judging materiality, regard should be had not merely to the net carrying amount of the investment in an associated company, but also to the scale of its operations in relation to those of the group.

29 The amount at which the investing group's interests in accumulated reserves is shown in the consolidated accounts should distinguish between profits retained by the group and profits retained by associated companies. If retained profits of associated companies overseas would be subject to further tax on distribution, this should be made clear. It will also be necessary to take account of and disclose movements on associated companies' other reserves, e.g. surplus on revaluation of fixed assets.

30 Where there has been permanent impairment in the value of any goodwill (including any premium paid on acquisition) attributable to an investment in an associated company, it should be written down. Because an impairment in the value of the underlying net assets would normally be reflected in the books of the associate, further provision against the investing company or group's share of these net assets should only be made in exceptional circumstances. A possible example is where there is no likelihood of the associated company being profitable in the future and the carrying value cannot be recovered.

31 Paragraph 5A of the Second Schedule to the Companies Act 1967 and paragraph 5A of the Second Schedule to the Companies (Northern Ireland) Order 1978 both include a reference to the use of the valuation basis for investments. Although this basis may be appropriate for trade investments its use for associated companies should be restricted in the consolidated accounts to the adjustments outlined in paragraph 30.

32 Any amounts written off during the period should be separately disclosed.

33 An investing company (other than a wholly owned subsidary) which does not prepare consolidated accounts, should show the above information by way of note to the balance sheet or by preparing a separate balance sheet.

Inclusion of associated companies' results in consolidated accounts of investing group

34 The accounts used for the purpose of including associated companies' results should be either coterminous with those of the investing company or made up to a date which is not more than six months before, or shortly after, the date of the investing group or company's accounts. In the case of associated companies which are listed on a recognised stock exchange, only published financial information should be disclosed in the accounts of the investing company.

35 Before incorporating results of an associated company based on accounts issued some appreciable time before the completion of the accounts of the investing company, care should be taken to ensure that later information has not materially affected the view shown by the accounts of the associated company. If accounts not coterminous with those of the investing company are used, the facts and the dates of year-ends should be disclosed.

36 Where the investing group or company holds 20% or more of the equity voting rights of any company other than a subsidiary and does not account for that company as an associated company, details of the accounting treatment adopted, and the reason for doing so, should be stated by way of note to the financial statements; conversely, where the investing group or company holds less than 20% of the equity voting rights of a company but accounts for that company as an associate, the basis on which significant influence is exercised should be stated.

Accounting adjustments

37 Wherever the effect is material, adjustments similar to those adopted for the purpose of presenting consolidated accounts should be made to exclude from the investing group's consolidated accounts such items as unrealised profits on stocks transferred to or from associated companies and to achieve reasonable consistency with the accounting practices adopted by the investing group.

Restrictions on distribution

38 If there are significant restrictions on the ability of an associated company to distribute its retained profits (other than those shown as non-distributable) because of statutory, contractual or exchange control restrictions the extent of the restrictions should be indicated.

Minority interests

39 Where the investment in an associated company is held by an investing company's subsidiary in which there are minority interests, the minority interests shown in the consolidated accounts of the investing company should include the minority share of the subsidiary's interest in the results and net assets of the associated companies.

Investments by associates

40 Where an associated company itself has subsidiary or associated companies, the profits or losses to be dealt with in the investing group's consolidated accounts are its attributable proportion of the profits or losses of the group of which the associated company is the parent.

Deficiency of net assets

41 Where an associated company has a deficiency of net assets but is still regarded as a long term investment it will usually have been supported by loans from the shareholders or by agreement, either formal or informal, to support it. In these circumstances, the investing company should reflect its share of the deficiency of net assets in its consolidated accounts.

Change of status

42 When an investment in a company ceases to fall within the definition of an associated company, an amount equal to the carrying value of that company treated as an associate at that date should be treated as the effective cost of the investment and no further account should be taken of the company's share of subsequent profits and losses. However, provision should be made against the investment if there has been any impairment in value.

Effective date of acquisition or disposal

43 The effective date for accounting for both acquisition and disposal of an associate should be the earlier of:
      (a) the date on which consideration passes; or
      (b) the date on which an offer becomes unconditional.
This applies even if the acquiring company has the right under the agreement to share in the profits of the acquired business from an earlier date.

Disclosure of particulars of associated companies

44 Subject to parts 4 and 5, the names of the principal associated companies should be disclosed in the group accounts showing for each of these associated companies:
      (a) the proportion of the nominal value of the issued shares of
          each class held by the group; and
      (b) an indication of the nature of its business.

Corresponding amounts

45 On first introduction of the amended standard method of accounting set out in this Statement the corresponding amounts for the preceding period should be appropriately stated on a comparable basis.

69

Date from which effective

46 The amended method of accounting for the results of associated companies set out in this Statement should be adopted as soon as possible and regarded as standard in respect of reports relating to accounting periods starting on or after (date to be inserted after exposure).

Part 4   Note on legal requirements in Great Britain

47 Paragraph 5A of Schedule 2 to the Companies Act 1967 requires certain information to be given about unlisted equity investments in the absence of a directors' valuation. The information required to be given by this Statement may not fully satisfy the requirements of the Act. To that extent it will be necessary either to re-arrange the information appropriately or, if this is impracticable, to provide it by way of a separate note.

48 In dealing with the results of associated companies, regard should be had to the provisions of paragraph 12(1)(g) of Schedule 2 to the Companies Act 1967, which requires the amounts respectively of income from listed investments and income from unlisted investments to be shown in the profit and loss account.

49 In the case of an associated company which is either incorporated outside the United Kingdom or carries on business outside the United Kingdom, Section 4(3) of the Companies Act 1967 provides that disclosure of a company's name and other particulars need not be made if in the opinion of the directors and with the concurrence of the Department of Trade such disclosures would be harmful.

50 The legal position may be affected by the eventual incorporation of EEC Directives into statute.

Part 5   Note on legal requirements in Ireland

A. Northern Ireland

51 Paragraph 5A of Schedule 2 to the Companies (Northern Ireland) Order 1978 requires certain information to be given about unlisted equity investments in the absence of a directors' valuation. The information required to be given by this statement may not fully satisfy the requirements of the Order. To that extent it will be necessary either to re-arrange the information appropriately or, if this is impracticable, to provide it by way of a separate note.

52 In dealing with the results of associated companies, regard should be had to the provisions of paragraph 12(1)(g) of Schedule 2 to the Companies (Northern Ireland) Order 1978, which requires the amounts respectively of income from listed investments and income from unlisted investments to be shown in the profit and loss account.

53 In the case of an associated company which is either incorporated outside the United Kingdom or carries on business outside the United Kingdom, Article 15(3) of the Companies (Northern Ireland) Order 1978 provides that disclosure of a company's name and other particulars need not be made if in the opinion of the directors and with the concurrence of the Department of Commerce such disclosures would be harmful.

54 The legal position may be affected by the eventual incorporation of EEC Directives into Statute.

N.B. The Companies (Northern Ireland) Order 1978 is coming into operation by stages. Paragraphs 51-53 above assume that the relevant Schedules/Articles will have been implemented by the time the standard becomes effective.

B. Republic of Ireland

55 The obligation to prepare group accounts is set out in section 150(1) of the Companies Act 1963, which refers only to public companies. It should be noted that SSAP 14 'Group Accounts' goes beyond this minimum legal requirement and applies also to private companies. Reference should be made to paragraphs 15 and 56 of SSAP 14.

56 Paragraph 22 of the Statement requires that additional information, including total turnover, should be given about associated companies in certain circumstances. Disclosure of total turnover, which is not mandatory under the Companies Act 1963, is recommended, however, in the interests of informative reporting.

57 The legal position may be affected by the eventual incorporation of the EEC Directives into Statute.

Part 6   Compliance with International Accounting Standard No. 3 'Consolidated Financial Statements'

58 The requirements of International Accounting Standard No. 3 'Consolidated Financial Statements' covering the basis of accounting for associated companies accord very closely with the content of the United Kingdom and Irish Accounting Standard No.   'Accounting for the Results of Associated Companies' and accordingly compliance with SSAP   will ensure compliance with IAS 3 in all material respects.

Appendix 1

Note: This Appendix does not form part of the Statement of Standard Accounting Practice. The method of presentation used is illustrative only and in no way prescriptive. Other methods of presentation may equally comply with the accounting standard set out in the Statement.

Example of consolidated profit and loss account for a company with subsidiaries

Consolidated profit and loss account of an investing company and subsidiaries, incorporating results of associated companies

	£'000	£'000
Turnover (of the investing company and subsidiaries)		2,000
Operating profit (after charging depreciation and all other trading expenses of the investing company and subsidiaries)		300
Share of profits less losses of associated companies		50
Profit before taxation		350
Taxation: Investing company and subsidiaries	85	
Associated companies	15	100
		250
Minority interests		50
Profit after taxation before extraordinary items		200
Extraordinary items (group proportion after taxation, after deducting minority interests and including share of associated companies' items)		20
Profit attributable to members of the investing company (See note)		180
Dividends		80
Net profit retained		100
Investing company		65
Subsidiaries		20
Associated companies		15
		100

Note: Of the profit attributable to members of the investing company, £115,000 is dealt with in the accounts of the investing company.

Appendix 2

Note: This Appendix does not form part of the Statement of Standard Accounting Practice. The method of presentation used is illustrative only and in no way prescriptive. Other methods of presentation may equally comply with the accounting standard set out in the Statement.

Example of profit and loss account for a company without subsidiaries

Profit and loss account of an investing company incorporating results of associated companies

	£'000	£'000
Turnover (of the investing company)		2,000
Operating profit (after charging depreciation and all other trading expenses of the investing company)		300
Share of profits less losses of associated companies		50
Profit before taxation		350
Taxation: Investing company	85	
Associated companies	15	
		100
Profit after taxation before extraordinary items		250
Extraordinary items (investing company and share of associated companies' items) after taxation		20
Profit attributable to members of the investing company comprising:		230
Profit of the investing company	215	
Profits retained in associated companies	15	
	230	
Dividends		80
Net profit retained		150
Investing company		135
Associated companies		15
		150

Appendix 3 ✓

Note: This Appendix does not form part of the Statement of Standard Accounting Practice. The method of presentation used is illustrative only and in no way prescriptive. Other methods of presentation may equally comply with the accounting standard set out in the Statement.

Example of consolidated balance sheet for a company with subsidiaries

Consolidated balance sheet of an investing company and subsidiaries, incorporating results of associated companies

	£'000	£'000
Assets employed:		
Fixed assets		1,500
Interest in associated companies (as shown in note below)		800
Current assets:		
Stocks and work in progress	1,200	
Debtors (including £90,000 due from associated companies)	600	
Bank balances and cash	100	
	1,900	
Current liabilities:		
Bank overdraft	650	
Creditors (including £60,000 due to associated companies)	400	
Taxation	70	
Dividends	80	
	1,200	
Net current assets		700
		3,000
Financed by:		
Share capital		200
Reserves (including £130,000 group share of associated company reserves)		1,000
		1,200
Minority interests in subsidiaries		600
Loan capital		1,000
Deferred tax		200
		3,000

Note: Interest in associated companies

Group's share of net assets other than goodwill	550
Goodwill and premium on acquisition	150
	700
Loans to associated companies	120
	820
Less: Loans from associated companies	20
	800

STATEMENT BY THE ACCOUNTING STANDARDS COMMITTEE ON THE PUBLICATION OF ED25 'ACCOUNTING FOR THE RESULTS OF ASSOCIATED COMPANIES'

In line with current ASC practice a statement has been issued detailing the changes introduced in the exposure draft. The statement is reproduced on the following pages for purposes of convenience only and it does not form part of the exposure draft on which comments are requested.

STATEMENT BY THE
ACCOUNTING STANDARDS COMMITTEE
ON THE PUBLICATION OF ED25
'ACCOUNTING FOR THE RESULTS
OF ASSOCIATED COMPANIES'

1 The first Statement of Standard Accounting Practice issued by the Accounting Standards (Steering) Committee, SSAP 1 'Accounting for the Results of Associated Companies', was published in January 1971.

2 SSAP 1 aimed at the introduction of a standard accounting treatment for companies which carry on a substantial part of their business through major holdings in companies other than subsidiaries. Where such business is carried on through subsidiaries, companies legislation requires group accounts, normally in the form of consolidated accounts. SSAP 1 introduced an amended form of this requirement for holdings of between 20% and 50%.

3 The standard defined an associated company as one in which the investing company's interest was either effectively that of a partner in a joint venture or consortium, or was long term and substantial and over which the investor exercised significant influence. 20% was specified as a minimum holding that should be considered as substantial. Where a company held such investments the standard required that it should include in its consolidated accounts the investing company or group's share of the profits, rather than just the dividends received, of its associated companies. This treatment (now generally known as equity accounting) produces similar results to consolidation except that:

    (a) the assets and liabilities of the associate are not allocated between categories in the investing company's consolidated balance sheet. Similarly, only the profit or loss and tax charge of the associate are reflected in the consolidated profit and loss account of the investing company, items such as turnover of the associate being excluded.

    (b) the investing company only accounts for its own share of the associated company's net assets and profit and consequently no minority interests arise in either the consolidated balance sheet or the consolidated profit and loss account.

4 Although SSAP 1 was at the time innovative, the principles it contains have since been incorporated into recommendations (or statements issued for comment) in several other countries.

5 In June 1976 International Accounting Standard Number 3 'Consolidated Financial Statements' was published. Although this includes accounting requirements for associated companies similar to those contained in SSAP 1, there exist some differences of emphasis in the exact application of the method and the definition of an associated company adopted.

6 The Accounting Standards Committee (ASC) is at present entering on a policy of review of the workings of existing standards. To this end a panel was established during the summer of 1978 to review SSAP 1. Comments on the working of the existing standard were requested in July 1978 to be received by 1 November 1978.

7 Comments were received from 67 organisations and individuals as follows:

Companies	21
Practising Firms	18
Representative Bodies of Accountants	12
Other Representative Bodies	10
Individuals	6
	67

8 It has not been possible to reply in detail to each respondent. However, as well as an acknowledgement, a copy of the full text of all comments received for which the author had not requested confidentiality was sent to each commentator. Copies of these comments were also placed in each of the libraries of the governing bodies of ASC. Comments may be inspected by any member of the public by arrangement with the librarian at the particular location.

9 To provide additional information a confidential two part questionnaire was sent to 500 major listed companies. Replies were received from 172 such companies detailing the treatment of over 650 companies in which they had invested. A number of these also included additional comments on the workings of SSAP 1.

10 The great majority of commentators appear to have been in favour of the treatment of associated companies outlined in SSAP 1, possibly with changes of emphasis in the wording or definitions used. A small number of commentators did, however, disagree with equity accounting as a concept on the grounds of prudence. In the light of general acceptance of the principles, ASC continues to support the basic approach of SSAP 1.

11 Careful consideration has been given to all submissions made, together with correspondence received over the years of operation of SSAP 1, and in the light of the comments and experience, SSAP 1 has been re-drafted. Details of the main points arising from the comments, together with details of changes made in the present exposure draft are given below.

12 The basic concepts of SSAP 1 have not been altered but some sections have been re-written to remove ambiguities from the principles or wording used. In addition, the layout and order of some paragraphs has been amended to be more in line with recent standards. Additional requirements have been introduced where such treatments were thought to convey useful information and be in line with modern needs and trends. In some instances requirements have been relaxed.

13 Three major areas for consideration were identified. These are the definition of an associated company, the profit and loss account treatment and the balance sheet treatment.

14 The amended standard is being issued as an exposure draft and persons interested in financial reporting are urged to submit their comments (critical and favourable) on the exposure draft and the amendments made as soon as possible and at the latest by 31 March 1980.

Definition of associated company

15 The aspect of SSAP 1 which attracted most comment was the definition of an associated company. Amongst the commentators on this subject there exists a complete gradation of views ranging from those in favour of a strict percentage definition (whether more or less than 20%) to those in favour of a definition based purely on significant influence. Most commentators seem agreed, however, that whatever definition is applied the terms used must be clearly explained.

16 ASC now proposes a definition based on significant influence but this has remained linked to a fixed percentage (20%). Holdings above this are presumed to give rise to significant influence unless clear evidence to the contrary can be demonstrated. Conversely, holdings of less than 20% are presumed not to give rise to such influence unless clear evidence to the contrary can be demonstrated and the associated company concurs with the investing company's view that significant influence exists. This represents a change from the previous standard as regards the definition of an associated company in the case of holdings of less than 20%. It is, however, essentially the same as the definitions contained in the International Standard and the American pronouncement (APB 18).

17 Clarification that holdings by a subsidiary of the investing company are to be aggregated with the investing company's own holding for the purposes of assessing whether or not 20% of the equity voting capital is held, is given in paragraph 15 of the exposure draft. Holdings by associates, or even a proportion of such holdings, should not be so aggregated.

18 References to a requirement that the accounts on which the amounts included for associated companies' results are based should be audited, have been deleted; this is an auditing matter rather than an accounting matter.

19 A requirement for disclosure of the reason for treating a less than 20% owned investment as an associate, or not so treating a greater than 20% owned investment, has been added.

20 As the only grounds upon which equity accounting should not be used for an associate in the consolidated accounts of the investing company in effect relate to the materiality of the associate's results to those of the investing company, and as materiality is covered in the Explanatory Foreword to accounting standards, it is proposed that any reference to such circumstances should be omitted.

21 Where a company has subsidiaries but does not prepare consolidated accounts by reason of being a wholly owned subsidiary, the requirement for that company to account for its associates on the equity accounting basis has been removed from the standard. This is a logical extension of the statutory exemption for subsidiaries and the treatment outlined in SSAP 14.

22 The term 'company' has been extended to include other non-corporate enterprises.

Profit and loss account treatment

23 Several commentators favoured the inclusion of the group's share of the associated companies' turnover within the group turnover. They argue that there is distortion in some turnover based ratios if the turnover of the associates is omitted; however, such distortions do not occur if the ratios are calculated on the basis of the group excluding the results of the associates. Other commentators argued for disclosure of the group's share of such items as depreciation and interest.

24 ASC considers that the group's share of the profits of an associate is of a different quality from those of the other constituents of the group and is best shown in the form of a single entry in the consolidated profit and loss account of the investing group. Specifically, it is inconsistent to show balance sheet related items such as depreciation when the carrying value is not sub-divided into items such as fixed assets. Consequently, ASC proposes that no change be made in this respect but has emphasised the need to disclose additional information concerning an associate where it is material.

25 The basis for judging materiality for such disclosure has been further defined so as to include the materiality of the scale of the operations of the associate as distinct from just the net amount of the group's share of its results or its carrying value.

26 As with subsidiaries, no credit should be taken in the investing company's own accounts for unrealised profits in the form of undistributed income of an associate. Consequently, the accounting adjustments required to reflect the investor's share of the retained profits of an associate should be made in the consolidated accounts and not in the parent company's own profit and loss account. Where an investing company (other than a wholly owned subsidiary) does not prepare consolidated accounts it will be necessary for it to adapt its own profit and loss account or to prepare an additional one to reflect the results of associated companies.

Balance sheet presentation

27 A requirement for the separation of the goodwill element of the cost of an associated company within the balance sheet has been introduced. This includes both goodwill retained in the associated company's own balance sheet and the premium (or discount) arising on acquisition of the associate. The latter should be calculated, where possible, after attributing fair values to the net assets of the associate. This requirement is consistent with the treatment specified for subsidiaries in paragraph 29 of SSAP 14 'Group Accounts'.

28 No accounting treatment has been specified for the goodwill so identified but it is envisaged that the treatment will be the same as that adopted for goodwill arising on consolidation.

29 As loans to associated companies from the investor (or vice versa) form part of the long term investment in the associates, a requirement has been included for any such amounts to be shown with the carrying value of the associated companies.

30 Similarly, it is felt that balances representing normal trading transactions should be disclosed if material. However, these should be shown as current items, not with the carrying value of the associated companies.

31 The basis on which materiality is judged with regard to disclosure of more detailed information of the associated companies' assets and liabilities has been extended to the individual items concerned.

32 Many commentators were in favour of the inclusion of a requirement to write down the carrying value of an associated company when it can be shown that there has been a reduction in fair value of the investment below the carrying value, which is other than temporary in nature.

33 ASC is of the opinion that any such adjustment should be made first against the goodwill element of the carrying value. As with subsidiaries a write down of the carrying value beyond the amount of the net assets is only likely to occur in exceptional circumstances such as the expectation of the absence of future profits of an associate.

34 Paragraph 5A of the Second Schedule to the Companies Act 1967 and paragraph 5A of the Second Schedule to the Companies (Northern Ireland) Order 1978 both include a reference to the use of the valuation basis for investments. ASC is of the opinion that, although this basis may be appropriate for the trade investments, its use for associated companies in consolidated accounts should be restricted to the adjustments outlined in paragraph 33 above (although details of a different valuation could be given by way of a note to the accounts). This is because the valuation basis is thought to be inconsistent with the principles of consolidation.

35 The proposed standard includes reference to the situation where there exists a deficiency of net assets in an associated company. In such a situation it will only be realistic to continue to consider that investment as long term (and consequently as an associate) if some means of support, either formal or informal, is provided in that company by the investing company. In these circumstances, the investing company should continue to reflect its share of the deficiency in its own accounts.

36 A consolidated balance sheet drawn up as an example of one possible method of presentation of the required information has been added as Appendix 3 to the standard. As with other appendices this does not form part of the standard and is not prescriptive.

37 Where an investor does not prepare consolidated accounts it should show the required information by way of note to the balance sheet or by preparing a separate balance sheet.

Procedure on first introduction of an amended standard

38 Where an associated company has been held for some time, it may not be possible to attribute fair values to the net assets acquired at the original date of acquisition, for the purposes of paragraph 25 of the exposure draft. In such a case it will be appropriate to use the book amounts at the time of acquisition and, as envisaged in paragraph 25, to show goodwill and premium paid on the acquisition as one aggregate amount.

Legal requirements in Ireland

39 A note on the legal requirements in Ireland has been added as part 5.

Compliance with international standards

40 Although the wording of the exposure draft differs in some respects from that included in IAS 3, ASC is of the opinion that compliance with an amended standard based on the draft would automatically ensure compliance in all material respects with the provisions covering the basis of accounting for associated companies contained in IAS 3.

Section Three
The texts of Technical Releases and other statements
published during the year to 1st June 1980 are
reproduced is this section.

Notice of public hearings 'Setting Accounting Standards'

(11 May 1979— TR341)

1. The Accounting Standards Committee (ASC) published a consultative document in September 1978 entitled *Setting Accounting Standards*. Persons interested in financial reporting were invited to submit their written comments to the ASC by 31st March 1979. 126 submissions have been received and the ASC is grateful to those who made them for the care they have taken and for the high quality of the submissions.

2. The ASC believes that public hearings should now be held. The purpose of these hearings is to give the members of the ASC an opportunity to gain a fuller understanding of the written submissions. This will be done by hearing short oral statements from interested persons and by questioning those persons on their submissions.

3. The public hearings will be held on Thursday, 5th July 1979 in Glasgow, Wednesday, 11th July 1979 in Dublin and Thursday, 19th July 1979 in London. The London hearing will continue if necessary on Friday, 20th July 1979. Hearings may be extended to such additional date or dates as the chairman of the hearings may in his discretion deem appropriate. The hearings will begin at 9.30 a.m.

4. Any individual or organisation may ask to be heard at the public hearing. As a general rule the ASC will accept the requests of only those individuals or organisations who have made written submissions on the consultative document. Any individual or organisation wishing to be heard should notify the Secretary of ASC, P.O. Box 433, Chartered Accountants' Hall, Moorgate Place, London EC2P 2BJ, not later than 8th June 1979. The notification should be in writing, should state whether the applicant wishes to be heard in Glasgow, Dublin or London, and should be accompanied by 10 copies of the proposed oral presentation or an outline of it.

5. The time alloted to each individual or organisation will be limited generally to 30 minutes. The chairman of the hearings may, however, allow more or less time at his discretion.

6. The ASC wishes to devote most of the time at the hearings to questioning those making oral presentations. Accordingly, not more than

10 minutes should be taken up with oral presentations, which should normally be confined to emphasising a point or points made in earlier written submissions or in commenting very briefly on submissions made by others. The ASC members at the hearings will be familiar with the written submissions already made by the presenter.

7. Each person making an oral presentation will be notified as soon as practicable after 8th June 1979, of the time it is expected that he or she will be called upon to make the presentation and the time expected to be allowed.

8. The public hearings will be open to the public including representatives of the press.

9. The public hearings will be conducted by one or more members of the ASC, one of whom will be chairman of the hearing. The chairman of the hearing has full authority with respect to its conduct including, without limitation, authority to adjourn and extend the hearings and to make all rulings he deems appropriate in his own discretion.

Notice of public hearings on ED24 Current cost Accounting
(3 August 1979— TR352)

1. The Accounting Standards Committee (ASC) published Exposure Draft 24 *Current Cost Accounting* on 30th April 1979. Persons interested in financial reporting are invited to submit their written comments on the exposure draft to the ASC by 31st October 1979.

2. The ASC believes that public hearings should now be held. The purpose of these hearings is to allow interested persons to present their views in public and to give members of the ASC an opportunity to gain a fuller understanding of these views.

3. The public hearings will be held on 4th, 5th and 8th October, 1979 in London, 30th October in Dublin and 1st November in Glasgow. Hearings may be extended to such additional date or dates as the chairman of the hearings may in his discretion deem appropriate. The hearings will begin at 9.30 a.m.

4. Any individual or organisation may ask to be heard at the public hearings. Those wishing to appear should notify the Secretary of ASC, P.O. Box 433, Chartered Accountants' Hall, Moorgate Place, London EC2P 2BJ, not later than 10th September 1979. The notification should be in writing and should state whether the applicant wishes to be heard in London, Dublin or Glasgow. On or before 19th September 1979, the applicant must deliver to the Secretary of the ASC (a) his written submission on ED24 or a preliminary submission in sufficient detail to enable his viewpoint to be understood, and (b) an outline of the proposed oral presentation. If the written submission and the outline presentation are not received by 19th September 1979, the request to be heard will be deemed to be cancelled.

5. The members of the panel hearing the submissions will be drawn from members of the ASC and the Inflation Accounting Steering Group. The time allotted to each individual or organisation will be limited generally to 30 minutes. The chairman of the hearings may, however, allow more or less time at his discretion.

6. The ASC wishes to devote most of the time at the hearings to questioning those making oral presentations. Accordingly, not more than 10 minutes should be taken up with oral presentations, which should normally be confined to emphasising a point or points made in earlier written submissions or in commenting very briefly on submissions made by others. The panel members at the hearings will be familiar with the written submissions already made by the presenter.

7. Each person making an oral presentation will be notified as soon as practicable after 10th September 1979, of the time it is expected that he or she will be called upon to make the presentation and the time expected to be allowed.

8. The hearings will be open to the public including representatives of the press.

9. The chairman of the hearing has full authority with respect to its conduct including, without limitation, authority to adjourn and extend the hearings and to make all rulings he deems appropriate in his own discretion.

Programme for public hearings on ED24 Current Cost Accounting

(15th October 1979 — TR363)

1. The full programme for the hearings which the Accounting Standards Committee is holding to allow interested persons to present their views in public on ED24 Current cost accounting will be as follows:

Dublin   Tue. 30 Oct. 1979 The Library
            9.30 a.m. (start)   The Institute of Chartered
                             Accountants in Ireland
                             7 Fitzwilliam Place
                             Dublin

Glasgow Thu. 1 Nov. 1979 The Central Hotel
            2.30 p.m. (start)   Gordon Street
                             Glasgow G1 3SP

London   Mon. 5 Nov. 1979 The Council Chamber
            Fri. 9 Nov. 1979   The Association of Certified Accountants
                             29 Lincoln's Inn Fields
            9.30 a.m. (start)   London WC2A 3EE

2. A list of the persons making presentations at each of the hearings, together with the approximate time at which they are expected to be heard, is shown on the attached schedule.

3. Any member of the public may attend the hearings, and tickets are not required.

4. The collected submissions and outlines of the oral presentations are now available for each day of the hearings, free of charge, from the Secretary of the Accounting Standards Committee.

Dublin   The Library, Institute of Chartered Accountants in Ireland, 7 Fitzwilliam Place, Dublin, Ireland.

            Tuesday 30 October 1979

ASC Panel
            T. R. Watts (Chairman)
            D. S. Morpeth
            N. MacMahon
            D. G. Sherriff

9.30	Jan de Jong	(Unilever)
10.00	V. Hilary-Hough	(Leinster Society of Certified Accountants)
10.30	E. A. Whiting	(Manchester Business School)
11.15	J. W. Miley	(Miley & Co.)
11.45	T. K. McGovern	(Financial Executives' Association)
12.15	J. P. Kavanagh	(Leinster Society of Chartered Accountants)
2.30	E. Grace	(Manchester Business School)
3.00	J. J. Hyland and	
	L. G. Quinn	(Institute of Chartered Accountants in Ireland)
3.45	A. Packenham-Walsh	(University of Dublin)

Glasgow   The Central Hotel, Gordon Street, Glasgow G1 35F

Thursday 1 November 1979

ASC Panel

T. R. Watts (Chairman)
D. S. Morpeth
I. M. Bowie
L. T. Miller

Presenters

2.30	J. Baillie	(Thomson McLintock & Co.)
3.00	Prof. R. B. Jack	(Law Society of Scotland)
3.45	R. K. Perkin	(Arthur Young McLelland Moores & Co.)
4.15	Prof. J. Grinyer	(Dundee University)
4.45	Dr. S. D. Howell	(Manchester Business School)

London   The Council Chamber, Association of Certified Accountants, 29 Lincoln's Inn Fields, London WC2A 3EE

Monday 5 November 1979

ASC Panel

T. R. Watts (Chairman)
D. S. Morpeth
W. Hyde (a.m.)
A. Morrison (a.m.)
P. M. D Gibbs (p.m.)
K. J. Sharp (p.m.)

Presenters

Time	Presenter	Affiliation
9.30	G. H. Stacy	(Price Waterhouse & Co.)
10.00	K. Percy	(Society of Investment Analysts)
10.30	S. Sedgwick	(London & Overseas Freighters Limited.
11.15	D. H. Cairns	(Stoy Hayward & Co.)
11.45	H. P. Gold and	
	Dr. J. M. Boersema	(Royal Dutch/Shell)
12.15	Dr. D. Rudd	(Chartered Engineer)
2.30	J. B. Stevenson	(Touche Ross & Co.)
3.00	K. A. Sherwood	(Chalmers Impey & Co.)
3.45	R. J. Foot	(Eddison Plant Limited)
4.15	P. J. Tombleson	—
4.45	D. Morley	(Engineering Employers' Federation)

Friday 9 November 1979

ASC Panel

T. R. Watts (Chairman)
D. S. Morpeth
H. C. Edey (a.m.)
B. D. G. Ogle (a.m.)
A. W. Nelson (p.m.)
K. G. Bishop (p.m.)

Presenters

Time	Presenter	Affiliation
9.30	P. R. Hinton	(Arthur Andersen & Co.)
10.00	Prof. D. R. Myddleton	(Cranfield School of Management)
10.30	D. Allen	(Cadbury Typhoo Limited)
11.15	Prof. G. H. Lawson	(Manchester Business School)
11.45	J. W. L. Nichols	(Richard Clay & Company Limited)
12.15	W. O'Farrell	(Young Chartered Accountants' Group)
2.30	P. R. W. Whyman	—
3.00	G. H. S. Archer	(London Business School)
3.45	M. N. Haslam and	
	K. D. Keymer	(Keymer Haslam & Co.)
4.15	A. N. Byford	(Chartered Engineer)

Statement by the Accounting Standards Committee on the publication of ED25 'Accounting for the Results of Associationed Companies'

(29th October 1979)

1. The first Statement of Standard Accounting Practice issued by the Accounting Standards (Steering) Committee, SSAP1 *Accounting for the results of associated companies,* was published in January 1971.

2. SSAP1 aimed at the introduction of a standard accounting treatment for companies which carry on a substantial part of their business through major holdings in companies other than subsidiaries. Where such business is carried on through subsidiaries, companies legislation requires group accounts, normally in the form of consolidated accounts. SSAP1 introduced an amended form of this requirement for holdings of between 20% and 50%.

3. The standard defined an associated company as one in which the investing company's interest was either effectively that of a partner in a joint venture or consortium, or was long term and substantial and over which the investor exercised significant influence. 20% was specified as a minimum holding that should be considered as substantial. Where a company held such investments the standard required that it should include in its consolidated accounts the investing company or group's share of the profits, rather than just the dividends received, of its associated companies. This treatment (now generally known as equity accounting) produces similar results to consolidation except that:

(a) the assets and liabilities of the associate are not allocated between categories in the investing company's consolidated balance sheet. Similarly, only the profit or loss and tax charge of the associate are reflected in the consolidated profit and loss account of the investing company, items such as turnover of the associate being excluded.

(b) the investing company only accounts for its own share of the associated company's net assets and profit and consequently no minority interests arise in either the consolidated balance sheet or the consolidated profit and loss account.

4. Although SSAP1 was at the time innovative, the principles it contains have since been incorporated into recommendations (or statements issued for comment) in several other countries.

5. In June 1976 International Accounting Standard Number 3 *Consolidated Financial Statements* was published. Although this includes accounting requirements for associated companies similar to those contained in SSAP1, there exist some differences of emphasis in the exact application of the method and the definition of an associated company adopted.

6. The Accounting Standards Committee (ASC) is at present entering on a policy of review of the workings of existing standards. To this end a panel was established during the summer of 1978 to review SSAP1. Comments on the working of the existing standard were requested in July 1978 to be received by 1 November 1978.

7. Comments were received from 67 organisations and individuals as follows:

Companies	21
Practising firms	18
Representative bodies of accountants	12
Other representative bodies	10
Individuals	6
	67

8. It has not been possible to reply in detail to each respondent. However, as well as an acknowledgement, a copy of the full text of all comments received for which the author had not requested confidentially was sent to each commentator. Copies of these comments were also placed in each of the libraries of the governing bodies of ASC. Comments may be inspected by any member of the public by arrangement with the librarian at the particular location.

9. To provide additional information a confidential two part questionnaire was sent to 500 major listed companies. Replies were received from 172 such companies detailing the treatment of over 650 companies in which they had invested. A number of these also included additional comments on the workings of SSAP1.

10. The great majority of commentators appear to have been in favour of the treatment of associated companies outlined in SSAP1, possibly with changes of emphasis in the wording or definitions used. A small number of commentators did, however, disagree with equity accounting as a concept on the grounds of prudence. In the light of general acceptance of the principles, ASC continues to support the basic approach of SSAP1.

11. Careful consideration has been given to all submissions made, together with correspondence received over the years of operation of SSAP1, and in the light of the comments and experience, SSAP1 has been re-drafted. Details of the main points arising from the comments, together with details of changes made in the present exposure draft are given below.

12. The basic concepts of SSAP1 have not been altered but some sections have been re-written to remove ambiguities from the principles or wording used. In addition, the layout and order of some paragraphs has been amended to be more in line with recent standards. Additional requirements have been introduced where such treatments were thought to convey useful information and be in line with modern needs and trends. In some instances requirements have been relaxed.

13. Three major areas for consideration were identified. These are the definition of an associated company, the profit and loss account treatment and the balance sheet treatment.

14. The amended standard is being issued as an exposure draft and persons interested in financial reporting are urged to submit their comments (critical and favourable) on the exposure draft and the amendments made as soon as possible and at the latest by 31 March 1980.

Definition of associated company
15. The aspect of SSAP1 which attracted most comment was the definition of an associated company. Amongst the commentators on this subject there exists a complete gradation of views ranging from those in favour of a strict percentage definition (whether more or less than 20%) to those in favour of a definition based purely on significant influence. Most commentators seem agreed, however, that whatever definition is applied the terms used must be clearly explained.

16. ASC now proposes a definition based on significant influence but this has remained linked to a fixed percentage (20%). Holdings above this are presumed to give rise to significant influence unless clear evidence to the contrary can be demonstrated. Conversely, holdings of less than 20% are presumed not to give rise to such influence unless clear evidence to the contrary can be demonstrated and the associated company concurs with the investing company's view that significant influence exists. This represents a change from the previous standard as regards the definition of an associated company in the case of holdings of less than

20%.It is, however, essentially the same as the definitions contained in the International Standard and the American pronouncement (APB 18).

17. Clarification that holdings by a subsidiary of the investing company are to be aggregated with the investing company's own holding for the purposes of assessing whether or not 20% of the equity voting capital is held, is given in paragraph 15 of the exposure draft. Holdings by associates, or even a proportion of such holdings, should not be so aggregated.

18. References to a requirement that the accounts on which the amounts included for associated companies' results are based should be audited, have been deleted; this is an auditing matter rather than an accounting matter.

19. A requirement for disclosure of the reason for treating a less than 20% owned investment as an associate, or not so treating a greater than 20% owned investment, has been added.

20. As the only grounds upon which equity accounting should not be used for an associate in the consolidated accounts of the investing company in effect relate to the materiality of the associate's results to those of the investing company, and as materiality is covered in the Explanatory Foreword to accounting standards, it is proposed that any reference to such circumstances should be omitted.

21. Where a company has subsidiaries but does not prepare consolidated accounts by reason of being a wholly owned subsidiary, the requirement for that company to account for its associates on the equity accounting basis has been removed from the standard. This is a logical extension of the statutory exemption for subsidiaries and the treatment outlined in SSAP14.

22. The term 'company' has been extended to include other non-corporate enterprises.

Profit and loss account treatment
23. Several commentators favoured the inclusion of the group's share of the associated companies' turnover within the group turnover. They argue that there is distortion in some turnover based ratios if the turnover of the associates is omitted; however, such distortions do not occur if the ratios are calculated on the basis of the group excluding the results of the associates. Other commentators argued for disclosure of the group's share of such items as depreciation and interest.

95

24. ASC considers that the group's share of the profits of an associate is of a different quality from those of the other constituents of the group and is best shown in the form of a single entry in the consolidated profit and loss account of the investing group. Specifically, it is inconsistent to show balance sheet related items such as depreciation when the carrying value is not sub-divided into items such as fixed assets. Consequently, ASC proposes that no change be made in this respect but has emphasised the need to disclose additional information concerning an associate where it is material.

25. The basis for judging materiality for such disclosure has been further defined so as to include the materiality of the scale of the operations of the associate as distinct from just the net amount of the group's share of its results or its carrying value.

26. As with subsidiaries, no credit should be taken in the investing company's own accounts for unrealised profits in the form of undistributed income of an associate. Consequently, the accounting adjustments required to reflect the investor's share of the retained profits of an associate should be made in the consolidated accounts and not in the parent company's own profit and loss account. Where an investing company (other than a wholly owned subsidiary) does not prepare consolidated accounts it will be necessary for it to adapt its own profit and loss account or to prepare an additional one to reflect the results of associated companies.

Balance sheet presentation
27. A requirement for the separation of the goodwill element of the cost of an associated company within the balance sheet has been introduced. This includes both goodwill retained in the associated company's own balance sheet and the premium (or discount) arising on acquisition of the associate. The latter should be calculated, where possible, after attributing fair values to the net assets of the associate. This requirement is consistent with the treatment specified for subsidiaries in paragraph 29 of SSAP14 *Group accounts*.

28. No accounting treatment has been specified for the goodwill so identified but it is envisaged that the treatment will be the same as that adopted for goodwill arising on consolidation.

29. As loans to associated companies from the investor (or vice versa) form part of the long term investment in the associates, a requirement has been included for any such amounts to be shown with the carrying value of the associated companies.

30. Similarly, it is felt that balances representing normal trading transactions should be disclosed if material. However, these should be shown as current items, not with the carrying value of the associated companies.

31. The basis on which materiality is judged with regard to disclosure of more detailed information of the associated companies' assets and liabilities has been extended to the individual items concerned.

32. Many commentators were in favour of the inclusion of a requirement to write down the carrying value of an associated company when it can be shown that there has been a reduction in fair value of the investment below the carrying value, which is other than temporary in nature.

33. ASC is of the opinion that any such adjustment should be made first against the goodwill element of the carrying value. As with subsidiaries a write down of the carrying value beyond the amount of the net assets is only likely to occur in exceptional circumstances such as the expectation of the absence of future profits of an associate.

34. Paragraph 5A of the Second Schedule to the Companies Act 1967 and paragraph 5A of the Second Schedule to the Companies (Northern Ireland) Order 1978 both include a reference to the use of the valuation basis for investments. ASC is of the opinion that, although this basis may be appropriate for the trade investments, its use for associated companies in consolidated accounts should be restricted to the adjustments outlined in paragraph 33 above (although details of a different valuation could be given by way of a note to the accounts). This is because the valuation basis is thought to be inconsistent with the principles of consolidation.

35. The proposed standard includes reference to the situation where there exists a deficiency of net assets in an associated company. In such a situation it will only be realistic to continue to consider that investment as long term (and consequently as an associate) if some means of support, either formal or informal, is provided in that company by the investing company. In these circumstances, the investing company should continue to reflect its share of the deficiency in its own accounts.

36. A consolidated balance sheet drawn up as an example of one possible method of presentation of the required information has been added as Appendix 3 to the standard. As with other appendices this does not form part of the standard and is not prescriptive.

37. Where an investor does not prepare consolidated accounts it should show the required information by way of note to the balance sheet or by preparing a separate balance sheet.

Procedure on first introduction of an amended standard
38. Where an associated company has been held for some time, it may not be possible to attribute fair values to the net assets acquired at the original date of acquisition, for the purposes of paragraph 25 of the exposure draft. In such a case it will be appropriate to use the book amounts at the time of acquisition and, as envisaged in paragraph 25, to show goodwill and premium paid on the acquisition as one aggregate amount.

Legal requirements in Ireland
39. A note on the legal requirements in Ireland has been added as part 5.

Compliance with international standards
40. Although the wording of the exposure draft differs in some respects from that included in IAS3, ASC is of the opinion that compliance with an amended standard based on the draft would automatically ensure compliance in all material respects with the provisions covering the basis of accounting for associated companies contained in IAS3.

Notice of public hearing on ED25—Accounting for the results of associated companies

(11 March 1980—TR378)

1. In July 1978 the Accounting Standards Committee (ASC) announced that it was reviewing the provisions of SSAP1 *Accounting for the results of associated companies* and invited comments on the standard from all persons concerned with financial reporting.

2. As a result of the review ASC published proposals for amending SSAP1 which were set out in ED25 *Accounting for the results of associated companies* issued in October 1979. The exposure draft remains open for comment until 31st March 1980.

3. In order that those interested persons who so wish may have an opportunity to present their views on the proposals in the exposure draft in public and to allow members of the ASC to gain fuller understanding of these views, it is intended that a public hearing should be held.

4. This hearing will be held on Friday 18th April 1980 in the Council Chamber of the Association of Certified Accountants, 29 Lincoln's Inn Fields, London. The hearing will begin at 10.30 a.m.

5. Any individual or organisation may ask to be heard at the public hearing. Those wishing to appear should notify the Secretary of ASC, P.O. Box 433, Chartered Accountants' Hall, Moorgate Place, London EC2P 2BJ, not later than 31st March 1980. The notification should be in writing. On or before 8th April, the applicant must deliver to the Secretary of the ASC:
(a) his written submission on ED25 and
(b) an outline of the proposed oral presentation.

If the written submission and the outline presentation are not received by 8th April 1980, the request to be heard will be deemed to be cancelled.

6. The members of the panel hearing the submission will be drawn from members of the ASC. The time allotted to each individual or organisation will be limited generally to 30 minutes. The Chairman of the hearings may, however, at his discretion allow more or less time.

7. The ASC wishes to devote most of the time at the hearing to questioning those making oral presentations. Accordingly, not more than 10 minutes should be taken up with oral presentations, which should normally be confined to emphasising a point or points made in earlier written submissions or in commenting very briefly on submissions made by others. The panel members at the hearing will be familiar with the written submissions already made by the presenter.

8. Each person making an oral presentation will be notified as soon as practicable after 31st March 1980, of the time it is expected that he or she will be called upon to make the presentation and the time expected to be allowed.

9. The hearings will be open to the public including representatives of the press.

10. The Chairman of the hearings has full authority with respect to its conduct including, without limitation, authority to adjourn and extend the hearings and to make all rulings he deems appropriate in his own discretion.

Statement by the Accounting Standards Committee on the publication of SSAP16—Current cost accounting

(31 March 1980—TR383)

Introduction

1. SSAP16 on Current cost accounting and the accompanying Guidance Notes are derived from the exposure draft (ED24 and its Guidance Notes) published on 30th April 1979. The original draft was broadly supported by most commentators. Accordingly, while the Standard and Guidance Notes have been amended to take account of the comments received, the substance of the original draft remains.

2. The primary purpose of this Technical Release is to state the way in which the main matters raised by commentators on the exposure draft have been dealt with in preparing SSAP16 and its Guidance Notes. An appendix gives a checklist of the amendments of substance from the drafts.

GENERAL MATTERS

Publication details

3. 14,600 copies of ED24 and 12,700 copies of the accompanying Guidance Notes were distributed during the exposure period. The text of the draft standard was reproduced in the professional and technical press.

Background papers

4. In September 1979, The Inflation Accounting Steering Group (IASG) published *Background Papers to ED24,* explaining how ED24 had been developed and linking it with the written comments on the earlier proposals in ED18, the *Interim Recommendation* and the general continuing debate. Some of the matters discussed in the Background Papers are now embodied in the Guidance Notes.

The exposure period and comments

5. During the exposure period the ASC received 248 written submissions and 38 people gave evidence at public hearings held in Dublin, Glasgow and London. Comments have also been received through the press, at public meetings and from other channels. Comments from all sources have been carefully considered by the IASG and ASC in preparing SSAP16 and its Guidance Notes.

6. Written comments were received from organisations and individuals as follows:

Companies	75
Professional firms of accountants	34
Representative bodies of accountants (including District Societies)	64
Other Representative Bodies	10
Individuals	65
	248

7. A copy of all the public written comments received has been placed in each of the libraries of the governing bodies of the ASC. Comments may be inspected by any member of the public by arrangement with the librarian in each location. In addition, a full text of the public written comments may be purchased from the Publications Department of the Institute of Chartered Accountants in England and Wales.

8. Not all commentators who had specific comments made their overall position wholly clear. The IASG secretariat contacted about one quarter of the written commentators in order to obtain further clarification. Those who were represented at public hearings were also questioned. As a result it became clear that, whilst most commentators had specific points they wanted considered, there was sufficient general support to proceed with a Standard. Over three quarters of the comments from (taken together) companies, representative bodies, accounting firms and groups of users broadly supported the proposals, and a further 10% supported them subject to an important point of substance (frequently gearing). The proportion of acceptance from those individuals who commented was lower although a majority were broadly supportive. Thus consideration turned to the comments on specific points.

MATTERS AFFECTING THE CONTENTS OF THE STANDARD

9. ED24 and SSAP16 both deal with four main matters:
(a) scope and status of current cost accounts;
(b) the objectives and principles to be followed when preparing current cost accounts;
(c) disclosure requirements; and
(d) operative date.

These are now dealt with in turn.

The scope and status of current cost accounts

10. ED24 applied to most listed and large companies, but offered exemption from mandatory compliance to about 99% of the accounts published in the UK. Exemption was offered to the following:

(a) smaller unlisted companies (a threshold at a turnover of £5 million was proposed);

(b) wholly owned subsidiaries of UK entities;

(c) entities where there is no long term profit objective; and

(d) entities where the principles of CCA, as proposed, are not wholly appropriate. This applies, for example, to Investment and Unit Trusts, insurers and property investment companies.

11. These exemption categories were broadly accepted by most commentators. Claims for exemption by certain companies, mainly on practical grounds, have been carefully considered but no changes have been made in response to these commentators.

12. Many considered it would be more appropriate if the threshold at which unlisted entities were explicitly included within the scope of the Standard coincided with the definition of 'large' companies in the EEC Fourth Directive, because this threshold will shortly have significance in relation to disclosure requirements in UK and Irish law. This proposal has been adopted so far as it is practicable to do so in advance of actual legislation. The change will have the effect of exempting a few hundred companies which would otherwise have been included such as those with high turnovers in relation to their assets or employees (SSAP16, paragraphs 1 and 46).

13. Although smaller unlisted businesses are not required to publish current cost accounts, they are not prohibited from doing so. The IASG and ASC plan to provide guidance to smaller companies who wish to produce current cost accounts voluntarily.

14. ED24 envisaged that annual financial statements would include HC accounts and CC accounts. Either could be the main accounts but both were required. Subsequently, however, in a Green Paper (Cmnd 7654), HM Government have stated that 'individual companies at present have discretion to adopt full CCA in their main accounts, not merely as additional statements'. The Green Paper also indicated that it is the intention of HM Government to take advantage of Article 33 when implementing the EEC Fourth Directive so as to continue to permit United Kingdom companies to adopt CC accounts as their main accounts (although there will still be no legal requirements for them to do so).

15. Consequent upon this and the advice in several submissions it seemed that, where a company chose to publish CC accounts as its main accounts, it would be inappropriate for SSAP16 also to require HC accounts when it was under no legal obligation to provide them. SSAP16 is now drafted to permit several options on presentation, from HC main accounts supplemented by prominent current cost accounts, to current cost main accounts supplemented by a minimum amount of HC information. (SSAP16, paragraphs 28, 47 and 48.)

16. Accounting standards on matters of disclosure (as opposed to measurement) have only previously applied to annual financial statements and have not applied to interim accounts, preliminary statements, etc. Despite several representations, the ASC has decided that SSAP16 should not depart from this practice. However, the ASC expects that entities, once they have published their first current cost accounts will publish current cost information with all financial statements. (SSAP16, paragraph 27.) The Stock Exchange have indicated their intentions to support this as far as concerns companies covered by their Listing Agreement.

The objectives and principles to be followed when preparing current cost accounts

17. ED24 contains statements on the objectives and principles to be followed when preparing current cost accounts, and the main methods necessary in order to achieve this. One innovation in ED24 was the monetary working capital adjustment (MWCA) which is necessary in order to identify the current cost operating profit. The idea of the MCMA has been accepted by most commentators, but many felt that the overall objectives and principles, (of which the MWCA is only a part) were still insufficiently clear. In consequence, the wording has been substantially revised. The changes do little more than clarify the original position, for example:

(a) the Standard now incorporates statements of the objective of CCA and definitions of the two levels of profit (SSAP16, paragraphs 5, 6, 7, 40 and 41);

(b) the MWCA is now much more closely identified with the cost of sales adjustment (COSA) as opposed to being part of a 'split' gearing adjustment; and

(c) the Standard now specifies more clearly that the current cost adjustments arise as a result of changes in input prices.

18. It is considered that these and other related textual changes will clarify the objectives when preparing current cost accounts and thus the methods to be adopted. This should help both preparers and users.

19. The main proposals of ED24 concerning the calculation of current cost operating profit were accepted by most commentators and the substance of the proposals in ED24 is now embodied in SSAP16. Three changes may be noted:

(a) many commentators thought the definition of monetary working capital was over restrictive in that the circumstances where part of a bank balance or overdraft should be included in monetary working capital (MWC) would be more numerous than implied by the ED24 definition of MWC. The wording has been changed, but the circumstances where part of bank balance or overdraft should be included in MWC has been carefully specified to minimise subjectivity in accounts preparation (SSAP16, paragraphs 13 and 44);

(b) the benefits of good buying (and the cost of errors) should be included in current cost operating profit. The position was unclear to many commentators but has now been discussed more fully, particularly in the Guidance Notes; and

(c) the treatment of currency translation differences previously appeared ambiguous in the Guidance Notes and has now been clarified (SSAP16, paragraph 25 and Guidance Notes).

However, as anticipated, the gearing adjustment was the aspect of ED24 that attracted most comments.

20. Several critics of the gearing adjustment were basing their criticism on their special circumstances. Special consideration is now given to entities with certain types of capital structure, e.g. Co-ops, wholly owned subsidiaries and Nationalised Industries, both in SSAP 16 (paragraph 21 and 51) and in the Guidance Notes. However, in other respects the substance of the original proposals has been retained and is definitive.

21. Most commentators accepted the gearing proposals as drafted. However, there were some who did not want any gearing adjustment, some who proposed a different method of calculating it, and there were others who proposed that companies should be free to choose the method they used. The IASG and ASC gave most careful consideration to all proposals made, consulted widely, and debated the subject at length.

22. The IASG and ASC concluded a gearing adjustment is necessary, and that to permit freedom of choice in this instance would be detrimental to the needs of users by failing to achieve adequate comparability (differences between the proposed methods could be very substantial). They further confirmed that the single method should be the ED24 method, a choice consistent with the views of the majority of commentators. Accordingly, they decided that the substance of the ED24 proposals on gearing should stand.

23. It is clear that the debate on gearing will continue. The ASC welcomes this debate and SSAP16 suggests that companies who wish to do so should give, by way of note, information about the effects of a gearing adjustment calculated by another method and should explain the reasons for doing so. Gearing is a subject which will be especially closely watched in the ASC's monitoring of the practical application of SSAP16.

24. A significant number of commentators thought that, if an entity had assets surplus to operating requirements and in excess of borrowing, these should be subject to a 'negative' gearing adjustment to recognise their fall in purchasing power. However, although the 'economic' case for this viewpoint is strong there can be severe practical difficulties. This problem is discussed (SSAP16, paragraph 22) but left for future consideration.

Disclosure requirements
25. ED24 proposed that the current cost accounts should include:
   A profit and loss account;
   A summarized balance sheet;
   An analysis of fixed assets;
   Movements on reserves;
   Explanatory notes; and
   Corresponding amounts (normally only after the first year) stated as shown last year.

The disclosure requirements were broadly accepted. Changes are of relative detail and the more important are listed below.

26. As a result of the inclusion of definitions of profit in the Standard, income of associated companies is normally to be included in arriving at group current cost operating profit. (SSAP16, paragraphs 38 and 40.)

27. Many commentators proposed a different presentation of the gearing adjustment to that presented in the appendix to ED24. Two formats are now illustrated and either would comply with the Standard. One format shows the gearing adjustment related to the interest on borrowing; in the other the gearing adjustment is separated from this interest and shown after taxation but before extraordinary items. (SSAP16, Appendix).

28. A note to the balance sheet is now proposed, setting out the totals of the net operating assets and net borrowing, and their main elements. (SSAP16, paragraph 57 and Appendix.)

29. Many commentators thought the name 'capital maintenance reserve' inappropriate and found the disclosure requirements unnecessarily onerous. The name has been changed to 'current cost reserve' and the disclosure requirements simplified. (SSAP16, paragraphs 24, 25, 26 and 54).

30. Many commentators considered more emphasis should be given to the Notes to the accounts and that, particularly in the first year, they should include explanations of the accounts to help the user interpret them. Modifications along these lines are incorporated (SSAP16, paragraphs 34 and 58 and an example in the Guidance Notes).

31. ED24 required corresponding amounts to be stated as shown in the previous year. It is recognised that such corresponding amounts are not truly comparable unless they are adjusted to a common price basis, and SSAP16 is more flexible to enable companies to give corresponding figures so adjusted if they wish (SSAP16, paragraphs 37 and 61). The ASC intends to develop an exposure draft on how corresponding amounts and figures presented in 5/10 year statements should be calculated.

32. The ASC encourages the provision of information in addition to the minimum disclosures. The following are particularly mentioned:
(a) 'updated' comparatives and 5/10 years statements, together with explanation (SSAP 16, paragraphs 37 and 58(g));
(b) a statement of source and application of funds compatible with the CC accounts (SSAP16, paragraphs 30 and 62 and example in the Guidance Notes);
(c) a statement of changes in the shareholders' equity interest after allowing for changes in the general purchasing power of money, together with explanation (SSAP16, paragraph 36 and example in the Guidance Notes);

(d) the effect of alternative forms of gearing adjustment, disclosed in the notes together with explanation (SSAP16, paragraph 35); and

(e) the ratio of CC operating profit to average net operating assets (SSAP16, Appendix).

33. Where a company chooses to publish current cost accounts as its main accounts (under SSAP16, paragraph 48), such accounts will have to comply with the requirements of Statute, other Accounting Standards and, if appropriate, the requirements of other bodies, e.g. The Stock Exchange.

Operative date

34. ED24 stated that the ASC believed that there was an urgent need to produce an Accounting Standard as soon as possible and that it should be operative for accounting periods beginning on or after 1st January 1980. Most commentators accepted this.

THE GUIDANCE NOTES

35. The Guidance Notes have been substantially revised consequent upon amendments to the Standard and comments received on the draft Guidance Notes. The main changes are set out in the appendix.

36. The Guidance Notes suggest how to comply with the principles and objectives of CCA set out in the Standard and ·described practical methods which will frequently be appropriate when complying with the Standard. The Guidance Notes are not mandatory, and should not be followed if, in the particular circumstances, they do not best meet the principles and objectives.

37. The ASC encourages the formation of industry groups to resolve common practical problems in a unified way. The ASC Secretariat will be pleased, where possible, to help in the resolution of problems identified. A joint committee is to be established with representatives of the ASC and the Accepting Houses Committee to examine their particular problems of implementation.

FUTURE DEVELOPMENTS

Stability

38. There has been a long period of debate on how accounts should be prepared in periods of substantial price level changes. This debate has been going on in many countries in the world. The publication of SSAP16

puts the UK and the Republic of Ireland ahead in the development of current cost accounting and its application to listed and large companies. Debate is, however, certain to continue in the UK and Republic of Ireland but the ASC believes that there is now a need for a period of stability. It is the intention of the ASC, as far as possible, to make no change to SSAP16 for three years so as to enable producers and users to gain experience in dealing with practical problems and interpreting the information. The ASC will maintain a standing sub-committee to monitor the ways in which SSAP16 is being implemented and the changes that may ultimately be needed.

39. However, it is likely that there will be developments in other Accounting Standards, e.g. leasing, and legislation arising from the EEC Directives on Company Law, which may affect the current cost accounts. Further, as mentioned above, the ASC intend to issue an exposure draft on the treatment of corresponding amounts in current cost accounts.

40. As noted in paragraph 13 above, the ASC plans to issue guidance on the voluntary application of CCA to smaller businesses.

41. Statements of Standard Accounting Practice do not normally include any recommendation as regards audit and audit reports. These matters are dealt with by the Auditing Practices Committee which, it is expected, will make a statement on the auditing implications of SSAP16 in due course.

IN CONCLUSION

42. It has taken many years to reach the stage of an Accounting Standard on price level accounting. It has taken all this time to clarify objectives, develop methods and reach reasonable agreement on the final Standard. Many people have given their time and effort voluntarily in the pursuit of this goal. Discussions will continue and, no doubt, there will be further developments in due course. Nevertheless, the publication of SSAP16 is a significant milestone in the development of the subject. The ASC and IASG thank all commentators on the various drafts throughout the years and all contributors to the debate for their help in reaching this position.

Major changes from ED24 to SSAP 16 and their respective 'Guidance Notes'

	Paragraph numbers	
GENERAL	Standard	Guidance Notes

Scope
Threshold to move towards that for
'large' company in EEC 4th Directive. 1 & 46

Status
ED24 required two sets of accounts.
SSAP16 says:
— if HC accounts are the main
   accounts, the CC accounts must be
   prominent
— but CC accounts alone
   (supplemented by certain HC
   information required by law) will
   comply.   28, 47 & 48

The objective
Definitions of the two levels of profit
are now incorporated in the standard,
thus clarifying certain matters
previously uncertain.   40 & 41

The standard is now clearer that it is
only changes in the input prices of
goods and services used and financed
by the business that give rise to the
current cost adjustments.   4, 11 & 12   Generally

DISCLOSURE

Balance sheet
Totals and analysis of net operating
assets required.   57 & Appendix

Current cost reserve (previously
capital maintenance reserve)
— may be combined with HC reserves 54
— companies are encouraged to
   disclose the analysis between the
   realised and unrealised components. 26 & Appendix

Profit and loss account

The gearing and interest on borrowing
of Nationalised Industries is
specifically dealt with.   21 & 51

—alternative presentation of gearing
   adjustment given   Appendix

—encouragement to show return on
   capital ratio (Operating profit:
   Net operating assets)   Appendix

—example of statement of retained
   profits/reserves given.   Appendix

Other disclosure

Corresponding amounts need not be as
shown last year, but if they are, a third
(updated) column is encouraged.   37 & 61

The following are encouraged:

—5/10 year statements with prior year
   figures updated, as the information
   becomes available,   37

—statements of source and application   Example
   of funds, based on current cost   Appendix (vi)
   accounts,   30 & 62

—a statement of changes in the
   shareholders' equity interest after
   allowing for the change in the   Example
   general purchasing power of money   36   Appendix (vi)

—interim and preliminary statements
   and prospectuses, etc., to include
   CC information.   27

METHODS

With few exceptions, the changes in
methods proposed are only changes in
emphasis. The major changes are as
follows:

Fixed assets

The balance sheet and depreciation
calculations must be based on realistic   7, 42, & 53   55-57

110

asset lives. Changes in estimates of
asset lives represent changes in
estimated service potential and are
thus reflected in a change in the net
current replacement cost in the
balance sheet and passed through the
profit and loss account.   11, 12 & 55-57

The use of HC for intangibles is no
longer advocated.   45

Stock
Fewer situations now suggested where
stock should be treated as if it were
monetary working capital.   Part II generally

Monetary Working Capital
Inter-relationship with stock (COSA)
strengthened and a movement away
from considering the MWCA as part of
a 'split gearing adjustment'.   49   Part II

Definition of MWC (cash and
overdrafts) changed.   13 & 44

Basis of adjustment on debtors
clarified.   96

Gearing
Formula more completely specified,
particularly:
—the proportion is to be obtained from
  the current cost balance sheet   50
—the treatment of asset lives are not
  the same in HC and CC accounts   116
—the treatment of preference shares
  and convertible debentures.   112

The application of the gearing
adjustment to certain Co-ops and
wholly owned subsidiaries is
specifically dealt with.   21 & 45   109 & 110

The treatment of interest is more fully discussed. — 40, 49 & 51 — 110, 119 & 120

Groups

The use of HC figures for associated companies is no longer suggested, even where CC figures cannot be obtained from the associated company. — 53(b) — 134

Profits of associated companies are normally included within the group CC operating profit. — 38, 40 & 52 — 131 & 132

Foreign currencies; differences arising on consolidation are more specifically dealt with. — 25 & 52 — 135-139

The Guidance Notes to SSAP16 also offer guidance on the following matters to a greater extent than in the exposure draft:

Fixed assets:	Technological change	25-27 & Appendix (i)
	Recoverable amount	13, 14, 28-31
	Asset lives	55-57
	Backlog depreciation	50-52
	Government grants	60-62
Stocks:	Commodities and metals	77
	Land held for development	85
	Purchasing skills and 'special purchases'	80-82
	The applicability of LIFO	Appendix (ii)
	Stocks held at recoverable amount	Appendix (lii)
Groups:	Associates	130-134
	Minorities	143 & 144

A worked example in the Guidance
Notes now includes fixed assets and
the current cost reserve.   Appendix (vii)

There is also an additional example of
disclosure of current cost accounts,
including an example of explanatory
notes.   Appendix (v)

Programme for public hearing on ED25 Accounting for the results of associated companies

(8 April 1980— TR387)

1. The Accounting Standards Committee will hold a public hearing to allow interested persons to present their views in public on ED25 *Accounting for the results of associated companies* on Friday, 18th April 1980. The hearing will be held in the Council Chamber, The Association of Certified Accountants, 29 Lincoln's Inn Fields, London WC2A 3EE commencing at 10.30 a.m.

2. The persons making a presentation at the hearing, together with the approximate times at which they are expected to be heard, are as follows:
10.30 a.m.   H. P. Gold   (Shell)
11.15 a.m.   P. J. Rutteman   (Arthur Young McClelland Moores & Co.)

3. The members of the ASC panel will be:
T. R. Watts (Chairman)
P. M. D. Gibbs
B. D. G. Ogle

4. Any member of the public may attend the hearing. Tickets are not required.

5. Copies of the submissions and outlines of the oral presentations may be obtained from the Secretary of the Accounting Standards Committee.

Section Four

The texts of Accounting Standards extant at 1st June 1980 are reproduced in full in this Section.

Explanatory foreword

Authority and scope
Statements of standard accounting practice ('accounting standards') describe methods   1
of accounting approved by the Council of The Institute of Chartered Accountants
in England and Wales (in association with the Councils of The Institute of Chartered
Accountants of Scotland, The Institute of Chartered Accountants in Ireland, The
Association of Certified Accountants and The Institute of Cost and Management
Accountants) for application to all financial accounts intended to give a true and fair
view of financial position and profit or loss.*

Disclosure of significant departures
Significant departures in financial accounts from applicable accounting standards   2
should be disclosed and explained. The financial effects should be estimated and
disclosed unless this would be impracticable or misleading in the context of giving a
true and fair view. If the financial effects of departures from standard are not disclosed,
the reasons should be stated.

Obligation for chartered accountants to observe
accounting standards or justify departures
The Council expects members of the Institute who assume responsibilities in respect of   3
financial accounts to observe accounting standards.

Where this responsibility is evidenced by the association of their names with such   4
accounts in the capacity of directors or other officers the onus will be on them to
ensure that the existence and purpose of standards are fully understood by non-
member directors and other officers. They should also use best endeavours to ensure
that standards are observed or, if they are not observed, that significant departures
from them are disclosed and explained in the accounts. The effect of such departures
should, if material, be disclosed unless this would be impracticable or misleading in the
context of giving a true and fair view.

Where members act as auditors or reporting accountants the onus will be on them not   5
only to ensure disclosure of significant departures but also, to the extent that their concurrence is stated or implied, to justify them.

The Council, through its Professional Standards Committee, may inquire into apparent   6
failures by members of the Institute to observe accounting standards or to disclose
departures therefrom.

Date from which effective
The date from which members are expected to observe accounting standards will be   7
declared in each statement of standard accounting practice.

---

* Any limitation of general scope will be made clear as necessary in the texts in the statements.

Exceptional and borderline cases

8   Accounting standards are not intended to be a comprehensive code of rigid rules. It would be impracticable to establish a code sufficiently elaborate to cater for all business situations and circumstances and every exceptional or marginal case. Nor could any code of rules provide in advance for innovations in business and financial practice.

9   Moreover it must be recognised that there may be situations in which for justifiable reasons accounting standards are not strictly applicable because they are impracticable or, exceptionally, having regard to the circumstances, would be inappropriate or give a misleading view.

10   In such cases modified or alternative treatments must be adopted and, as noted, departure from standard disclosed and explained. In judging exceptional or borderline cases it will be important to have regard to the spirit of accounting standards as well as to their precise terms, and to bear in mind the overriding requirement to give a true and fair view.

11   Where accounting standards prescribe specific information to be contained in accounts, such disclosure requirements do not override exemptions from disclosure requirements given to and utilised by special classes of companies under Statute. Examples of such special classes of company are contained, for example, in Part III of the Second Schedule to the Companies Act 1967.

Future developments

12   Methods of financial accounting evolve and alter in response to changing business and economic needs. From time to time new accounting standards will be drawn at progressive levels, and established standards will be reviewed with the object of improvement in the light of new needs and developments.

Status of accounting recommendations

13   In so far as they are not replaced by statements of standard accounting practice, the Council's 'Accounting Recommendations' will continue in effect as guidance statements and indicators of best practice. They are persuasive in intent and departures from them do not necessarily require disclosure as do departures from accounting standards.

Application of accounting standards overseas

14   Statements of standard accounting practice are not intended to apply to accounts prepared and audited in overseas territories for local purposes where different requirements of law or generally accepted practice prevail, but are intended to be applied where accounts of overseas subsidiaries and associated companies are incorporated in United Kingdom group accounts.

1

Accounting for the results of associated companies

Contents

Accounting for the results of associated companies

(Issued January 1971)

Income from investments in 50 per cent and less than 50 per cent owned companies has in the past normally been included in the investing group or company's accounts only to the extent of dividends received or receivable up to its accounting date. With the spread of trading through joint venture and other companies which are 50 per cent or less than 50 per cent owned there started to emerge the practice of bringing into the accounts of the investing group or company its share of the profits or losses of such companies. The purpose of the statement which follows is to establish a standard method of accounting for the results of associated companies.

The better to appreciate the accounting method proposed, there should be kept in mind the distinction between (a) a company's own accounts as a legal entity and (b) its group accounts in the form of consolidated accounts the objects of which are to show the results and state of affairs of the group so far as concerns members of the parent company.

Use of the term 'associated company' should in future be restricted to the meaning defined in this statement.

Part 1 – Explanatory note

1   It is accepted accounting practice for a company not to take credit in its own (i.e., non-consolidated) profit and loss account and balance sheet for its share of the profits of other companies (subsidiary or otherwise) which have not been distributed. The view is taken that the inclusion of undistributed profits would ignore the separate legal entities of the companies concerned and, as regards the investing company, be in breach of the principle that credit should not be taken for investment income until it is received or receivable.

2   However, where a company conducts an important part of its business through the medium of other companies, whether more or less than 50 per cent owned, the mere disclosure of dividend income (or mere inclusion of dividend income alone) is unlikely to be sufficient to give shareholders adequate information regarding the sources of their income and of the manner in which their funds are being employed.

3   At one time such operations were usually carried out through the medium of subsidiary companies. It was for this reason that the Companies Act 1948 required the preparation of group accounts, normally in the form of consolidated accounts. In recent years there have been two important developments. One has been the growing practice of companies to conduct parts of their business through other companies (frequently consortium or joint venture companies) in which they have a substantial but not a controlling interest. The other is the importance which investors have come to attach to earnings (as distinct from dividends), the price/earnings ratio (P/E ratio) and, increasingly, earnings per share. Thus, in order that the investing company's accounts as a whole

may give adequate information, and provide a total of earnings from which the most meaningful ratios can be calculated, it is considered necessary that the coverage of consolidated accounts be extended so that they shall include (within the framework of the existing law) the share of earnings or losses of companies which are described in this statement as associated companies (see paragraph 6).

This approach recognises a difference in principle between the nature of investments in   4
associated companies (as defined in this statement) and other forms of trade investment. The essence of the distinction is that the investing company actively participates in the commercial and policy decisions of its associated companies; it thus has a measure of direct responsibility for the return on its investment, and should account for its stewardship accordingly, whereas it will not normally seek to exert direct management influence over the operating policy of other companies in which it invests, and should continue to deal with them in accordance with traditional accounting methods.

The broad concept underlying the accounting treatment of the results of associated   5
companies here stated is the adoption in modified form of the consolidation procedures used for subsidiary companies. It follows from this that the investing group's share of associated companies' profits and losses will be reflected in its consolidated profit and loss account, and its share of their post-acquisition retained profits or surplus will be reflected in its consolidated balance sheet, though not in its own balance sheet as a legal entity.

Part 2 – Definition of 'associated company'

A company (not being a subsidiary of the investing group or company) is an associated   6
company of the investing group or company if:

(a) the investing group or company's interest in the associated company is effectively
that of a partner in a joint venture or consortium; or

(b) the investing group or company's interest in the associated company is for the
long term and is substantial (i.e., not less than 20 per cent of the equity voting
rights), and, having regard to the disposition of the other shareholdings, the
investing group or company is in a position to exercise a significant influence over
the associated company.

In both cases it is essential that the investing group or company participates (usually through representation on the board) in commercial and financial policy decisions of the associated company, including the distribution of profits.

Part 3 – Standard accounting practice

Bases of accounting for income of associated companies

7   Income from investments by a company or its subsidiaries in associated companies (as defined in paragraph 6 above) should be brought into account on the following bases:

   (a) *In the investing company's own accounts*
   (i) Dividends received up to the accounting date of the investing company; and
   (ii) dividends receivable in respect of accounting periods ending on or before that date and declared before the accounts of the investing company are approved by the directors.

   (b) *In the investing group's consolidated accounts (see paragraph 8)*
   The investing group's share of profits less losses of associated companies (see paragraph 12 for exceptions).

8   Where the investing company has no subsidiaries, or otherwise does not prepare consolidated accounts, it will be necessary for it to adapt its profit and loss account, suitably titled, to incorporate the additional information required by this statement (see Appendix 2). References in this statement to investing groups and consolidated accounts are to be taken as embracing such additional information in the case of investing companies which do not have subsidiaries or which do not otherwise prepare consolidated accounts.

9   Where an associated company itself has subsidiary or associated companies, the profits or losses to be dealt with in the investing group's consolidated accounts are its attributable proportion of the profits or losses of the group of which the associated company is parent.

Inclusion of associated companies' results in consolidated accounts of investing group

10   The investing group should include in its consolidated accounts its share of all material associated companies' results (whether profits or losses), subject to the exceptions stated in paragraph 12.

11   The accounts used for the purpose of including associated companies' results should be audited accounts either coterminous with those of the investing company or made up to a date which is not more than six months before, or shortly after, the date of the investing group or company's accounts. In the absence of such audited accounts (for which there should be justifiable cause), unaudited accounts may be used provided the investing group is satisfied as to their reliability. In the case of associated companies which are listed on a recognised stock exchange, only published financial information should be used for incorporation in the accounts of the investing company. Before incorporating results of an associated company based on accounts, whether audited or unaudited, issued some appreciable time before the completion of the accounts of the investing company, care should be taken to ensure that later information has not materially affected the view shown by the accounts of the associated company. If accounts not coterminous with those of the investing company, or unaudited accounts, are used, the facts and the dates of year-ends should be disclosed.

An associated company's results should be omitted from the consolidated accounts   12
only on the same grounds as those which would permit group accounts not to deal with
a subsidiary, notably if the inclusion of such results:

(a) would involve expense or delay out of proportion to the value to the members of
the investing company; or

(b) would be misleading.

The reason for omission should be stated.

Accounting adjustments

Wherever the effect is material, adjustments similar to those adopted for the purpose of   13
presenting consolidated accounts should be made to exclude from the investing group's
consolidated accounts such items as unrealised profits on stocks transferred to or from
associated companies and to achieve reasonable consistency with the accounting
practices adopted by the investing group.

Profit and loss account items*

Profits before tax. The investing group should include in its consolidated accounts the   14
aggregate of its share of before-tax profits less losses of associated companies. The item
should be shown separately and suitably described, for example as 'share of profits less
losses of associated companies'.

Taxation. The tax attributed to the share of profits of associated companies should be   15
disclosed separately within the group tax charge in the consolidated accounts.

Extraordinary items. The investing group's share of aggregate extraordinary items   16
dealt with in associated companies' accounts should be included with the group share
of extraordinary items, unless the amount is material in the context of the group's
results when it should be separately disclosed.

Net profit retained by associated companies. There should be shown separately the   17
investing group's share of aggregate net profits less losses retained by associated companies.

Other items. The investing group should not include its attributable share of associated   18
companies' items such as turnover and depreciation in the aggregate amounts of these
items disclosed in its consolidated accounts. If the results of one or more associated
companies are of such significance in the context of the investing group's accounts that
more detailed information about them would assist in giving a true and fair view, this
information should be given by separate disclosure of the total turnover of the
associated companies concerned, their total depreciation charge, their total profits less
losses before taxation, and the amounts of such profits attributable to the investing
group.

---

* Examples of profit and loss accounts drawn up to give the information required are shown in
Appendices 1 and 2.

Balance sheet items

19 Unless shown at a valuation, the amount at which the investing group's interests in associated companies should be shown in the consolidated balance sheet is:

(a) the cost of the investments less any amounts written off; and

(b) the investing company or group's share of the post-acquisition retained profits and reserves of the associated companies.

The investing company which has no subsidiaries, or which does not otherwise prepare consolidated accounts, should show its share of its associated companies' post-acquisition retained profits and reserves by way of note to its balance sheet.

Information regarding associated companies' tangible and intangible assets and liabilities should be given, if materially relevant for the appreciation by the members of the investing company of the nature of their investment.

20 The amount at which the investing group's interests in accumulated reserves is shown in the consolidated accounts should distinguish between profits retained by the group and profits retained by associated companies. If retained profits of associated companies overseas would be subject to further tax on distribution, this should be made clear. It will also be necessary to take account of and disclose movements on associated companies' other reserves, e.g., surplus on revaluation of fixed assets.

Disclosure of particulars of associated companies

21 The investing group or company should give particulars of the names of and its interests in companies treated as associated companies, and of any other companies in which it holds not less than 20 per cent of the equity voting rights but which are not treated as associated companies.

Corresponding amounts

22 On first introduction of the standard method of accounting set out in this statement the corresponding amounts for the preceding period should be appropriately stated on a comparable basis.

Date from which effective

23 The method of accounting for the results of associated companies set out in this statement should be adopted as soon as possible and regarded as standard in respect of reports relating to accounting periods starting on or after 1st January 1971.

Part 4 – Note on legal requirements

Paragraph 5 A of Schedule 2 to the Companies Act 1967 requires certain information 24
to be given about unquoted equity investments in the absence of a directors' valuation.
The information required to be given by this statement may not fully satisfy the
requirements of the Act. To that extent it will be necessary either to re-arrange the
information appropriately or, if this is impracticable, to provide it by way of a separate
note.

In dealing with the results of associated companies, regard should be had to the provi- 25
sions of paragraph 12 (1) (g) of Schedule 2 to the Companies Act 1967, which requires
the amounts respectively of income from quoted investments and income from
unquoted investments to be shown in the profit and loss account.

The disclosure requirements of this statement are not intended to override exemptions 26
from the disclosure requirements of the Companies Acts, available to and utilised by
special classes of company under Part III of the Second Schedule to the Companies
Act 1967, and applicable to companies incorporated outside the United Kingdom
under Section 4 (3) of the Companies Act 1967.

Appendix 1

Note. This Appendix does not form part of the statement of standard accounting practice. The method of presentation used is illustrative only and in no way prescriptive. Other methods of presentation may equally comply with the accounting standard set out in the statement.

EXAMPLE OF CONSOLIDATED PROFIT AND LOSS ACCOUNT FOR A COMPANY WITH SUBSIDIARIES

Consolidated profit and loss account of an investing company and subsidiaries, incorporating results of associated companies

		£
Turnover (of the investing company and subsidiaries)		X
Operating profit (after charging depreciation and all other trading expenses		£
of the investing company and subsidiaries)		X
Share of profits less losses of associated companies		X
Profit before taxation		X
Taxation: Investing company and subsidiaries	X	
Associated companies	X	X
		X
Minority interests		X
Profit after taxation before extraordinary items		X
Extraordinary items (group proportion after taxation, after deducting minority interests and including share of associated companies' items)		X
Profit attributable to members of (the investing company) (See note)		X
Dividends		X
Net profit retained		£X*

	£
By the investing company	X
By subsidiaries	X
In associated companies	X
	£X*

Note. Of the profit attributable to members of the investing company, £—is dealt with in the accounts of the investing company.

Appendix 2

Note. This Appendix does not form part of the statement of standard accounting practice. The method of presentation used is illustrative only and in no way prescriptive. Other methods of presentation may equally comply with the accounting standard set out in the statement.

EXAMPLE OF PROFIT AND LOSS ACCOUNT FOR A COMPANY WITHOUT SUBSIDIARIES

Profit and loss account of an investing company incorporating results of associated companies

	£	£
Turnover (of the investing company)		X
Operating profit (after charging depreciation and all other trading expenses of the investing company)		X
Share of profits less losses of associated companies		X
Profit before taxation		X
Taxation: Investing company	X	
Associated companies	X	
		X
Profit after taxation before extraordinary items		X
Extraordinary items (investing company and share of associated companies' items) after taxation		X
Profit attributable to members of the investing company comprising:		X*
Profit of the investing company	X	
Profits retained in associated companies	X	
		£X*
Dividends		X
Net profit retained		£X**

	£
By the investing company	X
In associated companies	X
	£X**

2

Disclosure of accounting policies

Contents

Disclosure of accounting policies

(Issued November 1971)

It is fundamental to the understanding and interpretation of financial accounts that those who use them should be aware of the main assumptions on which they are based. The purpose of the statement which follows is to assist such understanding by promoting improvement in the quality of information disclosed. It seeks to achieve this by establishing as standard accounting practice the disclosure in financial accounts of clear explanations of the accounting policies followed in so far as these are significant for the purpose of giving a true and fair view. The statement does not seek to establish accounting standards for individual items; these will be dealt with in separate statements of standard accounting practice issued from time to time.

Part 1 – Explanatory note

Fundamental accounting concepts, accounting bases and accounting policies

1   In accounting usage terms such as 'accounting principles', 'practices', 'rules', 'conventions', 'methods' or 'procedures' have often been treated as interchangeable.* For the purpose of this statement it is convenient to distinguish between *fundamental accounting concepts*, *accounting bases* and *accounting policies*.

2   *Fundamental accounting concepts* are here defined as broad basic assumptions which underlie the periodic financial accounts of business enterprises. It is expedient to single out for special mention four in particular: (a) the 'going concern' concept, (b) the 'accruals' concept, (c) the 'consistency' concept and (d) the 'prudence' concept.† The use of these concepts is not necessarily self-evident from an examination of accounts, but they have such general acceptance that they call for no explanation in published accounts and their observance is presumed unless stated otherwise. They are practical rules rather than theoretical ideals and are capable of variation and evolution as accounting thought and practice develop, but their present generally accepted meanings are restated in paragraph 14 below.

3   *Accounting bases* are the methods which have been developed for expressing or applying fundamental accounting concepts to financial transactions and items. By their nature accounting bases are more diverse and numerous than fundamental concepts, since they have evolved in response to the variety and complexity of types of business and business transactions, and for this reason there may justifiably exist more than one recognised accounting basis for dealing with particular items.

---

* In this series 'accounting practices' has been adopted as a generic term to encompass all aspects of financial accounting methods and presentation.

† It is emphasised that it is not the purpose of this statement to develop a basic theory of accounting. An exhaustive theoretical approach would take an entirely different form and would include, for instance, many more propositions than the four fundamental concepts referred to here. It is, however, expedient to recognise them as working assumptions having general acceptance at the present time.

Accounting policies are the specific accounting bases judged by business enterprises to be most appropriate to their circumstances and adopted by them for the purpose of preparing their financial accounts.

4

Particular problems in application of the fundamental concepts

The main difficulty in applying the fundamental accounting concepts arises from the fact that many business transactions have financial effects spreading over a number of years. Decisions have to be made on the extent to which expenditure incurred in one year can reasonably be expected to produce benefits in the form of revenue in other years and should therefore be carried forward, in whole or in part; that is, should be dealt with in the closing balance sheet, as distinct from being dealt with as an expense of the current year in the profit and loss account because the benefit has been exhausted in that year.

5

In some cases revenue is received for goods or services the production or supply of which will involve some later expenditure. In this case a decision must be made regarding how much of the revenue should be carried forward, to be dealt with in subsequent profit and loss accounts when the relevant costs are incurred.

6

All such decisions require consideration of future events of uncertain financial effect, and to this extent an element of commercial judgement is unavoidable in the assessment.

7

Examples of matters which give rise to particular difficulty are: the future benefits to be derived from stocks and all types of work in progress at the end of the year; the future benefits to be derived from fixed assets, and the period of years over which these will be fruitful; the extent to which expenditure on research and development can be expected to produce future benefits.

8

Purpose and limitations of accounting bases

In the course of practice there have developed a variety of accounting bases designed to provide consistent, fair and as nearly as possible objective solutions to these problems in particular circumstances; for instance bases for calculating such items as depreciation, the amounts at which stocks and work in progress are to be stated, and deferred taxation.

9

Accounting bases provide an orderly and consistent framework for periodic reporting of a concern's results and financial position, but they do not, and are not intended to, substitute for the exercise of commercial judgement in the preparation of financial reports. Where a choice of acceptable accounting bases is available judgement must be exercised in choosing those which are appropriate to the circumstances and are best suited to present fairly the concern's results and financial position; the bases thus adopted then become the concern's accounting policies. The significance of accounting bases is that they provide limits to the area subject to the exercise of judgement, and a check against arbitrary, excessive or unjustifiable adjustments where no other objective yardstick is available. By definition it is not possible to develop generalised rules for the exercise of judgement, though practical working rules may be evolved on a pragmatic basis for limited use in particular circumstances. Broadly, the longer a concern's normal business cycle – the period between initiation of business transactions and their

10

completion – the greater the area subject to judgement and its effect on periodic financial accounts, and the less its susceptibility to close regulation by accounting bases. These limitations to the regulating powers of accounting bases must be recognised.

Significance of disclosure of accounting policies

11   In circumstances where more than one accounting basis is acceptable in principle, the accounting policy followed can significantly affect a concern's reported results and financial position and the view presented can be properly appreciated only if the policies followed in dealing with material items are also explained. For this reason adequate disclosure of the accounting policies is essential to the fair presentation of financial accounts. As accounting standards become established through publication of statements of standard accounting practice, the choice of accounting bases regarded as generally available will diminish, but it has to be recognised that the complexity and diversity of business renders total and rigid uniformity of bases impracticable.

12   The items with which this statement is mainly concerned are those which are subject to the exercise of judgement as to how far they should be dealt with in the profit and loss account for the period under review or how far all or part should be carried forward in the balance sheet as attributable to the operations of future periods. The determination of the annual profit or loss of nearly every business substantially depends on a systematic approach to a few material items of this type. For the better appreciation of the view they give, annual accounts should include a clear explanation of the accounting policies followed for dealing with these few key items (some examples of which are given in paragraph 13 below). The intention and spirit of this statement are that management should identify those items of the type described which are judged material or critical for the purpose of determining and fully appreciating the company's profit or loss and its financial position, and should make clear the accounting policies followed for dealing with them.

Examples of matters for which different accounting bases are recognised

13   Significant matters for which different accounting bases are recognised and which may have a material effect on reported results and financial position include:

- depreciation of fixed assets
- treatment and amortisation of intangibles such as research and development expenditure, patents and trademarks
- stocks and work in progress
- long-term contracts
- deferred taxation
- hire-purchase or instalment transactions
- leasing and rental transactions
- conversion of foreign currencies
- repairs and renewals
- consolidation policies
- property development transactions
- warranties for products or services.

This list is not exhaustive, and may vary according to the nature of the operations conducted.

Part 2 – Definition of terms

Fundamental accounting concepts are the broad basic assumptions which underlie the periodic financial accounts of business enterprises. At the present time the four following fundamental concepts (the relative importance of which will vary according to the circumstances of the particular case) are regarded as having general acceptability: 14

(a) the 'going concern' concept: the enterprise will continue in operational existence for the foreseeable future. This means in particular that the profit and loss account and balance sheet assume no intention or necessity to liquidate or curtail significantly the scale of operation;

(b) the 'accruals' concept: revenue and costs are accrued (that is, recognised as they are earned or incurred, not as money is received or paid), matched with one another so far as their relationship can be established or justifiably assumed, and dealt with in the profit and loss account of the period to which they relate; provided that where the accruals concept is inconsistent with the 'prudence' concept (paragraph (d) below), the latter prevails. The accruals concept implies that the profit and loss account reflects changes in the amount of net assets that arise out of the transactions of the relevant period (other than distributions or subscriptions of capital and unrealised surpluses arising on revaluation of fixed assets). Revenue and profits dealt with in the profit and loss account are matched with associated costs and expenses by including in the same account the costs incurred in earning them (so far as these are material and identifiable);

(c) the 'consistency' concept: there is consistency of accounting treatment of like items within each accounting period and from one period to the next;

(d) the concept of 'prudence': revenue and profits are not anticipated, but are recognised by inclusion in the profit and loss account only when realised in the form either of cash or of other assets the ultimate cash realisation of which can be assessed with reasonable certainty; provision is made for all known liabilities (expenses and losses) whether the amount of these is known with certainty or is a best estimate in the light of the information available.

Accounting bases are the methods developed for applying fundamental accounting concepts to financial transactions and items, for the purpose of financial accounts, and in particular (a) for determining the accounting periods in which revenue and costs should be recognised in the profit and loss account and (b) for determining the amounts at which material items should be stated in the balance sheet.   15

Accounting policies are the specific accounting bases selected and consistently followed by a business enterprise as being, in the opinion of the management, appropriate to its circumstances and best suited to present fairly its results and financial position.   16

Part 3 – Standard accounting practice

Disclosure of adoption of concepts which differ from those generally accepted

17   If accounts are prepared on the basis of assumptions which differ in material respects from any of the generally accepted fundamental concepts defined in paragraph 14 above, the facts should be explained. In the absence of a clear statement to the contrary, there is a presumption that the four fundamental concepts have been observed.

Disclosure of accounting policies

18   The accounting policies (as defined in paragraph 16 above) followed for dealing with items which are judged material or critical in determining profit or loss for the year and in stating the financial position should be disclosed by way of note to the accounts. The explanations should be clear, fair, and as brief as possible.

Date from which effective

19   The accounting practices set out in this statement should be adopted as soon as possible and regarded as standard in respect of reports relating to accounting periods starting on or after 1st January 1972.

3

Earnings per share

Contents

Earnings per share

(Revised August 1974)

The original Statement of Standard Accounting Practice on Earnings Per Share *(SSAP No. 3) was issued in February 1972.*

Although little change is needed in the basic definition of Earnings Per Share (Part 2) or in the standard accounting practice (Part 3), other parts of the statement have been brought up to date to take account of:

(a) *The change in the basis of taxation in the United Kingdom from the former system of corporation tax to the imputation system;*

(b) *The issue by the Councils of the bodies participating in the Accounting Standards Steering Committee of a number of statements of accounting practice; in particular SSAP No. 8* The treatment of taxation under the imputation system in the accounts of companies.

The Council of the Stock Exchange states in note 28 of the listing agreement that it will 'expect the accounts of listed companies to be drawn up in accordance with the standards approved by these accountancy bodies'. This requirement to apply the accounting standard on earnings per share is extended by note 6 of the listing agreement to the computation of the figure of earnings per share to be shown in preliminary profits announcements for the year or other full accounting period.

This statement is intended to apply to the audited accounts of listed companies. The circumstances of smaller unlisted companies and the problems of computation (particularly when a company is financed by interest-free loans from directors) are often such that an earnings per share figure would not be meaningful.

Part 1 – Explanatory note

1   The original call for a standard accounting practice for the disclosure of earnings per share was based on the increasing use of the price-earnings ratio as a standard stock market indicator. Despite the complication introduced by the imputation system of corporation tax and the limitation of dividends by Government regulation in the United Kingdom, price-earnings ratios remain one of the most commonly used stock market indicators. Although they are not strictly comparable because of differences between one country's tax system and another's, they are, nevertheless, used on a world-wide basis.

2   The continued use of price-earnings ratios requires that the earnings per share on which that ratio is based, should be calculated and disclosed on a comparable basis as between one company and another and as between one financial period and another, so far as this is possible.

3   As between one company and another, the main problem arising from the imputation system of corporation tax is the treatment of irrecoverable Advance Corporation Tax

(ACT)*. After the transitional period, only a small proportion of listed companies is likely to have irrecoverable ACT (or unrelieved overseas tax arising from a dividend) included in their tax charge for the year. These companies will mainly be those whose earnings arise overseas, or who have large capital allowances for corporation tax, such as the oil, mining, plantation and shipping companies. The calculation of earnings per share when there is irrecoverable ACT is considered in paragraphs 7 to 9.

4 One of the features of the change from the former system to the imputation system of corporation tax is that, whereas before April 1973 earnings after corporation tax were available to cover gross dividends before deduction of income tax, the earnings after corporation tax under the new system are available to cover the actual cash dividends payable to the shareholders. The transitional arrangements also give rise to problems of comparison.

5 In calculating the earnings for the equity shareholders it is not the former gross dividend but the amount of the dividend declared and payable to the preference shareholders, which falls to be deducted from the profit after tax, since, under the imputation system, post-tax profits are available to cover cash dividends.

6 Before calculating earnings per share under the new system, it is necessary to examine carefully the charge for taxation to be deducted in arriving at the earnings figure. The tax charge will always include some elements which are constant, in that they will not vary with the proportion of the profit distributed by way of dividend; the charge may however include other elements which do vary according to the amount of profit distributed and which would be absent if no distributions were made. These components may be classified as follows:

Constant
Corporation tax on income.
Tax attributable to dividends received.
Overseas tax unrelieved because the rate of overseas tax exceeds the rate of UK corporation tax.

Variable
Irrecoverable ACT.
Overseas tax unrelieved because dividend payments restrict the double tax credit available.

7 Two alternative methods of computing earnings per share under the imputation system have been propounded. One would take account of all the elements of the taxation charge listed above, both constant and variable – this is called the 'net basis'. The other would recognise only the constant elements, and because it seeks to arrive at what the earnings would be if the distributions were nil, it is called the 'nil basis'. It can be expected that most companies, in normal circumstances, will not incur either of the variable elements of taxation, so that for them calculations on the net basis and the nil basis will produce the same result. The companies where the two methods are most

---

* Recoverable and Irrecoverable ACT are defined in SSAP No. 8 Part 2.

likely to produce divergent figures are those which have income taxed overseas, a significant proportion of which is distributed.

8   The advantage of the nil basis is that it produces a figure of earnings which is not dependent on the level of distribution, and so provides an indicator of one company's performance more closely comparable with that of another. The argument which is preferred is that the net basis takes account of all the relevant facts, including the additional tax liabilities inherent in the dividend policy pursued by the company, for which the directors should no less be accountable to shareholders. It is considered therefore that quoted companies should report in their accounts earnings per share primarily on the net basis.

9   Where, however, there is a material difference between earnings per share calculated on the net basis and on the nil distribution basis, it is most desirable that the latter also be shown although the disclosure requirements in respect of the treatment of taxation in accounts* will enable this earnings per share on a nil basis to be calculated by the user.

Part 2 – Definition of terms

Earnings per share
10   The profit in pence attributable to each equity share, based on the consolidated profit of the period after tax and after deducting minority interests and preference dividends, but before taking into account extraordinary items, divided by the number of equity shares in issue and ranking for dividend in respect of the period.

Net basis of calculating earnings per share
11   In determining earnings per share on the net basis, the charge for taxation used in determining earnings includes:

    (a) any irrecoverable advance corporation tax (ACT);

    (b) any unrelieved overseas tax arising from the payment or proposed payment of dividends.

Nil distribution basis of calculating earnings per share
12   In determining earnings per share on the nil basis, the charge for taxation used in determining earnings generally excludes (a) and (b) above (except in so far as these arise in respect of preference dividends).

---

* SSAP No. 8. *The treatment of taxation under the imputation system in the accounts of companies.*

Part 3 – Standard accounting practice

Applicable to listed companies

13 This accounting standard shall apply to companies having a listing on a recognised stock exchange for any class of equity, other than companies claiming exemption from the disclosure requirements under Part III of Schedule 2 of the Companies Act 1967.   13

14 In the audited accounts of such listed companies, the earnings per share should be shown on the face of the profit and loss account on the net basis both for the period under review and for the corresponding previous period. (The desirability of showing also the earnings per share on the nil distribution basis where materially different from those on the net basis is emphasised in paragraph 9.)   14

15 The basis of calculating earnings per share should be disclosed, either in the profit and loss account or in a note thereto. In particular, the amount of the earnings and the number of equity shares used in the calculation should be shown.   15

16 Where a company has at the balance sheet date contracted to issue further shares after the end of the period, or where it has already issued shares which will rank for dividend later, the effect may be to dilute future earnings per share. In addition, therefore, to the basic earnings per share, as set out above, the fully diluted earnings per share should be shown on the face of the profit and loss account of quoted companies in the following circumstances: 16

(a) where the company has issued a separate class of equity shares which do not rank for any dividend in the period under review, but which will do so in the future;

(b) where the company has issued debentures or loan stock (or preference shares) convertible into equity shares of the company;

(c) where the company has granted options or issued warrants to subscribe for equity shares of the company.

In each case:

(i) the basis of calculation of fully diluted earnings per share should be disclosed;

(ii) the fully diluted earnings per share need not be given unless the dilution is material. Dilution amounting to 5 per cent or more of the basic earnings per share is regarded as material for this purpose;

(iii) fully diluted earnings per share for the corresponding previous period should not be shown unless the assumptions on which it was based still apply;

(iv) equal prominence should be given to basic and fully diluted earnings per share wherever both are disclosed.

Date from which effective

17 The disclosure of earnings per share became an accounting standard in respect of accounts relating to periods starting on or after 1st January 1972. This standard has   17

been revised to take into account the imputation system of corporation tax which was introduced with effect from 6th April 1973.

Application in Republic of Ireland

18 The calculation of earnings per share should be based on the consolidated profits for the period after corporation profits tax and income tax and after deducting minority interests and preference dividends, but before taking into account extraordinary items.

19 Earnings per share should be described as follows: 'Earnings per share after deducting corporation profits tax and income tax.'

Appendix 1

This appendix is for general guidance and does not form part of the statement of standard accounting practice.

GUIDELINES FOR THE DETERMINATION OF EARNINGS PER SHARE

Primary considerations

Preliminary

In simple terms, the earnings per share figure is calculated by apportioning the total amount earned for the equity share capital in a financial period over the number of shares in issue and ranking for dividend in respect of that period. 1

Earnings for equity

The amount earned for equity should normally be the consolidated profit of the year after tax, minority interests and preference dividends, but before extraordinary items*. net of taxation and minority interests. It would include the earnings of associated companies – see Statement of Standard Accounting Practice *Accounting for the results of associated companies*, issued January 1971. 2

Preference dividends

Under the imputation system, the preference dividend has ceased to be the gross dividend but is now the cash amount declared and payable to the shareholder. This is the amount to be deducted from the profit after tax in calculating earnings per share. 3

Where the preference shares are cumulative, the dividend for the period should be taken into account, whether or not it has been earned or declared. Subject to this, arrears of preference dividend paid during the year should be ignored. In the case of a non-cumulative dividend the deduction should be the amount of the preferential dividend paid or proposed. 4

The fixed part of the dividend on participating preference shares should be treated in the same way as a preference dividend. If the participating element is limited (e.g., maximum 10 per cent) the whole dividend for the period may be deducted. If it is unlimited, then the appropriate proportion of the earnings for the period to allow for the participating element should be deducted before arriving at the earnings for the ordinary shares. 5

Losses

Where a loss is incurred or the amount earned for equity is a negative figure, the earnings per share should be determined in the normal manner and the result shown as a loss per share. 6

---

* Extraordinary items are defined in Statement of Standard Accounting Practice No. 6, issued April 1974.

7   Where the tax charge is reduced by losses brought forward, the tax charge for the year shown in the profit and loss account (rather than a notional tax charge) should be used in the calculation of earnings per share accompanied by an adequate explanation of the effects of the incidence of tax relief on earnings per share for the year under review and for the preceding year.

Sinking fund

8   Transfers to a loan redemption reserve or to a sinking fund (even though supported by a corresponding transfer of cash) merely divide the profits between those available for immediate distribution and those distributable later; they do not reduce the earnings of the period, and should not be deducted in calculating the earnings of the period.

Corresponding amounts for the previous period

9   Earnings per share for the corresponding previous period should be shown.

Equity share capital

10   Where there is only one class of equity share capital ranking for dividend, the calculation of earnings per share should be based on the number of such shares in issue during the period. Where there is more than one class of equity shares or where some of the shares are not fully paid, the earnings should be apportioned over the different classes of shares in accordance with their dividend rights or other right to participate in profits.

Subsequent changes in capital

11   Where there has been a change in the capital structure after the accounting date but before the preliminary announcement of the results of the period, the earnings per share shown in the profit and loss account should not take this into account; however, it is desirable that the effect on the basic earnings per share of any capitalisation issue, share split, or bonus element inherent in a rights issue should be disclosed.

Summary

12   Earnings per share should be calculated by apportioning the earnings (that is, normally, the consolidated profit of the period after taxation, minority interests and preference dividends but before extraordinary items – see paragraph 2 above) over the number of equity shares in issue and ranking for dividend during the period. A simple example is given below.

EXAMPLE 1

Simple capital structure

A   *Capital structure*
Issued share capital:
£500,000 in 10 per cent (now 7 per cent+tax credit)*
cumulative preference shares of £1 (issued before
6th April, 1973) £1,000,000 in ordinary shares of
25p=4,000,000 shares

---

* See paragraph 18 of SSAP No. 8. *Accounting for corporation tax under the imputation system.*

		Year ended 31st December	
		Year 2	Year 1
B	*Trading results*		
	Profit after tax	£535,000	£435,000

Assumptions
No change in the issued share capital during the two years

		Year 2	Year 1
C	*Calculation of earnings per share*	£	£
	Profit after tax	535,000	435,000
	Less Preference dividend	35,000	35,000
	Earnings	£500,000	£400,000
	Number of ordinary shares . . .	4,000,000	4,000,000

		Year ended 31st December	
D	*Illustration of presentation in the profit and loss account*	Year 2	Year 1
	Earnings per ordinary share of 25p . .	12$\frac{1}{2}$p	10p

Note. The calculation of earnings per share is based on earnings of £500,000 (Year 1 £400,000) and four million ordinary shares in issue throughout the two years ended 31st December, Year 2.

Treatment of changes in equity share capital

Where further equity shares have been issued during the financial year, they will probably have been issued by one of the following methods: 13

	Paragraphs
Issue at full market price	14
Capitalisation issue	15
Share exchange	16
Rights issue at less than full market price . . .	17–18

Each of these circumstances is likely to affect the method of determining the earnings per share and the effect is summarised below:

Issue at full market price

Most issues for cash in this country are in the form of rights issues rather than at full market price. If, however, new equity shares have been issued either for cash at full market price or as consideration for the acquisition of an asset the earnings should be apportioned over the average number of shares ranking for dividend during the period weighted on a time basis.   14

Capitalisation issue

Where new equity shares have been issued by way of capitalisation during the period, the earnings should be apportioned over the number of shares ranking for dividend   15 after the capitalisation. The corresponding figures for all earlier periods should be adjusted accordingly. Similar considerations apply where equity shares are split into shares of smaller nominal value.

Share exchange

16 Where shares (ranking for dividend) or loan stock have been issued during the period as consideration for shares in a new subsidiary, it should be assumed that, for the purpose of calculating the earnings per share, these securities were issued on the first day of the period for which the profits of the new subsidiary are included in the earnings of the group.

Rights issue at less than full market price

17 *Earnings per share for prior years* Where equity shares are issued by way of rights during the period it is recommended that the factor for adjustment of past earnings per share after a rights issue be based on the closing price* on the last day of quotation of the shares cum rights. The factor is therefore:

$$\frac{\text{Theoretical EX RIGHTS price}}{\text{Actual CUM RIGHTS price on the last day of quotation cum rights}}$$

Where a rights issue is made during the year under review, the earnings per share for the previous year, and for all earlier years, will need to be adjusted by the factor, calculated as above, to correct for the bonus element in the rights issue.

18 *Earnings per share for the year in which a rights issue is made* For the current year in which a rights issue is made it would be undesirable to split the earnings into two periods, one before the rights issue and one after this event. It is necessary to adjust the weighted average share capital by taking the proportion of the capital in issue before the rights issue, applying to this figure the reciprocal of the factor set out above, i.e., $\dfrac{\text{actual cum rights price}}{\text{theoretical ex rights price}}$, and adding the proportion in issue after the rights issue.

Fully diluted earnings per share

Introduction

19 The earnings per share calculations considered up to this point have been based on either the weighted average share capital ranking for dividend in the period or, in the case of a capitalisation issue, the equity share capital ranking for dividend at the financial year-end.

20 Where a listed company has outstanding:

a separate class of equity shares which do not rank for dividend in the period but will do so in the future (see paragraph 29 below); or

debentures or loan stock (or preference shares) convertible into equity shares of the company (see paragraph 30 below); or

---

* i.e., the official middle market quotation published on the following day.

options or warrants to subscribe for equity shares of the company (see paragraph 31 below);

the company has entered into obligations which may dilute the earnings per share in the future. In these circumstances, in addition to the basic earnings per share, the fully diluted earnings per share should be calculated and shown on the face of the profit and loss account in accordance with paragraph 16 of Part 3 and paragraphs 22 to 28 below.

In each of these cases, full information as to the rights of the holders (existing shareholders, convertible stockholders, preference shareholders or holders of options or warrants) should be set out in the accounts.   21

Depending on the terms of the conversion rights or the options to subscribe, it is possible that the calculation of an earnings per share figure, based on the assumption that these rights or options had been exercised at the beginning of the period, would result in increasing the earnings per share above the basic figure. In these circumstances, it is likely that the conversion rights or options would not be exercised. The resultant figure (i.e., increased earnings per share rather than diluted earnings per share) should not be shown if it is in excess of the basic earnings per share.   22

The fully diluted earnings per share need not be given if the dilution is not material, in which event that fact should be stated. Dilution amounting to 5 per cent or more of the basic earnings per share is regarded as material for this purpose.   23

The fully diluted earnings per share should not be shown when the basic earnings per share is a negative figure (i.e., a loss).   24

Since the fully diluted earnings per share is concerned with future dilution, a corresponding amount for the previous period may not be meaningful; it should not be shown unless the assumptions on which it was based are still applicable.   25

Where the dilution is material and the full diluted earnings per share is shown, the basis of calculation should be disclosed.   26

A listed company may, in any period, have more than one type of convertible debenture or loan stock (or preference shares), in issue with differing conversion rights, or may also have issued shares to rank in a future period or have granted options or warrants to subscribe. In this event, the fully diluted earnings per share should take into account only those 'convertibles' or shares or options or warrants which would have a diluting effect on the earnings per share and should disregard those which have no such diluting effect.   27

Wherever fully diluted earnings per share is disclosed in addition to the basic earnings per share, they should both be given equal prominence.   28

Another class of equity share ranking for dividend in the future

29   Where a listed company has in issue a class of equity shares* not yet ranking for dividend but which will do so in the future (by conversion or otherwise), in addition to the basic earnings per share (calculated on the equity shares ranking for all or any dividends in respect of the period), the fully diluted earnings per share should be calculated on the assumption that this class of shares ranked for dividend from the beginning of the period (or such later date as they were issued).

Convertible securities

30   Where a company has convertible loan stock in issue at any time during the period, in addition to the basic earnings per share, the fully diluted earnings per share should be calculated on the assumption that the maximum number of new equity shares had been issued on conversion and that this conversion had taken place on the first day of the period (or on the date of issue of the convertible loan stock if later). The earnings for the period should be adjusted by adding back the assumed saving of interest on the stock so converted, net of corporation tax.

Options or warrants to subscribe

31   Where a listed company has granted options or issued warrants to subscribe for equity shares of the company, in addition to the basic earnings per share, the fully diluted earnings per share should be calculated on the assumption that the maximum number of new shares had been issued under the terms of the options or warrants and that these had been exercised on the first day of the period (or the date of issue if later). The earnings for the period should be adjusted on the basis that the proceeds of subscription had been invested in $2\frac{1}{2}$ per cent Consolidated Stock on the first day of the period at the closing price of the previous day.

Exceptions

32   In the circumstances dealt with in paragraphs 29 to 31 above fully diluted earnings per share should be shown on the face of the profit and loss account subject to the exceptions stated in paragraphs 22 to 25 above.

Final conversion or subscription during the year

33   Where the convertible loan stock has been finally converted during the year (unless it was converted on the first day of the year and the shares issued have, therefore, ranked for dividend for the full year), it will still be necessary to show the fully diluted earnings per share in the accounts for the year in which that final conversion took place.

34   Similar considerations apply on final subscriptions in the case of options or warrants to subscribe.

---

* 'New' shares of the same class as existing equity shares, which are separately quoted for a time, only because they are transferable in a different form or because they rank for a later (e.g. final) but not for an earlier (e.g., interim) dividend in respect of the period under review, should not be treated as a separate class of shares.

Appendix 2

This appendix is for general guidance and does not form part of the statement of standard accounting practice.

Financial statistics in the historical summary

In order to present a fair comparison over the period of the historical summary the basic earnings per share figures will need to be adjusted for subsequent changes in capital on the basis set out in the three following paragraphs. The resultant figures should be described as the adjusted earnings per share and should be set out separately from the other financial data which is not so adjusted, e.g., in a separate box.   1

Adjustments for capitalisation issues
Where new equity shares have been issued by way of capitalisation of reserves during any financial year, or where shares have been split into shares of a lower nominal value, the earnings per share for all earlier years will need to be adjusted by the appropriate factor, i.e., the number of equity shares before the capitalisation divided by the number of such shares after the capitalisation.   2

Adjustments for rights issues
Where equity shares have been issued by way of rights in any financial year, the earning per share for all earlier years should be adjusted by the factor set out in paragraph 17 of Appendix 1 of this statement.   3

Cumulative adjustment
Where there is more than one capitalisation or rights issue, both these factors will operate cumulatively.   4

Dividends per share
Where there have been capitalisation or rights issues in the period covered by the summary a straight record of the equity dividends actually paid would not, however, be comparable with the adjusted earnings per share. It is therefore suggested that a record of the equity dividends should be set out in the form of pence per share, the dividends being adjusted by the same factors for capitalisation and rights issues (set out in paragraphs 2 to 4 above) as the earnings per share. This record should cover the same period, being described as the adjusted equity dividends, and should be set alongside the adjusted basic earnings per share (e.g., in the box referred to in paragraph 1).   5

Equity dividend cover
Dividend cover will normally be found by dividing earnings by dividends under the imputation system of taxation but this simple relationship will not always apply, since the payment of additional dividends may involve the company in the payment of further taxation either in the United Kingdom or overseas. It is the theoretical maximum dividend, after allowing for such additional taxation, which should then be divided by the actual dividend to give the cover.   6

The accounting treatment of government grants

(Issued April 1974)

The application of this statement is limited to grants made for the purchase of fixed assets in the United Kingdom and the Republic of Ireland.

Part 1 – Explanatory note

Introduction

The accounting treatment of government grants has varied as different grants schemes have been produced by successive governments. With the advent of regional development grants under the Industry Act 1972 it is desirable to standardise the accounting treatment of all capital-based grants.

1

Revenue-based grants

The Industry Act 1972 (and similar Acts in the Republic of Ireland and Northern Ireland) make provision for grants to be made by reference to specified categories of revenue expenditure. Such grants do not produce accounting problems as they clearly should be credited to revenue in the same period in which the revenue expenditure to which they relate is charged. If the amount receivable is not precisely ascertainable at the accounting date it is generally practicable to make a reasonable estimate.

2

Capital-based grants

The Industry Act 1972 (and similar Acts in the Republic of Ireland and Northern Ireland) also make provision for grants to be made by reference to certain types of capital expenditure. In the past, where expenditure on the acquisition of a fixed asset was eligible for a government grant, there have been different views about the choice of accounting treatments. Three principal treatments have been discussed:

3

   (a) to credit to profit and loss account the total amount of the grant immediately;

   (b) to credit the amount of the grant to a non-distributable reserve;

   (c) to credit the amount of the grant to revenue over the useful life of the asset by:

      (i) reducing the cost of the acquisition of the fixed asset by the amount of the grant; or

      (ii) treating the amount of the grant as a deferred credit, a portion of which is transferred to revenue annually.

The effect of the grant on the company's reported earnings under the methods listed in paragraph 3 would be:

4

   (a) immediate effect;

   (b) no effect;

   (c) progressive effect over the life of the asset.

5 Methods (a) and (b) provide no correlation between the accounting treatment of the grant and the accounting treatment of the expenditure to which the grant relates. Method (c) matches the application of the grant with the amortisation of the capital expenditure to which it relates and is therefore considered to be the most appropriate treatment.

6 Of the two ways in which (c) may be applied, the main argument in favour of the first alternative (reducing the cost of the fixed asset) is its simplicity. By crediting the grant to the cost of the asset the resulting reduced depreciation charge automatically credits the amount of the grant to revenue over the life of the asset.

7 The arguments in favour of the second alternative (crediting the amount of the grant to a deferred credit account, and releasing it to revenue over an extended period) are:

    (a) assets acquired at different times and locations are recorded on a uniform basis regardless of changes in government policy (such comparability is often important to management in establishing price structures and investment policies);

    (b) control over the ordering, construction and maintenance of assets is based on the gross value;

    (c) as capital allowances for tax purposes are normally calculated on the cost of an asset before deduction of the grant, adjustments of the depreciation charge shown in the accounts are avoided when computing the amount of deferred taxation.

Transitional arrangements

8 Where accounting practices other than those described in Part 2 of this statement have been adopted in respect of capital based grants received or receivable prior to its effective date, it is preferable but not a required standard accounting practice to restate them in a manner consistent with that afforded to grants to which the Statement applies.

Part 2 – Standard accounting practice

Accounting treatment and disclosure

9 Grants relating to fixed assets should be credited to revenue over the expected useful life of the asset. This may be achieved by:

    (a) reducing the cost of the acquisition of the fixed asset by the amount of the grant; or

    (b) treating the amount of the grant as a deferred credit, a portion of which is transferred to revenue annually.

If method (b) is selected, the amount of the deferred credit should, if material, be shown separately in the balance sheet. It should not be shown as part of shareholders' funds.

Date from which effective

10 The accounting practices set out in this statement should be adopted as soon as possible and regarded as standard in respect of financial statements relating to accounting periods beginning on or after 1st January 1974.

Accounting for value added tax

(Issued April 1974)

This statement seeks, by presenting a standard accounting practice, to achieve uniformity of accounting treatment of VAT in financial statements.

Part 1 – Explanatory note

General

VAT is a tax on the supply of goods and services which is eventually borne by the final consumer but collected at each stage of the production and distribution chain. As a general principle, therefore, the treatment of VAT in the accounts of a trader should reflect his role as a collector of the tax and VAT should not be included in income or in expenditure whether of a capital or of a revenue nature. There will however be circumstances, as noted below, in which a trader will himself bear VAT and in such circumstances the accounting treatment should reflect that fact.   1

Persons not accountable for VAT

Persons not accountable for VAT will suffer VAT on inputs. For them VAT will increase the cost of all goods and services to which it applies and should be included in such costs. In particular, the VAT on fixed assets should be added to the cost of the fixed assets concerned.   2

Accountable persons who also carry on exempted activities

In the case of persons who also carry on exempted activities there will be a residue of VAT, which will fall directly on the trader and which will normally be arrived at by division of his activities as between taxable outputs (including zero-rated) and those which are exempt. In such cases, the principle that such VAT will increase the costs to which it applies and should be included in such costs will be equally applicable. Hence the appropriate portion of the VAT allocable to fixed assets should, if irrecoverable, be added to the cost of the fixed assets concerned and the proportion allocable to other items should, if practicable and material, be included in such other items. In some cases, for example where financial and VAT accounting periods do not coincide, an estimate may be necessary.   3

Non-deductible inputs

All traders will bear tax in so far as it relates to non-deductible inputs (for example, motor-cars, other than for resale, and certain business entertaining expenses). Such tax should therefore be included as part of the cost of those items. A similar situation exists in the Republic of Ireland where traders dealing in products such as motor-cars, radios and television sets will bear some non-deductible VAT on the input cost of these items.   4

Amounts due to or from the revenue authorities

The net amount due to or from the revenue authorities in respect of VAT should be included as part of debtors or creditors and will not normally require separate disclosure.   5

Capital commitments

6   The estimated amount of capital commitments should include the appropriate amount, if any, of irrecoverable VAT.

Comparisons

7   Where it has been customary for purchase tax (or sales taxes in the Republic of Ireland) to be included in turnover, it may be desirable in the initial years of VAT to disclose the turnover of periods in which such tax applied both gross and net of tax so as to assist in comparisons. In some cases, for example retailers, it may not be possible to ascertain the amount of purchase tax (or sales taxes) included in turnover; in those cases an explanatory note will be desirable. Where customs or excise duties are included in turnover and such duties are reduced to take account of VAT, an explanatory note may be necessary.

Part 2 – Standard accounting practice

Turnover

8   Turnover shown in the profit and loss account should exclude VAT on taxable outputs. If it is desired to show also the gross turnover, the VAT relevant to that turnover should be shown as a deduction in arriving at the turnover exclusive of VAT.

Irrecoverable VAT

9   Irrecoverable VAT allocable to fixed assets and to other items disclosed separately in published accounts should be included in their cost where practicable and material.

Date from which effective

10   The accounting practices set out in this statement should be adopted as soon as possible and regarded as standard in respect of accounting periods starting on or after 1st January 1974.

6

Extraordinary items and prior year adjustments

Contents

Extraordinary items and prior year adjustments

(Issued April 1974. Part 5 added June 1978)

Accounting for extraordinary and prior year items through reserves or retained profits instead of through the profit and loss account can lead to anomalies in the reported annual results of a business and to disparities in the reported results of similar businesses. This statement requires all extraordinary and prior year items, with certain specified exceptions, to be accounted for through the profit and loss account of the year and not through reserves.

Part 1 – Explanatory note

1 There are currently two different points of view on the treatment of extraordinary and prior year items. One view is that in order to avoid distortion, the profit and loss account for the year should include only the normal recurring activities of the business. It should therefore exclude extraordinary and prior year items, which should be taken direct to reserves or adjusted against the opening balance of retained profits.

2 The other view, on which this statement is based, is that the profit and loss account for the year should include and show separately all extraordinary items which are recognised in that year and, with certain specified exceptions, all prior year items. The main reasons for accepting this view are that:

(a) inclusion and disclosure of extraordinary and prior year items will enable the profit and loss account for the year to give a better view of a company's profitability and progress;

(b) exclusion, being a matter of subjective judgement, could lead to variations and to a loss of comparability between the reported results of companies; and

(c) exclusion could result in extraordinary and prior year items being overlooked in any consideration of results over a series of years.

Extraordinary items

3 Extraordinary items are defined in paragraph 11 below. They derive from events outside the ordinary activities of the business; they do not include items of abnormal size and incidence which derive from the ordinary activities of the business. The classification of items as extraordinary will depend on the particular circumstances – what is extraordinary in one business will not necessarily be extraordinary in another. Subject to this, examples of extraordinary items could be the profits or losses arising from the following:

(a) the discontinuance of a significant part of a business;

(b) the sale of an investment not acquired with the intention of resale;

(c) writing off intangibles, including goodwill, because of unusual events or developments during the period; and

(d) the expropriation of assets.

In order to present fairly the results from the ordinary activities of the business, extraordinary items require to be disclosed in the profit and loss account after the ordinary results have been ascertained.

4

Items which, though abnormal in size and incidence, are not extraordinary items (as defined in paragraph 11) because they derive from the ordinary activities of the business would include:

5

(a) abnormal charges for bad debts and write-offs of stocks and work in progress and research and development expenditure;

(b) abnormal provisions for losses on long-term contracts; and

(c) most adjustments of prior year taxation provisions.

These items, because they derive from the ordinary activities, should be reflected in the ascertainment of profit before extraordinary items although, because of their unusual size and incidence, they may require disclosure if a true and fair view is to be given.

At a time of frequent movement of currency exchange rates, the accounting treatment of foreign currency transactions and conversions and the distinguishing of items that are extraordinary present many problems. These problems are currently under study with a view to the issue of a separate accounting standard. In the meantime, the accounting policies adopted should be disclosed and explained in accordance with Statement of Standard Accounting Practice No. 2 *Disclosure of accounting policies*.

6

Prior year adjustments

Prior year adjustments, that is prior year items which should be adjusted against the opening balance of retained profits or reserves, are rare and limited to items arising from changes in accounting policies and from the correction of fundamental errors. They are discussed in the paragraphs that follow. The majority of prior year items however should be dealt with in the profit and loss account of the year in which they are recognised and shown separately if material. They arise mainly from the corrections and adjustments which are the natural result of estimates inherent in accounting and more particularly in the periodic preparation of financial statements. Estimating future events and their effects requires the exercise of judgement and will require reappraisal as new events occur, as more experience is acquired or as additional information is obtained. Since a change in estimate arises from new information or developments it should not be given retrospective effect by a restatement of prior years. Sometimes a change in estimate may have the appearance of a change in accounting policy and care is necessary in order to avoid confusing the two. For example, the future benefits of a cost may have become doubtful and a change may be made from amortising the cost over the period of those benefits to writing it off when incurred. Such a change should be treated as a change in estimate and not as a change in accounting policy. Prior year items are not extraordinary merely because they relate to a prior year; their nature will determine their classification.

7

Changes in accounting policies

It is a fundamental accounting concept that there is consistency of accounting treatment within each accounting period and from one period to the next. A change in accounting policy should therefore not be made unless it can be justified on the ground

8

that the new policy is preferable to the one it replaces because it will give a fairer presentation of the results and of the financial position of the business. For example, the issue of a statement of standard accounting practice that creates a new accounting basis or expresses a preference for a basis not at present in use in the company is sufficient ground for making a change. It is a characteristic of a change in accounting policy that it is the result of a choice between two or more accounting bases. It therefore does not arise from the adoption or modification of an accounting basis necessitated by transactions or events that are clearly different in substance from those previously occurring. An example of a change in accounting policy would be a change in the method of computing the cost of stock and work in progress from one which includes no overheads to one which includes all production overheads. In the case of a change in accounting policy, the cumulative adjustments applicable to prior years have no bearing on the results of the current year and they should therefore not be included in arriving at the profit for the current year. They should be accounted for by restating prior years with the result that the opening balance of retained profits will be adjusted accordingly. The effect of the change should be disclosed where practicable by showing separately in the restatement of the previous year the amount involved.

Corrections of fundamental errors

9   In exceptional circumstances accounts may have been issued containing errors which are of such significance as to destroy the true and fair view and hence the validity of those accounts and which would have led to their withdrawal had the errors been recognised at the time. The corrections of such fundamental errors should be accounted for not by inclusion in the profit and loss account of the current year but by restating the prior year(s) with the result that the opening balance of retained profits will be adjusted accordingly.

Special cases

10   There are a few special instances where items of a revenue or expense nature are permitted or required, either by law or by a company's constitution, to be taken to reserves. For example, Section 56 of the Companies Act 1948 permits the preliminary expenses of a company or the expenses of, or the commission paid or discount allowed on, any issue of its shares or debentures to be written off against the share premium account. It also permits the share premium account to be used in providing for the premium payable on redemption of any redeemable preference shares or of any debentures of the company. Another example is the common requirement in the Articles of Association of many property and investment holding companies to take the profits on sale of properties or investments to capital reserve. So as to reflect the effect of all such items on the profit or loss for the year, they should be dealt with by taking them, on an amortised basis where appropriate, to the profit and loss account and by transferring an equivalent amount between reserves and the profit for the year.

(In the special circumstances of investment trust companies,* the major part of

---

* An investment trust company is:

  (a) a company approved as an investment trust under Section 359 of the Income and Corporation Taxes Act 1970; or

  (b) a company whose business is wholly or mainly the making and managing of a portfolio of marketable investments, whose income consists wholly or mainly of interest and dividends

whose assets consist of readily marketable securities, it may not be appropriate to deal with losses or gains whether realised or unrealised in the profit and loss account; in such cases realised and unrealised gains or losses should be shown prominently either in the balance sheet or in a note to the accounts.)

Part 2 – Definition of terms

Extraordinary items, for the purposes of this statement, are those items which derive from events or transactions outside the ordinary activities of the business and which are both material and expected not to recur frequently or regularly. They do not include items which, though exceptional on account of size and incidence (and which may therefore require separate disclosure), derive from the ordinary activities of the business. Neither do they include prior year items merely because they relate to a prior year.   11

Prior year adjustments are those material adjustments applicable to prior years arising from changes in accounting policies and from the correction of fundamental errors. They do not include the normal recurring corrections and adjustments of accounting estimates made in prior years.   12

Part 3 – Standard accounting practice

Profit after extraordinary items
The profit and loss account for the year should show a profit or loss after extraordinary items, reflecting all profits and losses recognised in the accounts of the year other than prior year adjustments as defined in Part 2 and unrealised surpluses on revaluation of fixed assets, which should be credited direct to reserves.   13

Items of an abnormal size and incidence which are derived from the ordinary activities of the business should be included in arriving at the profit for the year before taxation and extraordinary items, and their nature and size disclosed.   14

Extraordinary items
Extraordinary items as defined in Part 2 (less attributable taxation) should be shown separately in the profit and loss account for the year after the results derived from ordinary activities and their nature and size disclosed.   15

---

derived therefrom, and whose Memorandum or Articles of Association prohibit the distribution as dividend of surpluses arising from the realisation of investments; or

(c) a company whose Memorandum or Articles of Association prohibit the distribution as dividend of surpluses arising from the realisation of investments and whose business is wholly or mainly to invest in subsidiary or associated companies which are themselves investment trust companies as defined in (b) above.

Prior year adjustments

16   Prior year adjustments as defined in Part 2 (less attributable taxation) should be
      accounted for by restating prior years, with the result that the opening balance of
      retained profits will be adjusted accordingly. The effect of the change should be
      disclosed where practicable by showing separately in the restatement of the previous
      year the amount involved. Items which represent the normal recurring corrections and
      adjustments of accounting estimates made in prior years should be included in the
      profit and loss account for the year and, if material, their nature and size should be
      disclosed.

Profit and loss account presentation

17   As a result of the foregoing, the profit and loss account for the year should, if there are
      extraordinary items, include the following elements:

      – profit before extraordinary items;

      – extraordinary items (less taxation attributable thereto);

      – profit after extraordinary items.

      A statement of retained profits/reserves showing any prior year adjustments should
      immediately follow the profit and loss account for the year. An example of a statement
      of profit and loss for the year and a statement of retained profits/reserves is set out in
      the appendix.

Date from which effective

18   The accounting practices set out in this statement should be adopted as soon as
      possible and regarded as standard in respect of financial statements relating to
      accounting periods beginning on or after 1st January 1974.

Part 4 – Note on legal requirements

19   The application of the foregoing standard accounting practice will provide the
      disclosure required by paragraph 14 (6) (a) of Schedule 2 to the Companies Act 1967
      (paragraph 14 (7) (a) of Schedule 6 to the Companies Act 1963 Republic of Ireland
      and paragraph 14 (6) (a) of Schedule 6 to the Companies Act 1960 Northern Ireland)
      which requires the following to be stated by way of note if not otherwise shown:

      'Any material respects in which any items shown in the profit and loss account
      are affected –

      (a) by transactions of a sort not usually undertaken by the company or otherwise
          by circumstances of an exceptional or non-recurrent nature; or

      (b) by any change in the basis of accounting.'

Part 5 – Compliance with International Accounting Standard No. 8 'Unusual and prior period items and changes in accounting policies'

Compliance with the requirements of Statement of Standard Accounting Practice No. 6 *Extraordinary items and prior year adjustments* will automatically ensure compliance with International Accounting Standard No. 8 *Unusual and prior period items and changes in accounting policies*. 20

Appendix

This appendix is illustrative only and does not form part of the statement of standard accounting practice.

EXAMPLE OF A STATEMENT OF PROFIT AND LOSS FOR THE YEAR AND A STATEMENT OF RETAINED PROFITS/RESERVES

Statement of profit and loss for the year ended 31st December 1974

	1974 £000	1974 £000	1973 £000	1973 £000
Turnover		183,000		158,000
Operating profit after charging or including:		19,400		18,100
Depreciation	4,100		4,000	
Exceptional loss on major contract (see note 2)	1,000		–	
Other items	325		310	
Other income:				
Investment income		300		500
Profit before taxation and extraordinary items		19,700		18,600
Taxation		9,850		8,835
Profit before extraordinary items		9,850		9,765
Extraordinary items *less taxation* (see note 3)		835		850
Profit after extraordinary items		9,015		8,915
Dividends		4,410		4,200
Retained profit		4,605		4,715

Statement of retained profits/reserves

Retained profit for the year		4,605		4,715
Retained profits/reserves at beginning of year:				
As previously reported	48,890		44,000	
Prior year adjustment (see note 1)	450		275	
As restated		48,440		43,725
Retained profits/reserves at end of year		53,045		48,440

Notes

(1) The policy followed in accounting for research and development expenditure, which in prior years was written off over a period of four years, was changed during the year ended 31st December 1974 and such expenditure is now written off in the year in which it is incurred. It is considered that the new policy will give a fairer presentation of the results and the financial position of the company. Research and development expenditure carried forward at 31st December 1973 (less attributable

taxation £340,000) amounted to £450,000. In restating the results for 1973 on the basis of the new policy the charge for research and development in that year has been increased by £175,000 out of the expenditure carried forward at the end of 1973. The remainder, £275,000 relating to 1972 and earlier years, has been charged against retained profits at the beginning of 1973.

(2) Items within the normal activities of the company which require disclosure on account of their abnormal size and incidence.

(3) Description of actual items.

8

The treatment of taxation under the imputation system in the accounts of companies

Contents

The treatment of taxation under the imputation system in the accounts of companies

(Issued August 1974. Appendix 3 added December 1977)

The imputation system of company taxation started in the United Kingdom in April 1973 and in the Republic of Ireland in 1976. The purpose of this statement is to establish a standard treatment of taxation in company accounts, with particular reference to advance corporation tax and 'mainstream' corporation tax. This Statement has been prepared for use when the imputation system of corporation tax is fully implemented. It does not deal in detail with the problems arising in the transitional periods, which should be resolved in the light of the principles herein.

In order to obviate the need to amend the statement whenever there are changes in the rates of taxation the following have been assumed:

(a) corporation tax – 50 per cent;

(b) advance corporation tax – three-sevenths of the amount of qualifying distributions.

The small companies rate should be substituted where warranted by the circumstances.

The application of this statement to companies subject to taxation in the Republic of Ireland is dealt with in Appendix 3. (*December 1977*)

Part 1 – Explanatory note

Introduction

1   The principal features of the imputation system of corporation tax are broadly as follows. Corporation tax is charged at a single rate on a company's income whether distributed or undistributed; in the absence of a dividend the whole of the tax is payable on a date which may be a year or more after the end of the relevant accounting period. When in an accounting period a company makes a distribution to shareholders, it does not withhold income tax from the payment, but is required to make an advance payment of corporation tax (ACT). This ACT will normally be set off against the company's total liability for corporation tax on its income (but not on its chargeable gains) of the same accounting period. The resultant net liability is known as the mainstream corporation tax. The charge for corporation tax therefore comprises the mainstream corporation tax and the ACT. From the paying company's point of view the concept of 'gross' dividends and the deduction of income tax at source therefrom has disappeared. However, an individual shareholder receiving the dividend is chargeable to tax on an amount of income equivalent to the dividend plus the imputed tax credit. This tax credit (generally equivalent to the ACT paid by the company) will discharge the basic rate liability to income tax of a United Kingdom resident or would in certain circumstances

be recoverable. For corporate shareholders the concept of franked investment income continues.

The ACT set off against the final corporation tax bill is effectively restricted to 30 per cent (assuming a 50 per cent tax rate) of the company's taxable income. Any ACT thereby unrelieved (i.e., ACT on a distribution which together with the related ACT is in excess of taxable income) can be carried back for two years or forward without time limit (but cannot be set against corporation tax on income arising before 1st April 1973).   2

The main accounting problems arising from the imputation system are: 3

   (a) the treatment in the profit and loss account of outgoing dividends and the related ACT;

   (b) determining the recoverability of ACT;

   (c) the treatment of irrecoverable ACT and of unrelieved overseas tax arising from the payment or proposed payment of dividends;

   (d) the treatment in the balance sheet of taxation liabilities, recoverable ACT and dividends;

   (e) the treatment of franked investment income.

Dividends and the related ACT

The treatment in the profit and loss account of outgoing dividends and the related ACT,   4
is concerned with whether ACT should be treated as part of the cost of the dividend or whether it should be treated as part of tax on the company's profits. The right of a company to deduct income tax from dividends no longer applies. Whatever percentage or per-share dividend is declared, that is the amount which the company will pay to its members. The fact that the dividend will carry a tax credit is a matter affecting the recipient rather than the company's method of accounting for the dividend. Accordingly it is considered appropriate that dividends should be shown in the profit and loss account at the amount paid or payable to the shareholders and that neither the related ACT nor the imputed tax credit should be treated as part of the cost of the dividend. It follows that the charge for taxation in the profit and loss account should embrace the full amount of corporation tax, and not merely the mainstream liability.

Recoverability of ACT

ACT is primarily recovered by being set off against the corporation tax on the income   5
of the year in which the related distribution is made. In the case of dividends paid during the year under review, the taxable income of that year and of the two previous years will normally be available to absorb the relief. Where a proposed dividend is to be paid in the following year, then the related ACT falls to be set off against the corporation tax on the taxable income of the year of payment of the proposed dividend and in default of that, against the taxable income of the year under review or of the year previous to that. In both cases ACT can be carried forward indefinitely if necessary. In each year there is an overriding restriction on the use of ACT for set off, by reference to the taxable income of that year.

For accounting purposes it is necessary to decide whether recovery of the ACT is   6

[handwritten margin notes: Treatment of surplus or unrelieved ACT / Decide if can recover ACT or if it should be w/o in P&L a/c]

reasonably certain and foreseeable or whether it should be written off in the profit and loss account. If the taxable income of the year under review and the amounts available from the preceding year or years are insufficient to cover the ACT, then recoverability of ACT will depend on the extent to which income is earned in future periods in excess of dividends paid or on the existence of a deferred taxation account of adequate size (see paragraph 7). Although the relief remains available indefinitely it will be prudent to have regard only to the immediate and foreseeable future; how long this future period should be will depend upon the circumstances of each case, but it is suggested that where there is no deferred taxation account it should normally not extend beyond the next accounting period.

[handwritten margin note: If no deferred tax a/c then not extend beyond next acct'g period]

7   Where a deferred taxation account is maintained, the attitude to recoverability may be different. The balance on the deferred taxation account usually represents an amount which will be released to profit and loss account over the life of related fixed assets. Unrelieved ACT is available to offset against future taxable profits for an indefinite period. There is thus a similarity between unrelieved ACT and the balance on the deferred taxation account and it is therefore reasonable to regard unrelieved ACT as being available for deduction from the amount at which the deferred taxation account is stated in the accounts. Only a proportion of the balance on the account (at the rates assumed 30 per cent of the amount on which the credit balance of the account has been calculated) can be used for this purpose: this is the extent to which ACT can be set off against the corporation tax liability. It should be noted, however, that to the extent to which the deferred taxation account represents deferred chargeable gains, it is not available for this purpose. *[handwritten: If deferred tax a/c repr deferred chargeable gains, cannot set off unrelieved ACT vs it.]*

[handwritten margin note: can set off unrelieved ACT to deferred tax a/c set off 30% of amount in deferred tax a/c.]

Irrecoverable ACT

8   Any irrecoverable ACT (i.e. ACT the recoverability of which is not reasonably certain and foreseeable) should be written off in the profit and loss account in which the related dividend is shown.

9   There are two differing views on the presentation in the profit and loss account of irrecoverable ACT written off. One view is that irrecoverable ACT should be treated as part of the tax charge upon the company to be deducted in arriving at profits after tax; the other that the irrecoverable ACT, being a cost stemming from the payment of a dividend, should be treated as an appropriation like the dividend itself. Of the two methods the first is supported as the appropriate accounting treatment because unrelieved ACT constitutes tax upon the company or group, as opposed to tax on the shareholders, and is not an appropriation of profits. It is appreciated however that some readers or analysts of accounts may wish for their purposes to regard irrecoverable ACT in some other manner. The amount of irrecoverable ACT should therefore be separately disclosed if material.

10   The question remains whether irrecoverable ACT could appropriately be treated as an 'extraordinary item' as defined in SSAP No. 6*. The test laid down in that document needs to be applied to each individual case, but it is unlikely that a cost arising from the payment of a normal dividend would be derived from 'transactions outside the

---

* SSAP No. 6. *Extraordinary items and prior year adjustments.*

ordinary activities of the business', and accordingly irrecoverable ACT will normally constitute part of the ordinary tax charge.

Unrelieved overseas tax

Although for tax purposes unrelieved overseas tax cannot be carried forward, the accounting treatment of unrelieved overseas tax arising from the payment of a dividend is similar to that of irrecoverable ACT. This matter is dealt with more fully in Appendix 2.

11

Franked investment income

The concept of franked investment income established under earlier tax systems is continued under the imputation system. Franked investment income comprises the amount of a qualifying distribution received from another UK resident company with the addition of the related tax credit. The net amount can be redistributed to shareholders of the recipient company without payment of ACT and the related tax credit remains attached from the viewpoint of the shareholder.

12

There are several possible methods of dealing with franked investment income in accounts. The two main possibilities are:

13

(a) to bring into the profit and loss account the cash amount received or receivable (i.e. excluding the tax credit); or

(b) to bring in the amount of the franked investment income (i.e., including the tax credit, an equivalent amount then being treated as part of the charge for taxation).

The first method would involve treating the income either as an item of profit before taxation, or as an addition to the profit after taxation — both alternatives are open to objection. The second method would allow recognition of the income both at the pre-tax and at the after-tax stage in a way which is consistent with other elements of profit, and is therefore adopted as the standard accounting practice.

Mainstream corporation tax

Apart from ACT the dates of payments of corporation tax under the new system remain as before. Depending on the date to which a company makes up its accounts, the balance sheet should contain either (a) one liability for mainstream corporation tax, being that on the profit of the year, or (b) two liabilities. In the latter case they will be the mainstream corporation tax on the profits of the previous year payable within nine months of the balance sheet date, and mainstream corporation tax for the year under review payable twelve months later than the above liability. These liabilities should be separately disclosed, under current liabilities or otherwise as appropriate. If they are not shown under current liabilities, the due date of payment should be stated.

14

ACT

ACT on dividends paid will either have been paid by the balance sheet date or will be due for payment shortly afterwards. Where the ACT is regarded as recoverable then it will normally be deducted from the full corporation tax charge based on the profit of the period in arriving at the mainstream corporation tax liability shown in the balance sheet.

15

16   In the case of dividends proposed but not paid at the balance sheet date, the related ACT will become due for payment within about three months of the dividend itself, and should be shown as a current liability. The right of set-off, however (assuming the ACT is regarded as recoverable), will not arise for at least twenty-one months from the balance sheet date. This right is, therefore, in the nature of a deferred asset, and should be shown as such on the balance sheet, unless there is a deferred tax account from the balance of which the amount may be deducted.

17   If ACT on dividends paid or proposed is treated as irrecoverable (see paragraphs 8 to 10) there is no corresponding asset to be dealt with in the balance sheet.

Preference shares

18   Any dividend right established before 6th April 1973 at a gross rate or a gross amount was reduced by the Finance Act 1972, Schedule 23, paragraph 18* to seven-tenths of its former rate or amount. Steps should therefore be taken to distinguish, for example a 10 per cent preference share issued before 6th April 1973, on which the dividend is now 7 per cent, from such a preference share issued after that date. A change in the basic rate of income tax and a corresponding change in the rate of ACT would not affect this once-for-all 'netting down'. Thus a former 10 per cent preference share may in the future yield, with related tax credit, either more or less than 10 per cent on nominal value. The new rate of dividend on preference shares† should therefore be incorporated in the description of the shares in the balance sheet, e.g.:

	Authorised	Issued
100,000 10 per cent (now 7 per cent + tax credit) preference shares of £1	£100,000	£100,000

Appendices

19   Certain accounting considerations arising from the imputation system of corporation tax are considered to be supplementary to the main purpose of this statement. These considerations have been dealt with as follows:

Appendix 1 Examples of the taxation items to be disclosed.

Appendix 2 Further practical points:

    (a) unrelieved overseas tax;

    (b) earnings and dividends in the historical summary.

---

* Subsequent changes in the rate of ACT have varied the rate of tax credit but not the amount of the cash divided payable to shareholders.

†Including participating preference and preferred ordinary shares where the former rate of dividend forms part of the title.

Part 2 – Definition of terms

Recoverable ACT
That amount of the ACT paid or payable on outgoing dividends paid and proposed   20
which can be:

(a) set off against a corporation tax liability on the profits of the period under review
or of previous periods; or

(b) properly set off against a credit balance on deferred tax account; or

(c) expected to be recoverable taking into account expected profits and dividends –
normally those of the next accounting period only.

Irrecoverable ACT
ACT paid or payable on outgoing dividends paid and proposed other than recoverable   21
ACT.

Part 3 – Standard accounting practice

Profit and loss account
The following items should be included in the taxation charge in the profit and loss
account and, where material, should be separately disclosed: 22

(a) the amount of the United Kingdom corporation tax specifying:

(i) the charge for corporation tax on the income of the year (where such
corporation tax includes transfers between the deferred taxation account
and the profit and loss account these also should be separately disclosed
where material);

(ii) tax attributable to franked investment income;

(iii) irrecoverable ACT;

(iv) the relief for overseas taxation;

(b) the total overseas taxation, relieved and unrelieved, specifying that part of the
unrelieved overseas taxation which arises from the payment or proposed
payment of dividends.

If the rate of corporation tax is not known for the whole or part of the period covered   23
by the accounts, the latest known rate should be used and disclosed.

Outgoing dividends should not include either the related ACT or the attributable tax   24
credit.

Incoming dividends from United Kingdom resident companies should be included at   25
the amount of cash received or receivable plus the tax credit.

Balance sheet
Dividends proposed (or declared and not yet payable) should be included in current   26
liabilities, without the addition of the related ACT. The ACT on proposed dividends
(whether recoverable or irrecoverable) should be included as a current tax liability.

27   If the ACT on proposed dividends is regarded as recoverable, it should be deducted from the deferred tax account if such an account is available for this purpose. In the absence of a deferred taxation account ACT recoverable should be shown as a deferred asset.

28   Where the title of a class of preference shares (or participating or preferred ordinary shares) issued before 6th April 1973, includes a fixed rate of dividend, the new rate of dividend should be incorporated in the description of the shares in the balance sheet.

Date from which effective for companies subject to taxation in the United Kingdom

29   The accounting practices set out in this statement should be adopted as soon as possible and regarded as standard in respect of financial statements relating to accounting periods beginning on or after 1st January 1975.

Date from which effective for companies subject to taxation in the Republic of Ireland

30   The accounting practices set out in Appendix 3 relating to companies subject to taxation in the Republic of Ireland should be regarded as standard in respect of financial statements relating to accounting periods beginning on or after 1st January 1978.

Appendix 1

This appendix is for general guidance and does not form part of the statement of standard accounting practice.

> This example indicates one method of showing (by way of note) the taxation items required to be disclosed under the Companies Act 1967 and Part 3 of this standard. In simple cases taxation may be dealt with entirely within the profit and loss account.

	£'000
Corporation tax on income at x per cent (including £b transferred to/from deferred taxation account) .	a
Less relief for overseas taxation	c
	d
Overseas taxation*	e
Tax credit on UK dividends received	f
Irrecoverable advance corporation tax	g
	H

* Including £J arising from the payment of dividends |see paragraphs 1 and 2 of Appendix 2|.

Appendix 2

This appendix is for general guidance and does not form part of the statement of standard accounting practice.

FURTHER PRACTICAL POINTS

Unrelieved overseas tax

1   If the rate of overseas tax on the overseas income of a UK company exceeds the rate of UK mainstream corporation tax thereon, then part of the overseas tax will be unrelieved. If the company pays all or part of a dividend out of its overseas income (i.e., if it pays a dividend which, together with the related ACT is substantially in excess of its, or its group's, taxable UK income) then the ACT on the dividend paid out of overseas income will not be available for the purpose of calculating overseas tax credit. Thus, the payment of a dividend in these circumstances may give rise to unrelieved tax (depending on the rate of overseas tax) but this unrelieved tax, unlike the irrecoverable ACT, is not available for carry forward.

2   Following the same reasoning as applied to the accounting treatment of irrecoverable ACT, unrelieved overseas tax which arises from an outgoing dividend should be treated as part of the tax charge to be deducted in arriving at profits after tax. The amount should be separately disclosed, if material.

Earnings and dividends in the historical summary

3   The change to the imputation system destroyed the comparability, as between one period and another, of many of the figures in the historical records. For example, earnings were formerly available to cover gross dividends before deduction of income tax, but under the imputation system they are now available to cover the actual cash dividends payable to the preference or equity shareholders. Hence, in calculating earnings for equity under the imputation system, preference dividends should be deducted at the amount declared and payable to the shareholders – not at the former gross amount.

4   In general, it is likely to be either impracticable or unsatisfactory to attempt to adjust profits earned under one system of taxation to another tax system. Furthermore, if a company had been taxed differently, it might have taken different financial decisions. Most of the items in the historical summary should therefore be left as originally published.

5   Figures such as earnings and dividends based on the old system of taxation should, however, be carefully distinguished from those based on the new system. It may be helpful to describe dividends paid under the old system of taxation as 'gross dividends' to distinguish them from dividends paid under the new system.

6   The transitional period, which may cover more than one accounting year, presents particular problems. It would usually be preferable (where practicable) to show an overlap with the figures calculated both ways for the straddling period, or alternatively to indicate in some other manner the points where comparability has been destroyed by

a change in the system of taxation (i.e. 1965 and 1973). Figures relating to earlier periods can then be shown entirely on the old basis with subsequent figures being entirely on the new basis.

To calculate the gross dividends for the straddling year (for the purposes of historical summaries only) any dividends relating to that year paid on or after 6th April 1973 may be increased by the amount of the appropriate tax credits and added to any dividends paid before 6th April 1973. To calculate the equivalent 'new' dividends from gross dividends, the gross dividends may be reduced by 30 per cent.   7

Appendix 3

(This appendix was added in December 1977)

This appendix contains the statement of standard accounting practice for application to companies subject to taxation in the Republic of Ireland.

Part 1 – Explanatory note

Introduction

The principal features of Irish corporation tax, which is an imputation system, are as follows: 1

(a) Corporation tax is charged at a single rate on a company's income whether distributed or undistributed.

(b) When, in an accounting period, a company makes a distribution to shareholders, it does not withhold income tax from the payment. From the paying company's point of view the concept of 'gross' dividends and the deduction of income tax at source therefrom has disappeared. However, an individual shareholder receiving the dividend is chargeable to tax on an amount of income equivalent to the dividend plus imputed tax credit. This tax credit will discharge the basic rate liability to income tax of a Republic of Ireland resident or would in certain circumstances be recoverable.

(c) For corporate shareholders the concept of franked investment income will continue.

The main accounting problems arising from the imputation system are: 2

(a) The treatment in the profit and loss account of dividends payable and dividends receivable.

(b) The treatment in the profit and loss account of the charge for taxation.

(c) The treatment in the balance sheet of taxation liabilities and dividends.

Dividends payable

The right of a company to deduct income tax from dividends no longer applies.   3
Whatever percentage or per-share dividend is declared, that is the amount which the

company will pay to its members. The fact that the dividend will carry a tax credit is a matter affecting the recipient rather than the company's method of accounting for the dividend. Accordingly, it is considered appropriate that dividends should be shown in the profit and loss account at the amount paid or payable to the shareholders and the imputed tax credit should not be treated as part of the cost of the dividend.

4   The Corporation Tax Act 1976 (Section 178) provides that any dividend right established before 6th April 1976 at a gross rate or a gross amount will be reduced under the new tax system. Therefore, for example, the rate of dividend applicable to preference shares issued before 6th April 1976 has been reduced by statute to a rate equivalent to the gross amount less tax at the imputed rate of 35 per cent. A change in the rate of tax credit would not affect this once-for-all 'netting down'. The new rate of dividend on preference shares should therefore be incorporated in the description of the shares in the balance sheet, for example:

	Authorised £	Issued and fully paid £
Share capital		
100,000 6% (now 3.9% plus tax credit) preference shares of £1 each	100,000	100,000

Dividends receivable

5   The concept of franked investment income is continued under the imputation system of corporation tax. Franked investment income comprises the amount of a distribution received from another Irish resident company plus the related tax credit.

6   There are several possible methods of dealing with franked investment income in financial statements. The two main possibilities are:

    (a) to bring into profit and loss account the cash received or receivable (i.e. excluding the tax credit), or

    (b) to bring in the amount of the franked investment income (i.e. the cash amount received or receivable plus the related tax credit) and show the amount equivalent to the tax credit as part of the charge for taxation.

7   The first method suggested would involve treating the income either as an item of profit before taxation, or as an addition to the profit after taxation, and both these alternatives are open to objection. The second method would allow recognition of the income both at the pre-tax and at the after-tax stage in a manner which is consistent with other similar but unfranked income, and it is therefore adopted as the standard accounting practice.

8   Where franked investment income includes a tax credit at less than the normal amount, due to export sales or Shannon relief, the income should be grossed up at the rate of the imputed tax credit which would itself be shown as a component of the taxation charge in the accounts. If the amount of franked investment income from export sales relieved or Shannon exempt sources is material, the amount should be disclosed in the accounts.

Profit and loss account

9   In the case of export sales relieved or Shannon exempt companies, corporation tax at

the normal rate should be shown in the profit and loss account and a deduction specified for taxation relieved due to export sales relief or Shannon exemption. as appropriate.

Balance sheet

Corporation tax assessable on the profits of an accounting period. but unpaid at the end of the period. is a liability at the date of the balance sheet and should be shown as such.   10

Taxation liabilities should be shown as follows: 11

(a) Corporation tax due for payment within twelve months from the date of the balance sheet should be described as 'taxation' and should be shown under current liabilities.

(b) Corporation tax due for payment later than twelve months after the date of the balance sheet should be described as 'Corporation tax payable . . . (give date of payment)' and should be shown as a separate non-current liability.

(c) Corporation tax recoverable should be included in the balance sheet either as a current asset described as 'Taxation recoverable' or. if available for off-set. as a deduction from any liability to corporation tax.

Part 2 – Standard accounting practice

Profit and loss account

There should be included in the taxation charge on the income of the period in the profit and loss account the amount of corporation tax specifying. where material: 12

(1) the charge for corporation tax on the income of the period (where such corporation tax includes transfers between the deferred taxation account and the profit and loss account these should also be separately disclosed where material).

(2) the tax credit applicable to franked investment income.

(3) total overseas taxation, relieved and unrelieved.

If the rate of corporation tax is not known for the whole or part of the period covered by the financial statements. the latest known rate should be used and disclosed.   13

Outgoing dividends should not include the attributable tax credit.   14

Incoming dividends from Republic of Ireland resident companies should be included at the amount of cash received or receivable plus the tax credit.   15

Balance sheet

Dividends proposed (or declared and not yet payable) should be included in current liabilities.   16

Where the title of a class of preference shares issued before 6th April 1976 includes a fixed rate of dividend, the new rate of dividend should be incorporated in the description of the shares in the balance sheet.   17

9

Stocks and work in progress

Contents

Stocks and work in progress
(Issued May 1975)

No area of accounting has produced wider differences in practice than the computation of the amount at which stocks and work in progress are stated in financial accounts. This statement of standard accounting practice seeks to define the practices, to narrow the differences and variations in those practices and to ensure adequate disclosure in the accounts.

Part 1 – Explanatory note

Introduction

1 The determination of profit for an accounting year requires the matching of costs with related revenues. The cost of unsold or unconsumed stocks and work in progress will have been incurred in the expectation of future revenue, and when this will not arise until a later year it is appropriate to carry forward this cost to be matched with the revenue when it arises; the applicable concept is the matching of cost and revenue in the year in which the revenue arises rather than in the year in which the cost is incurred. If there is no reasonable expectation of sufficient future revenue to cover cost incurred (e.g., as a result of deterioration, obsolescence or a change in demand), the irrecoverable cost should be charged to revenue in the year under review. Thus, stocks and work in progress normally need to be stated at cost, or, if lower, at net realisable value.

2 The comparison of cost and net realisable value needs to be made in respect of each item of stock separately. Where this is impracticable, groups or categories of stock items which are similar will need to be taken together. To compare the total realisable value of stocks with the total cost could result in an unacceptable setting off of foreseeable losses against unrealised profit.

3 In order to match costs and revenue, 'costs' of stocks and work in progress should comprise that expenditure which has been incurred in the normal course of business in bringing the product or service to its present location and condition. Such costs will include all related production overheads, even though these may accrue on a time basis.

4 The methods used in allocating costs to stocks and work in progress need to be selected with a view to providing the fairest possible approximation to the expenditure actually incurred in bringing the product to its present location and condition. For example, in the case of retail stores holding a large number of rapidly changing individual items, stocks on the shelves have often been stated at current selling prices less the normal gross profit margin. In these particular circumstances this may be acceptable as being the only practical method of arriving at a figure which approximates to cost.

Net realisable value

5 Net realisable value is the amount at which it is expected that items of stocks and work in progress can be disposed of without creating either profit or loss in the year of sale,

i.e., the estimated proceeds of sale less all further costs to completion and less all costs to be incurred in marketing, selling and distributing directly related to the items in question.

Replacement cost

Items of stock and work in progress have sometimes been stated in accounts at estimated replacement cost where this is lower than net realisable value. Where the effect is to take account of a loss greater than that which is expected to be incurred, the use of replacement cost is not regarded as acceptable. However, in some circumstances (e.g., in the case of materials whose price has fluctuated considerably and which have not become the subject of firm sales contracts by the time the accounts are prepared) replacement cost may be the best measure of net realisable value.   6

Long-term contract work in progress *7–11, 13, 22–24, 27, 30, App. 1 21–27.*

Separate consideration needs to be given to work in progress arising from long-term contracts. Owing to the length of time taken to complete such contracts, to defer taking profit into account until completion may result in the profit and loss account reflecting not so much a fair view of the activity of the company during the year but rather the results relating to contracts which have been completed by the year end. It is therefore appropriate to take credit for ascertainable profit while contracts are in progress, subject to the limitations in paragraph 8 below. *Take profit while contract in progress.*   7

The profit, if any, taken up needs to reflect the proportion of the work carried out at the accounting date and to take into account any known inequalities of profitability in the various stages of a contract. Many businesses, however, carry out contracts where the outcome cannot reasonably be assessed before the conclusion of the contract and in such cases it is prudent not to take up any profit. Where the business carries out contracts and it is considered that their outcome can be assessed with reasonable certainty before their conclusion, then the attributable profit should be taken up, but the judgement involved should be exercised with prudence. *Profits take into a/c × % work carried to date of a/c. If consider outcome with reas. certainty before conclusn*   8

If, however, it is expected that there will be a loss on a contract as a whole, provision needs to be made (in accordance with the prudence concept), for the whole of the loss as soon as it is recognised. This has the effect of reducing the work done to date to its net realisable value. Where unprofitable contracts are of such magnitude that they can be expected to absorb a considerable part of the company's capacity for a substantial period, related administration overheads to be incurred during the period to the completion of those contracts should also be included in the calculation of the provision for losses. *If expected to will be loss on contract, make prov. for whole loss. as soon as recognised. Add admin o/hds to loss. Provision = ×ls of loss of cost less progress payments received × receivable.* *take 9 profit If outcome cannot be assessed not take profit.*   9

Thus, the gross amount of long-term contract work in progress should be stated in accounts at cost plus attributable profits (if any) less foreseeable losses (if any). In arriving at a decision as to whether there are attributable profits, a company should consider whether having regard to the nature of the contracts undertaken it is reasonable to foresee profits in advance of the completion of the contracts. *take WIP at cost + foreseeab attributable profits less foreseeable losses and progress payments received × receivable.*   10

Disclosure in accounts

A suitable description of the amount at which stocks and work in progress are stated in accounts might be 'at the lower of cost and net realisable value' or, in the case of long-   11 term contract work in progress, 'at cost plus attributable profit (if any) less foreseeable losses (if any) and progress payments received and receivable'.

12   In order to give an adequate explanation of the affairs of the company the accounting policies followed in arriving at the amount at which stocks and work in progress are stated in the accounts should be set out in a note. Where differing bases have been adopted for different types of stocks and work in progress the amount included in the accounts in respect of each type will need to be stated.

13   In the case of long-term contract work in progress the terms of a contract usually involve progress payments which reduce the amount at which the contract is stated in the accounts. The financial position of a company may be materially dependent on the outcome of such contracts, despite this lessening of their apparent significance. A related note should, therefore, indicate the amount of progress payments received and receivable separately from the net amount of cost plus attributable profit, less foreseeable losses as appropriate.

Further practical considerations

14   The basic considerations which must be taken into account in determining costs and net realisable value in relation to stocks and work in progress are set out in Parts 2 and 3 of this statement. The majority of problems which arise in practice in determining both the cost and the net realisable value of stocks and work in progress result from considerations which are relevant to particular businesses and are not of such universal application that they can be the subject of a statement of standard accounting practice. Accordingly, Appendix 1 sets out in more detail some general guidelines which may be of assistance in determining cost and net realisable value and in identifying those situations in which net realisable value is likely to be less than cost. Appendix 1 also sets out considerations which need to be borne in mind in calculating the amount of profit to be taken into account in respect of long-term contracts.

Part 2 – Definition of terms

15   The following definitions of terms are used for the purpose of this statement.

16   *Stocks and work in progress* comprise:

    (a) goods or other assets purchased for resale;

    (b) consumable stores;

    (c) raw materials and components purchased for incorporation into products for sale;

    (d) products and services in intermediate stages of completion;

    (e) finished goods.

17   *Cost* is defined in relation to the different categories of stocks and work in progress as being that expenditure which has been incurred in the normal course of business in bringing the product or service to its present location and condition. This expenditure should include, in addition to cost of purchase (as defined in paragraph 18) such costs

of conversion (as defined in paragraph 19) as are appropriate to that location and condition.

Cost of purchase comprises purchase price including import duties, transport and handling costs and any other directly attributable costs, less trade discounts, rebates and subsidies.   18

Cost of conversion comprises: 19

    (a) costs which are specifically attributable to units of production, i.e., direct labour, direct expenses and sub-contracted work;

    (b) production overheads (as defined in paragraph 20);

    (c) other overheads, if any, attributable in the particular circumstances of the business to bringing the product or service to its present location and condition.

Production overheads: overheads incurred in respect of materials, labour or services   20
for production, based on the normal level of activity, taking one year with another. For this purpose each overhead should be classified according to function (e.g., production, selling or administration) so as to ensure the inclusion in cost of conversion of those overheads (including depreciation) which relate to production, notwithstanding that these may accrue wholly or partly on a time basis.

Net realisable value: the actual or estimated selling price (net of trade but before settle-   21
ment discounts) less:

    (a) all further costs to completion; and

    (b) all costs to be incurred in marketing, selling and distributing.

Long-term contract: a contract entered into for manufacture or building of a single   22
substantial entity or the provision of a service where the time taken to manufacture, build or provide is such that a substantial proportion of all such contract work will extend for a period exceeding one year.

Attributable profit: that part of the total profit currently estimated to arise over the   23
duration of the contract (after allowing for likely increases in costs so far as not recoverable under the terms of the contract) which fairly reflects the profit attributable to that part of the work performed at the accounting date. (There can be no attributable profit until the outcome of the contract can be assessed with reasonable certainty.)

Foreseeable losses: losses which are currently estimated to arise over the duration of   24
the contract (after allowing for estimated remedial and maintenance costs, and increases in costs so far as not recoverable under the terms of the contract). This estimate is required irrespective of:

    (a) whether or not work has yet commenced on such contracts;

    (b) the proportion of work carried out at the accounting date;

    (c) the amount of profits expected to arise on other contracts.

Part 3 – Standard accounting practice

25   The expressions used in this statement of standard accounting practice are defined in Part 2.

Stocks and work in progress other than long-term contract work in progress

26   The amount at which stocks and work in progress, other than long-term contract work in progress, is stated in periodic financial statements should be the total of the lower of cost and net realisable value of the separate items of stock and work in progress or of groups of similar items.

Long-term contract work in progress

27   The amount at which long-term contract work in progress is stated in periodic financial statements should be cost plus any attributable profit, less any foreseeable losses and progress payments received and receivable. If, however, anticipated losses on individual contracts exceed cost incurred to date less progress payments received and receivable, such excesses should be shown separately as provisions.

Disclosure in financial statements

28   The accounting policies which have been used in calculating cost, net realisable value, attributable profit and foreseeable losses (as appropriate) should be stated.

29   Stocks and work in progress should be sub-classified in balance sheets or in notes to the financial statements in a manner which is appropriate to the business and so as to indicate the amounts held in each of the main categories.

30   In relation to the amount at which long-term contracts are stated in the balance sheet there should be stated:

 (a) the amount of work in progress at cost plus attributable profit, less foreseeable losses;

 (b) cash received and receivable at the accounting date as progress payments on account of contracts in progress.

Date from which effective

31   The accounting practice set out in this statement should be adopted as soon as possible and regarded as standard in respect of accounts relating to accounting periods starting on or after 1st January 1976.

Appendix 1

This appendix is for general guidance and does not form part of the statement of standard accounting practice.

FURTHER PRACTICAL CONSIDERATIONS

Many of the problems involved in arriving at the amount at which stocks and work in progress are stated in accounts are of a practical nature rather than resulting from matters of principle. This appendix discusses some particular areas in which difficulty may be encountered.

The allocation of overheads

Production overheads are included in cost of conversion (as defined in Part 2) together with direct labour, direct expenses and sub-contracted work. This inclusion is a necessary corollary of the principle that expenditure should be included to the extent to which it has been incurred in bringing the product 'to its present location and condition' (paragraph 17 of Part 2). All abnormal conversion costs, however (such as exceptional spoilage, idle capacity and other losses), which are avoidable under normal operating conditions need, for the same reason, to be excluded.   1

Where firm sales contracts have been entered into for the provision of goods or services to customer's specification, overheads relating to design, and marketing and selling costs incurred before manufacture may be included in arriving at cost.   2

The costing methods adopted by a business are usually designed to ensure that all direct material, direct labour, direct expenses and sub-contracted work are identified and charged on a reasonable and consistent basis, but problems arise on the allocation of overheads which must usually involve the exercise of personal judgement in the selection of an appropriate convention.   3

The classification of overheads necessary to achieve this allocation takes the function of the overhead as its distinguishing characteristic (e.g. whether it is a function of production, marketing, selling or administration), rather than whether the overhead tends to vary with time or with volume.   4

The costs of general management, as distinct from functional management, are not directly related to current production and are, therefore, excluded from cost of conversion and hence from the cost of stocks and work in progress.   5

In the case of smaller organisations whose management may be involved in the daily administration of each of the various functions, particular problems may arise in practice in distinguishing these general management overheads. In such organisations the cost of management may fairly be allocated on suitable bases to the functions of production, marketing, selling and administration.   6

Problems may also arise in allocating the costs of central service departments, the allocation of which should depend on the function or functions that the department is serving. For example the accounts department will normally support the following functions: 7

(a) production — by paying production direct and indirect wages and salaries, by controlling purchases and by preparing periodic accounts for the production units;

(b) marketing and distribution — by analysing sales and by controlling the sales ledger;

(c) general administration — by preparing management and annual accounts and budgets, by controlling cash resources and by planning investments.

Only those costs of the accounts department that can reasonably be allocated to the production function fall to be included in the cost of conversion.

8   The allocation of overheads included in the valuation of stocks and work in progress needs to be based on the company's normal level of activity, taking one year with another. The governing factor is that the cost of unused capacity should be written off in the current year. In determining what constitutes 'normal' the following factors need to be considered:

(a) the volume of production which the production facilities are intended by their designers and by management to produce under the working conditions (e.g. single or double shift) prevailing during the year;

(b) the budgeted level of activity for the year under review and for the ensuing year;

(c) the level of activity achieved both in the year under review and in previous years.

Although temporary changes in the load of activity may be ignored, persistent variation should lead to a revision of the previous norm.

9   Where management accounts are prepared on a marginal cost basis, it will be necessary to add to the figure of stock so arrived at the appropriate proportion of those production overheads not already included in the marginal cost.

10   The adoption of a conservative approach to the valuation of stocks and work in progress has sometimes been used as one of the reasons for omitting selected production overheads. In so far as the circumstances of the business require an element of prudence in determining the amount at which stocks and work in progress are stated, this needs to be taken into account in the determination of net realisable value and not by the exclusion from cost of selected overheads.

Methods of costing

11   It is frequently not practicable to relate expenditure to specific units of stocks and work in progress. The ascertainment of the nearest approximation to cost gives rise to two problems:

(a) the selection of an appropriate method for relating costs to stocks and work in progress (e.g. job costing, batch costing, process costing, standard costing);

(b) the selection of an appropriate method for calculating the related cost where a number of identical items have been purchased or made at different times (e.g. unit cost, average cost or FIFO).

In selecting the methods referred to in paragraphs 11 (a) and (b) above, management must exercise judgement to ensure that the methods chosen provide the fairest practicable approximation to 'actual cost'. Furthermore, where standard costs are used they need to be reviewed frequently to ensure that they bear a reasonable relationship to actual costs obtaining during the period. Methods such as base stock and LIFO do not usually bear such a relationship.

12

The method of arriving at cost by applying the latest purchase price to the total number of units in stock is unacceptable in principle because it is not necessarily the same as actual cost and, in times of rising prices, will result in the taking of a profit which has not been realised.

13

One method of arriving at cost, in the absence of a satisfactory costing system, is the use of selling price less an estimated profit margin. This is acceptable only if it can be demonstrated that the method gives a reasonable approximation of the actual cost.

14

In industries where the cost of minor by-products is not separable from the cost of the principal products, stocks of such by-products may be stated in accounts at their net realisable value. In this case the costs of the main products are calculated after deducting the net realisable value of the by-products.

15

The determination of net realisable value
The initial calculation of provisions to reduce stocks from cost to net realisable value may often be made by the use of formulae based on predetermined criteria. The formulae normally take account of the age, movements during the past, expected future movements and estimated scrap values of the stock, as appropriate. Whilst the use of such formulae establishes a basis for making a provision which can be consistently applied, it is still necessary for the results to be reviewed in the light of any special circumstances which cannot be anticipated in the formulae, such as changes in the state of the order book.

16

Where a provision is required to reduce the value of finished goods below cost, the stocks of the parts and sub-assemblies held for the purpose of the manufacture of such products, together with stocks on order, need to be reviewed to determine if provision is also required against such items.

17

Where stocks of spares are held for sale special consideration of the factors in paragraph 16 of this appendix will be required in the context of:

18

(a) the number of units sold to which they are applicable;

(b) the estimated frequency with which a replacement spare is required;

(c) the expected useful life of the unit to which they are applicable.

Events occurring between the balance sheet date and the date of completion of the accounts need to be considered in arriving at the net realisable value at the balance sheet date (e.g. a subsequent reduction in selling prices). However, no reduction falls to be made when the realisable value of material stocks is less than the purchase price provided that the goods into which the materials are to be incorporated can still be sold at a profit after incorporating the materials at cost price.

19

The application of net realisable value

20   The principal situations in which net realisable value is likely to be less than cost are where there has been:

(a) an increase in costs or a fall in selling price;

(b) physical deterioration of stocks;

(c) obsolescence of products;

(d) a decision as part of a company's marketing strategy to manufacture and sell products at a loss;

(e) errors in production or purchasing.

Furthermore, when stocks are held which are unlikely to be sold within the turnover period normal in that company (i.e. excess stocks), the impending delay in realisation increases the risk that the situations outlined in (a) to (c) above may occur before the stocks are sold and needs to be taken into account in assessing net realisable value.

Long-term contract work in progress

21   In ascertaining cost of long-term contract work in progress it is not normally appropriate to include interest payable on borrowed money. However, in those infrequent circumstances where sums borrowed can be identified as financing specific long-term contracts, it may be appropriate to include such related interest in cost, in which circumstances the facts should be clearly stated.

22   In some businesses, long-term contracts for the supply of services or manufacture and supply of goods exist where the prices are determined and invoiced according to separate parts of the contract. In these businesses the most appropriate method of reflecting profits on each contract is usually to match costs against performance of the separable parts of the contract, treating each such separable part as a separate contract. In such instances, however, future revenues from the contract need to be compared with future estimated costs and provision made for any foreseen loss.

23   In determining whether there is attributable profit to be included in the amount at which long-term contract work in progress is stated in the accounts, and in calculating such attributable profit, account should be taken of the type of business concerned. It is necessary to define the earliest point for each particular contract before which no profit is taken up, the overriding principle being that there can be no attributable profit until the outcome of a contract can reasonably be foreseen. Of the profit which in the light of all the circumstances can be foreseen with a reasonable degree of certainty to arise on completion of the contract, there should be regarded as earned to date only that part which prudently reflects the amount of work performed to date. The method used for taking up such profits needs to be consistently applied.

24   In calculating the total estimated profit on the contract, it is necessary to take into account not only the total costs to date and the total estimated further costs to completion (calculated by reference to the same principles as were applied to cost to date) but also the estimated future costs of rectification and guarantee work, and any other future work to be undertaken under the terms of the contract. These are then compared with the total sales value of the contract. In considering future costs it is necessary to

In cost b/o a/c df^{Prices} in wages, raw mats & o/H not recoverable from customer under terms of contract.

have regard to likely increases in wages and salaries, to likely increases in the price of raw materials and to rises in general overheads so far as these items are not recoverable from the customer under the terms of the contract.

Where approved variations have been made to a contract in the course of it and the   25
amount to be received in respect of these variations has not yet been settled and is likely to be a material factor in the outcome, it is necessary to make a conservative estimate of the amount likely to be received and this is then treated as part of the total sales value. On the other hand, provision needs to be made for foreseen claims or penalties payable arising out of delays in completion or from other causes.

The settlement of claims arising from circumstances not envisaged in the contract or   26
arising as an indirect consequence of approved variations is subject to a high level of uncertainty relating to the outcome of future negotiations. In view of this, it is generally prudent to make provision for receipts in respect of such claims only when negotiations have reached an advanced stage and there is evidence in writing of the acceptability of the claim in principle to the purchaser, an indication of the magnitude of the sum involved also being available.

The amount to be reflected in the year's profit and loss account will be the appropriate   27
proportion of this total profit by reference to the work done to date, less any profit already taken up in prior years. The estimated outcome of a contract which extends over several accounting years will nearly always vary in the light of changes in circumstances and for this reason the result of the year will not necessarily represent the proportion of the total profit on the contract which is appropriate to the amount of work carried out in the period: it may also reflect the effect of changes in circumstances during the year which affect the total profit estimated to accrue on completion.

charge to P&L a/c = prop. of total profit to date less any profit taken in prior yrs.

Appendix 2

This appendix is for general guidance and does not form part of the statement of standard accounting practice.

GLOSSARY OF TERMS

The use of the following terms in describing the accounting policies adopted in arriving at the amount at which stocks and work in progress are stated in accounts should be restricted in conformity with the definitions given to each. Where these definitions are inapplicable, alternative expressions should be used and explained.

Unit cost: the cost of purchasing or manufacturing identifiable units of stock.   1

Average cost: the calculation of the cost of stocks and work in progress on the bases of   2
the application to the unit of stocks on hand of an average price computed by dividing the total cost of units by the total number of such units. This average price may be arrived at by means of a continuous calculation, a periodic calculation or a moving periodic calculation.

3   *FIFO (first in, first out):* the calculation of the cost of stocks and work in progress on the basis that the quantities in hand represent the latest purchases or production.

4   *LIFO (last in, first out):* the calculation of the cost of stocks and work in progress on the basis that the quantities in hand represent the earliest purchases or production.

5   *Base stock:* the calculation of the cost of stocks and work in progress on the basis that a fixed unit value is ascribed to a predetermined number of units of stock, any excess over this number being valued on the basis of some other method. If the number of units in stock is less than the predetermined minimum, the fixed unit value is applied to the number in stock.

6   *Replacement cost:* the cost at which an identical asset could be purchased or manufactured.

7   *Standard cost:* the calculation of the cost of stocks and work in progress on the basis of periodically predetermined costs calculated from management's estimates of expected levels of costs and of operations and operational efficiency and the related expenditure.

8   *Completed long-term contract:* a long-term contract on which no further work, apart from maintenance work, is expected to take place.

Appendix 3

This appendix is for general guidance and does not form part of the statement of standard accounting practice.

STOCK-IN-TRADE AND WORK IN PROGRESS

Inland Revenue practice with regard to a change in the basis of stock valuation on the adoption of SSAP 9 (Statement 2.109).

References in this statement to 'N22' relate to a Council recommendation *Treatment of stock-in-trade and work in progress in financial statements* which was withdrawn from the *Members' Handbook* on the introduction of SSAP 9.

At meetings on 7th May 1975 and 2nd August 1978 the Council authorised the publication of the following statement and supplementary statement, respectively:

Statement of 7th May 1975

Changes in basis of valuation
1. After the publication of **N22**, the Revenue explained their practice with regard to changes in the basis of valuation in a statement published in *The Accountant* on 17th

November 1962. The practice set out in that statement applies to changes made as a result of the adoption of SSAP 9 in the following way. References to stock-in-trade cover manufacturing work in progress but not professional work in progress or work under long-term contracts.

2. First, the basis set out in SSAP 9 will be regarded as a valid basis, and will be accepted as a good reason for a change from a previously valid basis. Therefore on such a change the opening stock of the year of change is to be valued on the same basis as the closing stock of that year. Whether the change is to a higher or lower level, the valuations of previous years will not be revised. Further assessments for past years will not therefore be raised nor will relief under the 'error or mistake' provisions be admitted on this account.

3. Where the existing basis of stock valuation is valid under recommendation **N22** and is such that the adoption of the new standard could be argued to be merely a refinement and not a change of basis, the Revenue will be prepared to accept a valuation of the opening stock in the year of change by reference to the new standard, i.e., the argument that there has only been a refinement, so that the opening valuation should be the same as the closing valuation of the preceding year, will not be used.

4. Where stock has been brought into accounts in the past on a basis which was not a valid basis under recommendation **N22**, the Revenue must reserve the right to review past liabilities. However, where there is no question of past irregularities (i.e. fraud, wilful default or neglect), the Revenue would not in any event seek to recover tax for past years on an amount greater than that involved in the uplift of the closed valuation of the year preceding the year of change to a valid basis within the old code.

5. These comments are made on the basis of existing law and practice. The Revenue reserve the right to reconsider their attitude in the event of any change in the law, and in any case, at the expiry of 3 years.

Discounted selling price

6. Where stock is valued at current selling prices less the normal gross profit margin in the circumstances described in paragraph 4 of Part 1 of the statement, the valuation will be acceptable only if the further test set out in paragraph 14 of Appendix 1 to the statement is clearly satisfied.

It is considered that the selling price to be used for the purpose of discounting should normally be the original price fixed for the article determined by operating the normal mark-up on the original cost price.

Replacement cost

7. Where the value of the raw material content forms a high proportion of the total value of stock in process of production and the price of the raw materials is liable to considerable fluctuation, it is common practice to make rapid changes in selling prices to accord with the changes in the price of the raw material. In cases of this kind the replacement cost basis may be extended to cover stock in process of production and finished stock as well as to the stocks of raw material.

Long-term contracts

8. Where a loss on a contract as a whole is foreseen, a proportion of the overall loss, calculated either by reference to time normally up to the due completion date under the terms of the contract, or to expenditure incurred, may normally be taken into account year by year during the remainder of the contract period so long as all contracts, profitable or otherwise, are dealt with similarly. Further, when the work on a long-term contract has been substantially completed, so that it is possible to assess the financial outcome of the contract with reasonable certainty, the Inland Revenue do not normally object to account being taken, at that point, of the foreseeable further expenditure representing obligations arising out of the contract up to the time of final delivery and also of a reasonable provision to allow for expenditure under any guarantee or warranties included in the contract. Beyond these limits it is not permissible for tax purposes to take account of expenditure which has not then been incurred. It follows that a provision for an expected future loss made in accordance with paragraph 9 of Part 1 of the statement would be disallowed for tax purposes to the extent that it is in excess of the amount determined above.

9. Where there is a change in the basis for treatment of long-term contracts, the opening figure in the year of change must, for taxation purposes, be the same as the closing figure for the preceding year.

The Inland Revenue will not accept a claim for a tax-free uplift based on the grounds that the opening and closing figures in the year of change must be on the same basis. Alternatively, the Inland Revenue would accept the continuance of the existing basis for long-term contracts current at the beginning of the year of change, with the new basis being applied only to contracts entered into in or after the year of change.

Supplementary Statement of 2nd August 1978

10. The Inland Revenue confirm that even if the taxpayer has prepared his accounts for the year of change on a basis that values all long-term contracts in accordance with SSAP9, he may nevertheless make an adjustment in his tax computation for that year to give effect to the concluding sentence of paragraph (9) above. Therefore any uplift on an existing valuation made solely to conform to SSAP9 either at the commencement of the year of change or during that year in respect of contracts in existence at the commencement of that year will be ignored for tax purposes. The profit on those contracts will be brought into charge for tax purposes on whatever basis the taxpayer has hitherto adopted, and this will therefore mean similar adjustments in subsequent years until those contracts are run off.

11. A change in the basis of valuation of stock or work in progress will normally lead to a revision of stock relief (Finance Act 1976, Schedule 5, paragraph 24). However, the Inland Revenue also confirm that they will not seek to apply paragraph 24 where a taxpayer changes his basis of valuation of long-term contracts in order to comply with SSAP9, but, at least so far as his tax computation is concerned, does so in accordance with paragraph (10) above. There will, therefore, be no restriction of stock relief in those circumstances.

12. Therefore in these circumstances old contracts would be run off as explained in paragraph (10) above, and there will be no restriction of stock relief in the case of new contracts.

13. The Inland Revenue confirm that the above comments apply to the accounting period in which a change is made to comply with SSAP9 (and to any subsequent accounting period in which old contracts are still being run off), provided that the accounting period commences on or after 1st January 1976 (when SSAP9 became standard practice). This, however, is subject to compliance with the existing time limits for claiming stock relief.

10

Statements of source and application of funds

Contents

Statements of source and application of funds

(Issued July 1975. Part 4 added June 1978)

The object of this statement is to establish the practice of providing source and application of funds statements as a part of audited accounts and to lay down a minimum standard of disclosure in such statements.

Part 1 – Explanatory note

1   The profit and loss account and the balance sheet of a company show, *inter alia*, the amount of profit made during the year and the disposition of the company's resources at the beginning and the end of that year. However, for a fuller understanding of a company's affairs it is necessary also to identify the movements in assets, liabilities and capital which have taken place during the year and the resultant effect on net liquid funds. This information is not specifically disclosed by a profit and loss account and balance sheet but can be made available in the form of a statement of source and application of funds (a 'funds statement').

2   The funds statement is in no way a replacement for the profit and loss account and balance sheet although the information which it contains is a selection, reclassification and summarisation of information contained in those two statements. The objective of such a statement is to show the manner in which the operations of a company have been financed and in which its financial resources have been used and the format selected should be designed to achieve this objective. A funds statement does not purport to indicate the requirements of a business for capital nor the extent of seasonal peaks of stocks, debtors, etc.

3   A funds statement should show the sources from which funds have flowed into the company and the way in which they have been used. It should show clearly the funds generated or absorbed by the operations of the business and the manner in which any resulting surplus of liquid assets has been applied or any deficiency of such assets has been financed, distinguishing the long term from the short term. The statement should distinguish the use of funds for the purchase of new fixed assets from funds used in increasing the working capital of the company.

4   The funds statement will provide a link between the balance sheet at the beginning of the period, the profit and loss account for the period and the balance sheet at the end of the period. A minimum of 'netting off' should take place as this may tend to mask the significance of individually important figures; for example, the sale of one building and the purchase of another should generally be kept separate in a funds statement. The figures from which a funds statement is constructed should generally be identifiable in the profit and loss account, balance sheet and related notes. If adjustments to those published figures are necessary, details should be given to enable the related figures to be rapidly located.

5   Funds statements should, in the case of companies with subsidiaries, be based on the

group accounts. They should reflect any purchases or disposals of subsidiary companies either (a) as separate items, or (b) by reflecting the effects on the separate assets and liabilities dealt with in the statement, so that the acquisition of a subsidiary company would be dealt with as an application of funds in acquiring the fixed assets (including goodwill) of that subsidiary and as a change in working capital. In either case, in the interests of clarity, it will generally also be necessary to summarise the effects of the acquisition or disposal by way of a footnote indicating, in the case of an acquisition, how much of the purchase price has been discharged in cash and how much by the issue of shares. Examples of the alternative treatments are shown in examples 2 and 3 in the Appendix.

A funds statement should form part of the audited accounts of a company. 6

Although this accounting standard is for application to all enterprises other than small enterprises with a turnover or gross income less than £25,000 per annum, consideration should nevertheless be given to the particular circumstances of such enterprises with a view to furnishing the funds statement wherever it is desirable. 7

Part 2 – Definition of terms

Net liquid funds: cash at bank and in hand and cash equivalents (e.g. investments held as current assets) less bank overdrafts and other borrowings repayable within one year of the accounting date. 8

Part 3 – Standard accounting practice

This accounting standard shall apply to all financial accounts intended to give a true and fair view of financial position and profit or loss other than those of enterprises with turnover or gross income of less than £25,000 per annum. 9

Audited financial accounts should, subject to paragraph 9 above, include a statement of source and application of funds both for the period under review and for the corresponding previous period. 10

The statement should show the profit or loss for the period together with the adjustments required for items which did not use (or provide) funds in the period. The following other sources and applications of funds should, where material, also be shown: 11

(a) dividends paid;

(b) acquisitions and disposals of fixed and other non-current assets;

(c) funds raised by increasing, or expended in repaying or redeeming, medium or long-term loans or the issued capital of the company;

(d) increase or decrease in working capital sub-divided into its components, and movements in net liquid funds.

12   Where the accounts are those of a group, the statement of source and application of funds should be so framed as to reflect the operations of the group.

Date from which effective
13   The accounting practices set out in this statement should be adopted as soon as possible and regarded as standard in respect of financial statements relating to accounting periods beginning on or after 1st January 1976.

Part 4 – Compliance with International Accounting Standard No. 7 'Statement of changes in financial position'

14   Compliance with the requirements of Statement of Standard Accounting Practice No. 10 *Statements of source and application of funds* will automatically ensure compliance with International Accounting Standard No. 7 *Statement of changes in financial position*.

Appendix

The appendix is for general guidance and does not form part of the statement of standard accounting practice.

The methods of presentation used are illustrative only and in no way prescriptive and other methods of presentation may equally comply with the accounting standard. The format used should be selected with a view to demonstrating clearly the manner in which the operations of the company have been financed and in which its financial resources have been utilised.

EXAMPLE 1

Company without subsidiaries Ltd
Statement of source and application of funds

	This Year		Last Year			
	£'000	£'000	£'000	£'000	£'000	£'000
Source of funds						
Profit before tax		1,430				440
Adjustments for items not involving the movement of funds:						
Depreciation		380				325
Total generated from operations .		1,810				765
Funds from other sources						
Issue of shares for cash . . .		100				80
		1,910				845
Application of funds						
Dividends paid	(400)			(400)		
Tax paid	(690)			(230)		
Purchase of fixed assets . . .	(460)			(236)		
		(1,550)				(866)
		360				(21)
Increase/decrease in working capital						
Increase in stocks	80			114		
Increase in debtors	120			22		
(Increase) decrease in creditors – excluding taxation and proposed dividends	115			(107)		
Movement in net liquid funds:						
Increase (decrease) in:						
Cash balances	(5)			35		
Short-term investments . .	50			(85)		
		45			(50)	
		360				(21)

197

EXAMPLE 2

Groups Limited
Statement of source and application of funds

(based on the accounts of the group and showing the effects of acquiring a subsidiary on the separate assets and liabilities of the group).

	This Year		Last Year		
	£'000 £'000	£'000	£'000 £'000	£'000	
Source of funds					
Profit before tax and extraordinary items, less minority interests		2,025		2,610	
Extraordinary items		450		(170)	
		2,475		2,440	
Adjustments for items not involving the movement of funds:					
Minority interests in the retained profits of the year		25		30	
Depreciation		345		295	
Profits retained in associated companies		(40)		—	
Total generated from operations		2,805		2,765	
Funds from other sources					
Shares issued in part consideration of the acquisition of subsidiary*		290		—	
Capital raised under executive option scheme		100		80	
		3,195		2,845	
Application of funds					
Dividends paid	(650)		(650)		
Tax paid	(770)		(970)		
Purchase of fixed assets*	(660)		(736)		
Purchase of goodwill on acquisition of subsidiary*	(30)		—		
Debentures redeemed	(890)	(3,000)	—	(2,356)	
		195		489	
Increase/decrease in working capital					
Increase in stocks*	120		166		
Increase in debtors*	100		122		
Decrease in creditors – excluding taxation and proposed dividends*	75		17		
Movement in net liquid funds:					
Increase(decrease) in cash balance*	(35)		10		
Increase(decrease) in short-term investments	(65)	(100)	174	184	
		195		489	

* See page 199.

Summary of the effects of the acquisition of Subsidiary Limited

Net assets acquired		Discharged by	
Fixed assets	290	Shares issued	290
Goodwill	30	Cash paid	60
Stocks	40		
Debtors	30		
Creditors	(40)		
	350		350

EXAMPLE 3

Groups Limited
Statement of source and application of funds

(based on the accounts of the group and showing the acquisition of a subsidiary as a separate item).

| | This Year | | | Last Year | | |
	£'000	£'000	£'000	£'000	£'000	£'000
Source of funds						
Profit before tax and extraordinary items. less minority interests		2,025			2,610	
Extraordinary items		450			(170)	
		2,475			2,440	
Adjustments for items not involving the movement of funds:						
Minority interests in the retained profits of the year		25			30	
Depreciation		345			295	
Profits retained in associated companies		(40)			—	
Total generated from operations		2,805			2,765	
Funds from other sources						
Shares issued in part consideration of the acquisition of subsidiary*		290			—	
Capital raised under executive option scheme		100			80	
		3,195			2,845	
Application of funds						
Dividends paid	(650)			(650)		
Tax paid	(770)			(970)		
Purchase of fixed assets	(370)			(736)		
Purchase of Subsidiary Ltd*	(350)			—		
Debentures redeemed	(890)			—		
		(3,030)			(2,356)	
		165			489	
Increase/decrease in working capital						
Increase in stocks		80			166	
Increase in debtors		70			122	
Decrease in creditors — excluding taxation and proposed dividends		115			17	
Movement in net liquid funds:						
Increase(decrease) in cash balance*	(35)			10		
Increase(decrease) in short-term investments	(65)			174		
		(100)			184	
		165			489	

* See page 201.

Analysis of the acquisition of Subsidiary Limited

Net assets acquired		Discharged by	
Fixed assets	290	Shares issued	290
Goodwill	30	Cash paid	60
Stocks	40		
Debtors	30		
Creditors	(40)		
	350		350

12

Accounting for depreciation

Contents

Accounting for depreciation

(*Issued December 1977*)

Part 1 – Explanatory note

1 Depreciation is a measure of the wearing out, consumption or other loss of value of a fixed asset whether arising from use, effluxion of time or obsolescence through technology and market changes. Depreciation should be allocated to accounting periods so as to charge a fair proportion to each accounting period during the expected useful life of the asset. Depreciation includes amortisation of fixed assets whose useful life is pre-determined (e.g. leases) and depletion of wasting assets (e.g. mines).

2 Assessment of depreciation, and its allocation to accounting periods, involves in the first instance consideration of three factors:

   (a) cost (or valuation when an asset has been revalued in the financial statements);

   (b) the nature of the asset and the length of its expected useful life to the business having due regard to the incidence of obsolescence;

   (c) estimated residual value.

3 An asset's useful life may be:

   (a) pre-determined, as in leaseholds;

   (b) directly governed by extraction or consumption;

   (c) dependent on the extent of use;

   (d) reduced by obsolescence or physical deterioration.

4 The precise assessment of residual value is normally a difficult matter. Where it is likely to be small in relation to cost, it is convenient to regard it as 'nil' and to deal with any proceeds on eventual disposal in the same way as depreciation over-provided on disposal as referred to in paragraph 6 below.

5 The allocation of depreciation to accounting periods involves the exercise of judgement by management in the light of technical, commercial and accounting considerations and accordingly requires annual review. When, as the result of experience or of changed circumstances, it is considered that the original estimate of useful life of an asset requires to be revised, the unamortised cost of the asset should be charged to revenue over the revised remaining useful life. If at any time the unamortised cost is seen to be irrecoverable in full (perhaps as a result of obsolescence or a fall in demand for a product), it should be written down immediately to the estimated recoverable amount which should be charged over the remaining useful life.

6 Where fixed assets are disposed of for an amount which is greater or less than their book value, the surplus or deficiency should be reflected in the results of the year and disclosed separately if material.

The management of a business has a duty to allocate depreciation as fairly as possible to the periods expected to benefit from the use of the asset and should select the method regarded as most appropriate to the type of asset and its use in the business. 7

A change from one method of providing depreciation to another is permissible only on the grounds that the new method will give a fairer presentation of the results and of the financial position. In these circumstances the unamortised cost should be written off over the remaining useful life commencing with the period in which the change is made. 8

Where assets are revalued and effect is given to the revaluation in the financial state-ments, the charge for depreciation thereafter should be based on the revalued amount and, in the year of change, there should be disclosed by way of note to the financial statements the subdivision of the charge between that applicable to original cost (or valuation if previously revalued) and that applicable to the change in value on the current revaluation, if material. 9

It is not appropriate to omit charging depreciation of a fixed asset on the grounds that its market value is greater than its net book value. If account is taken of such increased value by writing up the net book value of a fixed asset then, as indicated in paragraph 9, an increased charge for depreciation will become necessary. 10

Freehold land, unless subject to depletion by, for example, the extraction of minerals or to reduction in value due to other circumstances, will not normally require a provision for depreciation. However, the value of freehold land may be adversely affected by considerations such as the desirability of its location either socially or in relation to available sources of materials, labour or sales and in these circumstances it should be written down. 11

Buildings have a limited life which may be materially affected by technological and environmental changes and they should be depreciated having regard to the same criteria as in the case of other fixed assets. 12

As in the case of other assets an increase in the value of land or buildings does not remove the necessity for charging depreciation on the buildings whenever any of the causes mentioned in paragraph 1 are applicable, whether or not the value of the asset has increased in the past. 13

Transitional arrangements
Where existing buildings are depreciated for the first time under the terms of this standard it will represent a change in accounting policy and therefore the amount of depreciation charged which relates to prior years should properly be treated as a prior year adjustment and charged against the opening balance of retained profits. 14

Part 2 – Definition of terms

15   The following definition is used for the purpose of this statement: *Depreciation* is the measure of the wearing out, consumption or other loss of value of a fixed asset whether arising from use, effluxion of time or obsolescence through technology and market changes.

Part 3 – Standard accounting practice

Accounting treatment

16   Provision for depreciation of fixed assets having a finite useful life should be made by allocating the cost (or revalued amount) less estimated residual values of the assets as fairly as possible to the periods expected to benefit from their use.

17   Where there is a revision of the estimated useful life of an asset, the unamortised cost should be charged over the revised remaining useful life.

18   However, if at any time the unamortised cost of an asset is seen to be irrecoverable in full, it should be written down immediately to the estimated recoverable amount which should be charged over the remaining useful life.

19   Where there is a change from one method of depreciation to another, the unamortised cost of the asset should be written off over the remaining useful life on the new basis commencing with the period in which the change is made. The effect should be disclosed in the year of change, if material.

20   Where assets are revalued in the financial statements, the provision for depreciation should be based on the revalued amount and current estimate of remaining useful life, with disclosure in the year of change, of the effect of the revaluation, if material.

Disclosure

21   The following should be disclosed in the financial statements for each major class of depreciable asset:

(a) the depreciation methods used;

(b) the useful lives or the depreciation rates used;

(c) total depreciation allocated for the period;

(d) the gross amount of depreciable assets and the related accumulated depreciation.

Date from which effective

22   The accounting and disclosure requirements set out in this statement should be adopted as soon as possible and regarded as standard in respect of financial statements relating to periods starting on or after 1st January 1978, except that the provisions of the standard need not be applied to investment properties in respect of periods starting before 1st January 1980.

Part 4 – Compliance with International Accounting Standard No. 4 'Depreciation accounting'

Compliance with the requirements of Statement of Standard Accounting Practice No.   23
12 *Accounting for Depreciation* will automatically ensure compliance with International Accounting Standard No. 4 *Depreciation Accounting.*

Amendment issued 7 December, 1978

Part 1 – Explanatory note
The Accounting Standards Committee is reviewing the application of SSAP12 to   24
investment properties.

SSAP12 is due to become effective for investment properties in respect of financial   25
statements relating to accounting periods beginning on or after 1st January 1979.

It will not be possible for the Accounting Standards Committee to complete its review   26
before the 31st December 1978. Members of the Accounting Standards Committee
are continuing discussions with persons concerned with the financial statements issued
by companies which own investment properties. It would be inappropriate to allow the
Standard to come into force before the process of consultation was completed and
appropriate recommendations formulated. The Councils of the governing bodies of the
Accounting Standards Committee have therefore accepted the Accounting Standards
Committee's recommendation that the date from which the standard becomes effective
in regard to investment properties should be deferred until the 1st January 1980.

Part 2 – Standard Accounting Practice (Amendment)
In Paragraph 22 of SSAP12 the date '1st January 1979' should be deleted and   7
replaced by '1st January 1980'.

13

Accounting for research and development

Contents

Accounting for research and development

(Issued December 1977)

Part 1 – Explanatory note

Basic concepts

1 The accounting policies to be followed in respect of research and development expenditure must have regard to the fundamental accounting concepts including the 'accruals' concept by which revenue and costs are accrued, matched and dealt with in the period to which they relate and the 'prudence' concept by which revenue and profits are not anticipated but are recognised only when realised in the form either of cash or of other assets the ultimate cash realisation of which can be established with reasonable certainty. It is a corollary of the prudence concept that expenditure should be written off in the period in which it arises unless its relationship to the revenue of a future period can be established with reasonable certainty.

The different types of research and development expenditure

2 The term 'research and development' is currently used to cover a wide range of activities. Classification of the related expenditure is often dependent on the type of business and its organisation. However, it is generally possible to recognise three broad categories of activity, namely, pure research (work directed primarily towards the advancement of knowledge), applied research (work directed primarily towards exploiting pure research other than work defined as development expenditure), and development (work directed towards the introduction or improvement of specific products or processes).

3 The definitions of the different types of research and development used in this statement have been based on those used by the Organisation for Economic Co-operation and Development which are used on a world-wide basis for the purposes of collecting data on this subject.

4 The dividing line between these categories of expenditure will often be indistinct and particular expenditure may have characteristics of more than one category. This is particularly apparent when new products are developed through research and development to production, when the activities may have characteristics of both development and production.

The accounting treatment of research and development

5 Expenditure incurred on pure and applied research can be regarded as part of a continuing operation required to maintain a company's business and its competitive position. In general, one particular period rather than another will not be expected to benefit and therefore it is appropriate that these costs should be written off as they are incurred.

6 The development of new and improved products is, however, distinguishable from pure and applied research. Expenditure on such development is normally undertaken with a reasonable expectation of specific commercial success and of future benefits arising

210

from the work, either from increased revenue and related profits or from reduced costs. On these grounds it may be argued that such expenditure should be deferred to be matched against the future revenue.

It will only be practicable to evaluate the potential future benefits of development expenditure if: 7

(a) there is a clearly defined project; and

(b) the related expenditure is separately identifiable.

The outcome of such a project would then need to be examined for: 8

(a) its technical feasibility; and

(b) its ultimate commercial viability considered in the light of factors such as:

(i) likely market conditions (including competing products);

(ii) public opinion;

(iii) consumer and environmental legislation.

Furthermore a project will only be of value: 9

(a) if further development costs to be incurred on the same project together with related production, selling and administration costs will be more than covered by related future revenues; and

(b) adequate resources exist, or are reasonably expected to be available, to enable the project to be completed and to provide any consequential increases in working capital.

The elements of uncertainty inherent in the considerations set out in paragraphs 8 and 9 are considerable. There will be a need for different persons having differing levels of judgement to be involved in assessing the technical, commercial and financial viability of the project. Combinations of the possible different assessments which they might validly make can produce widely differing assessments of the existence and amounts of future benefits. 10

If these uncertainties are viewed in the context of the concept of prudence, the future benefits of most development projects would be too uncertain to justify carrying the expenditure forward. Nevertheless, in certain industries it is considered that there are numbers of major development projects that satisfy the stringent criteria set out in paragraphs 7 to 9. Accordingly, where expenditure on development projects is judged on a prudent view of available evidence to satisfy these criteria, it may be carried forward and amortised over the period expected to benefit. 11

At each accounting date the unamortised balance of development expenditure should be examined project by project to ensure that it still fulfils the criteria in paragraphs 7 to 9. Where any doubt exists as to the continuation of those circumstances the balance should be written off. 12

Fixed assets may be acquired or constructed in order to provide facilities for research and/or development activities. The use of such fixed assets will usually extend over a 13 number of accounting periods and accordingly they should be capitalised and written off over their useful life. The depreciation so written off should be included as part of the expenditure on research and development and should also be included in the amount of depreciation disclosed under paragraph 12 (1) (a) of the 2nd Schedule of the Companies Act 1967.

Exceptions

14   Where companies enter into a firm contract

  (a) to carry out development work on behalf of third parties on such terms that the related expenditure is to be fully reimbursed, or

  (b) to develop and manufacture at an agreed price which has been calculated to reimburse expenditure on development as well as on manufacture,

any such expenditure which has not been reimbursed at the balance sheet date should be included in work in progress. *listed as current assets*

15   Expenditure incurred in locating and exploiting mineral deposits in the extractive industries does not fall within the definition of research and development used in this accounting standard. *exclude a money spent on exploration by oil co's.*

Market research

16   The definitions of research and development expenditure given in paragraph 18 are based on those used by the Organisation for Economic Co-operation and Development and do not encompass expenditure on market research. Nevertheless the accounting treatment for expenditure on market research could generally be expected to follow that for research and development expenditure. Thus it would generally be appropriate to write off such expenditure as incurred: but where market research is carried out to ascertain the factors set out in paragraph 8 (b) in respect of a product which in all other respects satisfies the criteria set out in paragraphs 7 to 9, the related expenditure may reasonably be carried forward but should be separately disclosed.

Disclosure

17   The uncertainties inherent in development projects suggest that there is a case for disclosure, for example of the nature, status and costs of individual research and development projects whether written off or not. It is, however, thought that to call for such detailed disclosure would raise considerable problems of definition. Accordingly it is proposed that disclosure should be limited to the movements of unamortised development expenditure during the year.

Part 2 – Definition of terms

The following definition is used for the purpose of this statement: 18

Research and development expenditure means expenditure falling into one or more of the following broad categories (except to the extent that it relates to locating or exploiting mineral deposits or is reimbursable by third parties either directly or under the terms of a firm contract to develop and manufacture at an agreed price which has been calculated to reimburse both elements of expenditure):

(a) Pure (or basic) research: original investigation undertaken in order to gain new scientific or technical knowledge and understanding. Basic research is not primarily directed towards any specific practical aim or application;

(b) Applied research: original investigation undertaken in order to gain new scientific or technical knowledge and directed towards a specific practical aim or objective;

(c) Development: the use of scientific or technical knowledge in order to produce new or substantially improved materials, devices, products, processes, systems or services prior to the commencement of commercial production.

Part 3 – Standard accounting practice

Accounting treatment

The cost of fixed assets acquired or constructed in order to provide facilities for research and development activities over a number of accounting periods should be capitalised and written off over their useful life. 19

Expenditure on pure and applied research (other than that referred to in paragraph 19) should be written off in the year of expenditure. 20

Development expenditure should be written off in the year of expenditure except in the following circumstances when it may be deferred to future periods: 21

(a) there is a clearly defined project, and

(b) the related expenditure is separately identifiable, and

(c) the outcome of such a project has been assessed with reasonable certainty as to

   (i) its technical feasibility, and

   (ii) its ultimate commercial viability considered in the light of factors such as likely market conditions (including competing products), public opinion, consumer and environmental legislation, and

(d) if further development costs are to be incurred on the same project the aggregate of such costs together with related production, selling and administration costs are reasonably expected to be more than covered by related future revenues, and

(e) adequate resources exist, or are reasonably expected to be available, to enable the project to be completed and to provide any consequential increases in working capital.

22   In the foregoing circumstances development expenditure may be deferred to the extent that its recovery can reasonably be regarded as assured.

23   The criteria for determining whether development expenditure may be deferred should be applied consistently.

24   If development costs are deferred to future periods, their amortisation should commence with the commercial production of the product or process and should be allocated on a systematic basis to each accounting period, by reference to either the sale or use of the product or process or the period over which the product or process is expected to be sold or used.

25   Deferred development expenditure should be reviewed at the end of each accounting period and where the circumstances which have justified the deferral of the expenditure (see paragraph 21) no longer apply, or are considered doubtful, the expenditure, to the extent to which it is considered to be irrecoverable, should be written off immediately.

26   Development expenditure once written off should not be reinstated even though the uncertainties which had led to its being written off no longer apply.

Disclosure

27   Movements on deferred development expenditure and the amount carried forward at the beginning and the end of the period should be disclosed.

28   Deferred development expenditure should be separately disclosed and should not be included in current assets.

29   The accounting policy followed should be clearly explained.

Date from which effective

30   The accounting and disclosure requirements set out in this statement should be adopted as soon as possible and regarded as standard in respect of financial statements relating to periods starting on or after 1st January 1978.

14

Group accounts

Contents

Group accounts

(Issued September 1978)

This standard deals with the presentation of group accounts for a group of companies. The practice of preparing group accounts for a company and its subsidiaries, usually in the form of consolidated financial statements, has become well established in the United Kingdom and Ireland since 1948 and there has therefore been no urgent need for an accounting standard on the subject. However, the issue of International Accounting Standard No. 3 'Consolidated Financial Statements' (IAS3) which, while generally in accordance with the law and practice in the United Kingdom and Ireland, differs in some respects, has made it desirable for there to be a domestic standard on the subject.

Compliance with this standard will result in compliance with IAS3 so far as it relates to consolidated financial statements as indicated in paragraph 65. IAS3 also deals with the equity basis of accounting for associated companies which is the subject of a separate accounting standard, SSAP1 'Accounting for the Results of Associated Companies'.

The provisions of this statement of standard accounting practice should be read in conjunction with the Explanatory Foreword to accounting standards and need not be applied to immaterial items.

Part 1 – Explanatory note

1   Group accounts showing the state of affairs and profit or loss of a holding company and its subsidiaries have been required by law in most instances in the United Kingdom and Ireland for many years. In practice the group accounts usually take the form of consolidated financial statements which present the information contained in the separate financial statements of the holding company and its subsidiaries as if they were the financial statements of a single entity. Alternative forms of presentation are, however, permitted by the Companies Acts under certain conditions.

2   It is generally accepted that consolidated financial statements are usually the best means of achieving the objective of group accounts which is to give a true and fair view of the profit or loss and of the state of affairs of the group. This accounting standard recognises, therefore, that only exceptionally will alternative forms of group accounts give a better view than consolidated financial statements.

3   The method of preparation of consolidated financial statements on an item-by-item basis, eliminating intra-group balances and transactions and unrealised intra-group profit, is well understood in the United Kingdom and Ireland and this statement is not intended to be a detailed text on the subject.

4   Except to a limited extent this statement does not deal with the subjects of acquisitions and mergers or goodwill, which are closely related to the subject of consolidated financial statements but are better dealt with as separate accounting standards.

The standard has been drafted to apply to companies incorporated under the Companies Acts. The principles laid down in it are nevertheless applicable to the financial statements of any entity, whether incorporated or not, which controls another entity or entities and which wishes or is required to present financial statements reflecting the activities of the undertaking as a whole. 5

In giving a true and fair view of the profit or loss and of the state of affairs of the group as a whole, the same principles apply to consolidated financial statements as would apply to the financial statements of a single entity. Disclosure should therefore be made in the consolidated financial statements of any matters which would be required to be disclosed in the financial statements of a single entity such as, for instance, any exceptional risks which may have an impact on items in the consolidated financial statements. 6

Part 2 − Definition of terms

Subsidiary company. A company shall be deemed to be a subsidiary of another if but only if, 7

  (a) that other either:

    (i) is a member of it and controls the composition of its board of directors; or

    (ii) holds more than half in nominal value of its equity share capital; or

  (b) the first mentioned company is a subsidiary of any company which is that other's subsidiary,

and it otherwise comes within the terms of Section 154 of the Companies Act 1948. This definition differs slightly from the definition of a subsidiary company in the Republic of Ireland (see paragraph 61).

Holding company. A company is a holding company of another if but only if that other is its subsidiary as defined above. 8

Group. A holding company and its subsidiaries. 9

Financial statements. Balance sheets, profit and loss accounts, statement of source and application of funds, notes and other statements, which collectively are intended to give a true and fair view of financial position and profit or loss. 10

Group accounts. Financial statements of a group. 11

Consolidated financial statements. One form of group accounts which presents the information contained in the separate financial statements of a holding company and its subsidiaries as if they were the financial statements of a single entity. 12

Equity share capital. Issued share capital of a company excluding any part thereof which, neither as respects dividends nor as respects capital, carries any right to participate beyond a specified amount in a distribution. 13

14   *Equity method of accounting.* A method of accounting under which the investment in
      a company is shown in the consolidated balance sheet at:

      (a) the cost of the investment; and

      (b) the investing company or group's share of the post-acquisition retained profits
          and reserves of the company; less

      (c) any amounts written off in respect of (a) and (b) above;

      and under which the investing company accounts separately in its profit and loss
      account for its share of the profits before tax, taxation and extraordinary items of the
      company concerned. This method is usually applied to associated companies under the
      provisions of SSAP1 *Accounting for results of associated companies.*

Part 3 – Standard accounting practice

Consolidated financial statements
15   A holding company should prepare group accounts in the form of a single set of con-
      solidated financial statements covering the holding company and its subsidiary com-
      panies, at home and overseas. The only exceptions to this practice are in the
      circumstances set out in paragraphs 19 to 22 below. A description of the bases on
      which subsidiary companies have been dealt with in the group accounts should be
      given.

Uniform accounting policies
16   Uniform group accounting policies should be followed by a holding company in pre-
      paring its consolidated financial statements. Where such group accounting policies are
      not adopted in the financial statements of a subsidiary, appropriate adjustments should
      be made in the consolidated financial statements. In exceptional cases where this is
      impracticable, different accounting policies may be used provided they are generally
      acceptable and there is disclosure of:

      (a) the different accounting policies used;

      (b) an indication of the amounts of the assets and liabilities involved, and where
          practicable, an indication of the effect on results and net assets of the adoption of
          policies different from those of the group;

      (c) the reasons for the different treatment.

Group accounting periods and dates
17   For the purposes of consolidated financial statements the financial statements of all
      subsidiaries should wherever practicable be prepared:

      (a) to the same accounting date; and

      (b) for identical accounting periods as the holding company.

18   If a subsidiary does not prepare its formal financial statements to the same date as the
      holding company and if it is not practicable to use for consolidation purposes special

financial statements drawn up to the same date as those of the holding company (Department of Trade or other Government consent having been obtained as necessary), appropriate adjustments should be made to the consolidated financial statements for any abnormal transactions in the intervening period. The following additional information should be given for each principal subsidiary with a different accounting date:

(a) its name; and

(b) its accounting date; and

(c) the reason for using a different accounting date.

Where the accounting period of a principal subsidiary was of a different length from that of the holding company the accounting period involved should be stated.

Exclusion of subsidiaries from group accounts and consolidation
Group accounts need not be prepared, unless required by law, where the holding company itself is at the end of its financial year a wholly owned subsidiary.   19

When a company is not a wholly owned subsidiary and it does not prepare group accounts dealing with all its subsidiaries for one of the other reasons permitted under the Companies Acts, the reason for the exclusion of any subsidiary must be stated. Consideration will need to be given to whether the resulting financial statements give a true and fair view of the position of the group as a whole.   20

A subsidiary should be excluded from consolidation if: 21

(a) its activities are so dissimilar from those of other companies within the group that consolidated financial statements would be misleading and that information for the holding company's shareholders and other users of the statements would be better provided by presenting separate financial statements for such a subsidiary; or

(b) the holding company, although owning directly or through other subsidiaries more than half the equity share capital of the subsidiary, either:

 (i) does not own share capital carrying more than half the votes; or

 (ii) has contractual or other restrictions imposed on its ability to appoint the majority of the board of directors; or

(c) the subsidiary operates under severe restrictions which significantly impair control by the holding company over the subsidiary's assets and operations for the foreseeable future; or

(d) control is intended to be temporary.

If a group prepares group accounts in a form other than consolidated financial statements in circumstances different from those set out in paragraph 21, the onus is on the directors to justify and state the reasons for reaching the conclusion that the resulting group accounts give a fairer view of the financial position of the group as a whole. Similar considerations apply where consolidated financial statements are prepared dealing with a subsidiary which comes within the scope of the circumstances set out in paragraph 21.   22

Accounting treatment of subsidiaries excluded from consolidation

23   Where a subsidiary is excluded from consolidation on the grounds set out in paragraph 21 (a) because of dissimilar activities, the group accounts should include separate financial statements for that subsidiary. They may be combined with the financial statements of other subsidiaries with similar operations, if appropriate. The separate financial statements should include the following information:

(a) a note of the holding company's interest;

(b) particulars of intra-group balances;

(c) the nature of transactions with the rest of the group; and

(d) a reconciliation with the amount included in the consolidated financial statements for the group's investment in the subsidiary which should be stated under the equity method of accounting.

24   Where a subsidiary is excluded from consolidation on the grounds of lack of effective control as set out in paragraph 21 (b), it should be dealt with in the consolidated financial statements:

either

(a) under the equity method of accounting if in all other respects it satisfies the criteria for treatment as an associated company under SSAP1;

or, if these conditions are not met,

(b) as an investment at cost or valuation less any provision required.

In either event, separate financial information about it should be included in the group accounts to meet the requirements of the Companies Acts.

25   Where a subsidiary is excluded from consolidation on the grounds set out in paragraph 21 (c), because of severe restrictions, the amount of the group's investment in the subsidiary should be stated in the consolidated balance sheet at the amount at which it would have been included under the equity method of accounting at the date the restrictions came into force. No further accruals should be made for its profits or losses. However, if the amount at which the investment it stated in the consolidated financial statements on this basis has been impaired by a decline in value of the investment (other than temporarily) provision for the loss should be made through the consolidated profit and loss account. For this purpose, investments should be considered individually and not in the aggregate.

26   Where a subsidiary is excluded from consolidation on the grounds set out in paragraph 21 (c) the following information should be disclosed in the group accounts:

(a) its net assets;

(b) its profits or losses for the period;

(c) any amounts included in the consolidated profit and loss account in respect of:

(i) dividends received;

(ii) writing down of the investment.

Where a subsidiary is excluded from consolidation on the grounds set out in paragraph 21 (d) that control is intended to be temporary, the temporary investment in the subsidiary should be stated in the consolidated balance sheet as a current asset at the lower of cost and net realisable value.   27

Disclosure in respect of subsidiaries excluded from consolidation

In respect of subsidiaries excluded from consolidation, the following information should be disclosed in the group accounts: 28

  (a) the reasons for excluding a subsidiary from consolidation;

  (b) the names of the principal subsidiaries excluded;

  (c) any premium or discount on acquisition (in comparison with the fair value of assets acquired) to the extent not written off; and

  (d) any further detailed information required by the Companies Acts.

Changes in composition of the group

When subsidiaries are purchased, the purchase consideration should be allocated between the underlying net tangible and intangible assets other than goodwill on the basis of the fair value to the acquiring company. If this is not done by means of adjusting the values in the books of the acquired company, it should be done on consolidation. Any difference between the purchase consideration and the value ascribed to net tangible assets and identifiable intangible assets such as trade marks, patents or development expenditure, will represent premium or discount on acquisition.   29

In the case of material additions to or disposals from the group, the consolidated financial statements should contain sufficient information about the results of the subsidiaries acquired or sold to enable shareholders to appreciate the effect on the consolidated results.   30

Where there is a material disposal, the consolidated profit and loss account should include: 31

  (a) the subsidiary's results up to the date of disposal; and

  (b) the gain or loss on the sale of the investment, being the difference at the time of the sale between:

    (i) proceeds of the sale and

    (ii) the holding company's share of its net assets together with any premium (less any amounts written off) or discount on acquisition.

Effective date of acquisition or disposal

The effective date for accounting for both acquisition and disposal of a subsidiary should be the earlier of: 32

  (a) the date on which consideration passes; or

  (b) the date on which an offer becomes or is declared unconditional.

This applies even if the acquiring company has the right under the agreement to share in the profits of the acquired business from an earlier date.

Disclosure of principal subsidiaries

33   The names of the principal subsidiaries should be disclosed in the group accounts, showing for each of these subsidiaries:

(a) the proportion of the nominal value of the issued shares of each class held by the group; and

(b) an indication of the nature of its business.

Outside or minority interests

34   Outside or minority interests in the share capital and reserves of companies consolidated should be disclosed as a separate amount in the consolidated balance sheet and should not be shown as part of the shareholders' funds; debit balances should be recognised only if there is a binding obligation on minority shareholders to make good losses incurred which they are able to meet.

35   Similarly, the profits or losses of such companies attributable to outside interests should be shown separately in the consolidated profit and loss account after arriving at group profit or loss after tax but before extraordinary items. Minority interests in extraordinary items should be deducted from the related amounts in the consolidated profit and loss account.

Restrictions on distributions

36   If there are significant restrictions on the ability of the holding company to distribute the retained profits of the group (other than those shown as non-distributable) because of statutory, contractual or exchange control restrictions the extent of the restrictions should be indicated.

Date from which effective

37   The accounting and disclosure requirements set out in this statement should be adopted as soon as possible and regarded as standard in respect of group accounts relating to periods starting on or after 1st January 1979.

Part 4 – Note of legal requirements in Great Britain

References to companies legislation have been abbreviated as follows:

The 1948 Act – Companies Act 1948
The 1967 Act – Companies Act 1967
The 1976 Act – Companies Act 1976

38   The obligation to lay group accounts before the members of a holding company in general meeting is set out in Section 150 (1) of the 1948 Act as amended by the 1976 Act. In general terms the form and content of group accounts are dealt with *inter alia* in Sections 151 and 152 of the 1948 Act as amended by the 1976 Act and in Schedule 8 to the 1948 Act as amended by the 1967 Act.

Under Section 150 (2) (a) of the 1948 Act group accounts shall not be required where   39
the holding company is at the end of its financial year the wholly owned subsidiary of
another body corporate incorporated in Great Britain. Paragraph 19 of the standard
encompasses this exemption.

Section 150 (2) (b) of the 1948 Act also allows group accounts (subject to approval   40
of the Department of Trade in certain instances) not to deal with a subsidiary if the
company's directors are of the opinion that:
  (i) it is impracticable, or would be of no real value to members of the company, in
      view of the insignificant amounts involved, or would involve expense or delay
      out of proportion to the value to members of the company; or
  (ii) the result would be misleading, or harmful to the business of the company or
      any of its subsidiaries; or
  (iii) the business of the holding company and that of the subsidiary are so different
      that they cannot reasonably be treated as a single undertaking.

It should be noted that, where subsidiaries are not dealt with in group accounts or are   41
being dealt with in a form of group accounts other than consolidated financial statements, information may still be required by law about the results of these subsidiaries
and the extent to which they have been dealt with in the accounts of the holding
company (paragraphs 21 and 15 (4) of Schedule 8 of the 1948 Act, as amended by the
1967 Act).

In the case of a subsidiary excluded from consolidation under paragraph 21 (a), the   42
information set out in paragraph 23 should satisfy the requirements of the Companies
Acts about group accounts provided adequate detail is given. Where a subsidiary is
excluded from consolidation on the grounds set out in paragraphs 21 (b) to 21 (d) of
the standard, additional information to that set out in paragraphs 24 to 27 may be
needed in order to satisfy the requirements of the Companies Acts about group
accounts.

The definition of a subsidiary company given in paragraph 7 of this statement con-   43
forms with the statutory definition given in Section 154 of the 1948 Act.

Section 153 (1) of the 1948 Act states that a holding company's directors shall secure   44
that, except where in their opinion there are good reasons against it, the financial year
of each of its subsidiaries shall coincide with the company's own financial year.
Paragraph 18 of the standard specifies the action to be taken in preparing consolidated
accounts where the accounting periods do not coincide.

Under the provision of Section 152 (2) of the 1948 Act the consent of the Department   45
of Trade will be required to the use of special financial statements of subsidiaries where
used under paragraph 18 of the standard.

Section 3 (3) of the 1967 Act provides that disclosure of the name of a subsidiary   46
which is either incorporated outside the United Kingdom or carries on business outside
the United Kingdom need not be made if in the opinion of the directors and with the
concurrence of the Department of Trade such disclosure would be harmful.

Part 5 – Note of legal requirements in Ireland

Section A – Northern Ireland

References to companies legislation have been abbreviated as follows:

The 1960 Act – Companies Act (Northern Ireland) 1960

The 1978 Order – Companies Order (Northern Ireland) 1978.

47   The obligation to lay group accounts before the members of a holding company in general meeting is set out in Section 144 (1) of the 1960 Act as amended by the 1978 Order. In general terms the form and content of group accounts are dealt with *inter alia* in Sections 145 and 146 of the 1960 Act as amended by the 1978 Order and in Schedule 6 to the 1960 Act as amended by the 1978 Order.

48   Under Section 144 (2) (a) of the 1960 Act group accounts shall not be required where the holding company is at the end of its financial year the wholly owned subsidiary of another body corporate incorporated in Northern Ireland. Paragraph 19 of the standard encompasses this exemption.

49   Section 144 (2) of the 1960 Act also allows group accounts (subject to approval of the Department of Commerce in certain instances) not to deal with a subsidiary if the company's directors are of the opinion that:

　　(i) it is impracticable, or would be of no real value to members of the company, in view of the insignificant amounts involved, or would involve expense or delay out of proportion to the value to members of the company; or

　　(ii) the result would be misleading, or harmful to the business of the company or any of its subsidiaries; or

　　(iii) the business of the holding company and that of the subsidiary are so different that they cannot reasonably be treated as a single undertaking.

50   It should be noted that, where subsidiaries are not dealt with in group accounts or are being dealt with in a form of group accounts other than consolidated financial statements, information may still be required by law about the results of these subsidiaries and the extent to which they have been dealt with in the accounts of the holding company (paragraphs 21 and 15 (4) of Schedule 6 of the 1960 Act, as amended by the 1978 Order).

51   In the case of a subsidiary excluded from consolidation under paragraph 21 (a), the information set out in paragraph 23 should satisfy the requirements of the Companies Acts about group accounts provided adequate detail is given. Where a subsidiary is excluded from consolidation on the grounds set out in paragraphs 21 (b) to 21 (d) of the standard, additional information to that set out in paragraphs 24 to 27 may be needed in order to satisfy the requirements of the Companies Acts (Northern Ireland) about group accounts.

52   The definition of a subsidiary company given in paragraph 7 of this statement conforms with the statutory definition given in Section 154 of the 1960 Act, as amended by the 1978 Order.

Section 147 (1) of the 1960 Act states that a holding company's directors shall secure   53
that, except where in their opinion there are good reasons against it, the financial year
of each of its subsidiaries shall coincide with the company's own financial year.
Paragraph 18 of the standard specifies the action to be taken in preparing consolidated
accounts where accounting periods do not coincide.

Under the provision of Section 146 (2) of the 1960 Act the consent of the Department   54
of Commerce will be required to the use of special financial statements of subsidiaries
where used under paragraph 18 of the standard.

Section 15 (3) of the 1978 Order provides that disclosure of the name of a subsidiary   55
which is either incorporated outside the United Kingdom or carries on business outside
the United Kingdom need not be made if in the opinion of the directors and with the
concurrence of the Department of Commerce such disclosure would be harmful.

Section B – Republic of Ireland
References to companies legislation have been abbreviated as follows:

The 1963 Act – Companies Act 1963 (Republic of Ireland).

The obligation to lay group accounts before the members of a holding company in   56
general meeting is set out in Section 150 (1) of the 1963 Act. While the latter Section
refers to public companies only, it should be noted that the standard applies also to
private companies. In general terms the form and content of group accounts are dealt
with *inter alia* in Sections 151–152 and in Schedule 6 of the 1963 Act.

Under Section 150 (2) (a) of the 1963 Act group accounts shall not be required where   57
the holding company is at the end of its financial year the wholly-owned subsidiary of
another body corporate incorporated in the Republic of Ireland. Paragraph 19 of the
standard encompasses this exemption.

Section 150 (2) of the 1963 Act allows group accounts not to deal with a subsidiary if   58
the company's directors are of the opinion that:
  (i) it is impracticable or would be of no real value to members of the company in
      view of the insignificant amounts involved; or
  (ii) it would involve expense or delay out of proportion to the value to the members
      of the company; or
  (iii) the result would be misleading.

It should be noted, that where subsidiaries are not dealt with in group accounts or are   59
being dealt with in a form of group accounts other than consolidated financial statements, information may still be required by law about the results of these subsidiaries
and the extent to which they have been dealt with in the accounts of the holding
company (paragraphs 15 (4) and 21 of Schedule 6 of the 1963 Act).

In the case of a subsidiary excluded from consolidation under paragraph 21 (a), the   60
information set out in paragraph 23 should satisfy the requirements of the 1963 Act
about group accounts provided adequate detail is given. Where a subsidiary is excluded

from consolidation on the grounds set out in paragraphs 21 (b) to 21 (d) of the standard, additional information to that set out in paragraphs 24 to 27 may be needed in order to satisfy the requirements of the 1963 Act about group accounts.

61   Subsidiaries are statutorily defined in Section 155 (1) of the 1963 Act. The definition of a subsidiary given in paragraph 7 conforms with the statutory definition except that a company in which the holding company holds more than half of the shares carrying voting rights, as distinct from more than half of the equity share capital, is also included. Such companies will however normally come within the definition of paragraph 7 because holding more than half of the shares with voting rights will be equivalent to controlling the composition of the Board.

62   Section 153 (1) of the 1963 Act states that a holding company's directors shall secure that, except where in their opinion there are good reasons against it, the financial year of each of its subsidiaries shall coincide with the company's own financial year. Paragraph 18 of the standard specifies the action to be taken in preparing consolidated accounts where accounting periods do not coincide.

63   Under Section 152 (2) of the 1963 Act there is no provision for the use of special accounts of subsidiaries in consolidated accounts and accordingly the financial statements for the latest financial year must be used.

64   In the case of Republic of Ireland registered companies the provisions of paragraph 32 of the standard relating to the effective date of acquisition should be interpreted in the light of Section 149 (5) of the 1963 Act.

Part 6 – Compliance with International Accounting Standard No. 3 'Consolidated financial statements'

65   Compliance with the requirements of Statement of Standard Accounting Practice No. 14 *Group Accounts* will automatically ensure compliance with International Accounting Standard No. 3 *Consolidated Financial Statements* excluding paragraphs 40 to 42 (which cover the basis of accounting for associated companies dealt with in SSAP1 *Accounting for the results of associated companies*).

15

Accounting for deferred taxation

Contents

Accounting for deferred taxation

(Issued October 1978)

The provisions of this statement of standard accounting practice should be read in conjunction with the Explanatory Foreword to accounting standards and need not be applied to immaterial items.

Part 1 – Explanatory note

Background

1   The amount of taxation payable on the profits of a particular period often bears little relationship to the amount of income and expenditure appearing in the profit and loss account. This results from the different basis on which profits are arrived at for the purpose of computing taxation as opposed to the basis on which profits are stated in financial statements.

2   This different basis of arriving at profits for taxation purposes derives from two main sources. Firstly, the fact that certain types of income may be tax-free or that certain expenditure is disallowable, giving rise to 'permanent differences' between taxable and accounting profits. Secondly, the existence of items which are included in the financial statements of a period different from that in which they are dealt with for taxation, giving rise to 'timing differences'; stock appreciation relief, to the extent to which it is subject to withdrawal, comes into this category.

3   The effect of timing differences on taxation liabilities in relation to reported profits would be of little significance if taxation was not regarded as relevant to the performance of the business for the period, and the only accepted indicator was the profit before taxation. The view is widely held, however, that the profit after taxation is an important indicator of performance being the fund of earnings which supports (or perhaps does not support) the distribution of profit by way of dividend.

4   So far as the balance sheet is concerned, the relationship between funds provided by shareholders and other sources of finance may be distorted if provision is made for deferred taxation which can be demonstrated with reasonable probability not to be needed.

Timing differences

5   There is wide agreement on the need to identify timing differences and to disclose in financial statements the amounts by which the taxation assessed on a company has been affected by those differences. Paragraph 7A Schedule 2 of the UK Companies Act 1967 and of the Companies (Northern Ireland) Order 1978 require disclosure of amounts set aside to prevent undue fluctuations in charges for taxation and Paragraph 14 (3A) Schedule 2 of the Act and of the Order require disclosure of special circumstances which affect liability in respect of taxation in the current or succeeding financial years. Although there is no similar legislation in the Republic of Ireland the need for information along these lines is generally recognised.

Timing differences arise under five main categories:

    (a) short-term timing differences from the use of the receipts and payments basis for taxation purposes and the accruals basis in financial statements: these differences normally reverse in the next accounting period;

    (b) availability of capital allowances in taxation computations which are in excess of the related depreciation charges in financial statements;

    (c) availability of stock appreciation relief in taxation computations for which there is no equivalent charge in financial statements;

    (d) revaluation surpluses on fixed assets for which a taxation charge does not arise until the gain is realised on disposal;

    (e) surpluses on disposals of fixed assets which are subject to rollover relief.

In determining whether a deferred taxation provision is required the elements which give rise to timing differences should be calculated separately, although any charge or credit would be based on the net position taking into account all differences.

Short term timing differences
It is generally accepted that deferred taxation should be fully provided for on short-term timing differences.

Accelerated capital allowances
In many businesses timing differences arising from accelerated capital allowances are of a recurring nature, and reversing differences are themselves offset, wholly or partially, or are exceeded, by new originating differences, thereby giving rise to continuing tax reductions or the indefinite postponement of any liability attributable to the tax benefits received. An example of a recurring timing difference is that arising when a company having a relatively stable or growing investment in depreciable assets takes tax relief year by year on capital expenditure of an amount which equals or exceeds the additional taxation which would otherwise have been payable in consequence of the reversal of the original timing difference. There may on the contrary be cases where timing differences are not recurring e.g., because of a spasmodic, declining or highly irregular pattern of capital expenditure, which may indicate that a liability in subsequent years should be provided for in full.

It is therefore appropriate that in the case of accelerated capital allowances, provision be made for deferred taxation except in so far as the tax benefit can be expected with reasonable probability to be retained in the future in consequence of recurring timing differences of the same type. The assessment of reasonable probability in these cases should be made in the light of the current intentions of the directors and of the company's expectations and plans for the future viewed in relation to the historical pattern of capital expenditure.

Stock appreciation relief
Stock appreciation relief arises from both volume and price increases in stocks and work in progress between two balance sheet dates. Full provision for deferred taxation should be made in respect of stock appreciation relief except to the extent that it can be

demonstrated with reasonable probability that stock values will not be reduced in the future by reason of lower volumes or prices or that the relief is unlikely to be reclaimed by the Government by reason of any time limits for recovery which may be introduced. The risk of a fall in stock values is of particular importance in the case of stocks which are seasonal in production or subject to sharp fluctuations in price.

Revaluations and disposals of fixed assets

12   A charge for taxation does not arise when a fixed asset is revalued. Normally a taxation charge only arises when an asset is disposed of at a price in excess of its original cost or tax written down value and no rollover or similar relief is available. Provision for taxation payable on the disposal of a fixed asset which has been revalued should be made out of the revaluation surplus as soon as a liability is foreseen based on the value at which the fixed asset is carried in the balance sheet. A liability would usually be foreseen (in the absence of rollover relief) at the time a company decides in principle to dispose of the asset.

Debit balances arising from timing differences

13   Debit balances on deferred taxation account arising from timing differences should be carried forward only if there is reasonable certainty of their recovery in future periods.

Trading losses

14   While trading losses give rise to timing differences, prudence dictates that they should not be recognised through the deferred taxation account, since there can be no certainty that future profits will be earned of sufficient amount to absorb them.

15   Credit for the tax effects of a trading loss should only be taken when the loss is utilised for tax purposes, unless there is a credit balance on deferred taxation account at the time when the loss carry-forward arises.

16   In such circumstances credit balances on deferred taxation account should be released to profit and loss account to the extent of the notional tax relief attributable to the loss, but not exceeding that part of the deferred taxation account which represents tax on income which can properly be offset against the loss for tax purposes. When trading profits are subsequently earned a deferred taxation account balance may require to be reinstated to the extent of the tax relief resulting from the loss, but not exceeding tax on the equivalent amount of timing differences previously released when the losses were carried forward.

Advance corporation tax (ACT)

17   The minimum tax charge in the profit and loss account in any accounting period should normally be the amount payable as ACT (net of any recovery) plus any amounts charged in respect of overseas taxation. As noted in paragraph 7 of Statement of Standard Accounting Practice No. 8 *The treatment of taxation under the imputation system in the accounts of companies*, ACT which cannot be recovered out of the corporation tax liability on the income of the year but which is carried forward to be recovered out of the corporation tax liability on the income of future periods, may be deducted from the balance on the deferred taxation account subject to certain limitations set out in SSAP8. Where in an accounting period ACT is payable in respect of a

dividend, but there is no mainstream corporation tax payable, the ACT if deemed irrecoverable is required by SSAP8 to be included in the tax charge for the year.

Transitional arrangements

Companies which have heretofore taken account of timing differences in a deferred   18
taxation account should, at the time when they change over to this standard, release to
reserve any part of the deferred tax balance which is not required. Such changes would
be dealt with as a prior year adjustment (change of accounting policy) under Statement
of Standard Accounting Practice No. 6 *Extraordinary items and prior year
adjustments*. Thereafter, any transfers to or from the deferred taxation account, other
than those relating to revaluation surpluses, should be passed through the profit and
loss account as part of the tax charge for the year or, to the extent that they relate to
extraordinary items, as part of the extraordinary items.

Part 2 – Definition of terms

Timing differences are differences between profits as computed for taxation purposes   19
and profits as stated in financial statements which result from the inclusion of items of
income and expenditure in taxation computations in periods different from those in
which they are included in financial statements. Timing differences originate in one
period and are capable of reversal in one or more subsequent periods. Stock appreciation relief, to the extent to which it is subject to withdrawal, comes into this category.
The revaluation of an asset is regarded as creating a timing difference when it is
incorporated in financial statements.

Originating timing differences are timing differences which arise in an accounting   20
period when a transaction or event is treated differently in financial statements from the
treatment accorded to the same transaction or event for taxation purposes.

Short term timing differences are originating timing differences which arise from the   21
use of the receipts and payments basis for tax purposes and the accruals basis in
financial statements. They can be identified with specific transactions and normally
reverse in the next accounting period.

Deferred taxation is the taxation attributable to timing differences.   22

Financial statements are balance sheets, profit and loss accounts, statements of source   23
and application of funds, notes and other statements, which collectively are intended to
give a true and fair view of financial position and profit or loss.

Company includes any enterprise which comes within the scope of statements of   24
standard accounting practice.

Directors include the corresponding officers of organisations which do not have   25
directors.

Part 3 – Standard accounting practice

26   Deferred taxation should be accounted for on all short-term timing differences.

27   Deferred taxation should be accounted for in respect of the tax effects arising from all other originating timing differences of material amount other than any tax effects which, based on the criteria set out in paragraphs 28 to 30, can be demonstrated with reasonable probability to continue in the future. This may be by reason of recurring or continuing timing differences or, in the case of revalued assets, by the continuing use of the assets or the postponement of liability on their sale.

28   It will be reasonable to assume that timing differences will not reverse and tax liabilities will therefore not crystallise if, but only if, the company is a going concern and:

(a) the directors are able to foresee on reasonable evidence that no liability is likely to arise as a result of reversal of timing differences for some considerable period (at least three years) ahead; and

(b) there is no indication that after this period the situation is likely to change so as to crystallise the liabilities.

29   Where the criteria in paragraph 28 are satisfied it will be reasonable to assume that the period which can be foreseen sets the pattern for the indefinite future, and accordingly the deferred tax provision relating to such timing differences can be eliminated. The position should be reviewed each year and regard should be had to the past pattern of capital expenditure and stock levels and whether forecasts made in the past have proved to be reliable.

30   Where the criteria in paragraph 28 are not fully satisfied it may be appropriate to provide only part of the full potential deferred taxation. The partial amount not provided should be based on substantiated calculations and assumptions which are explained in the financial statements.

31   Where the criteria in paragraph 28 are not satisfied the directors will have no basis for assuming that timing differences will not reverse and accordingly deferred taxation should be provided.

32   Notwithstanding the provisions of paragraphs 26 and 27 debit balances on deferred taxation account arising from either timing differences or the payment of ACT should be carried forward only if there is reasonable certainty of their recovery in future periods.

33   The potential amount of deferred tax for all timing differences should be disclosed by way of note, distinguishing between the various principal categories of deferred tax and showing for each category the amount that has been provided within the accounts.

Profit and loss account

34   Deferred taxation dealt with in the profit and loss account should be shown separately as a component of the total tax charge or credit in the profit and loss account or by way of note to the financial statements.

The profit and loss account or a note to the financial statements should indicate the 35 extent to which the taxation charge for the period has been reduced by accelerated capital allowances, stock appreciation relief and other timing differences.

Adjustments to the deferred taxation account resulting from a change in the rate of 36 taxation should be separately disclosed as part of the taxation charge for the period, unless the change in rate is associated with a fundamental change in the basis of taxation, in which case the adjustment should be treated as an extraordinary item. Deferred taxation charges or credits which relate to extraordinary items should themselves be shown separately as part of such items.

Balance sheet
Deferred taxation account balances should be shown separately in the balance sheet 37 and described as 'deferred taxation'. They should not be shown as part of shareholders' funds. A note in the financial statements should indicate the nature and amount of the major elements of which the net balance is composed and a description of the method of calculation adopted.

Where amounts of deferred taxation arise which relate to movements on reserves (e.g., 38 resulting from a revaluation of assets) the amounts transferred to or from deferred taxation account should be shown separately as part of such movements.

Where the value of an asset is shown by way of note on the face of or annexed to the 39 financial statements and that the value differs from the book value of the asset, the note should also show, if material, the tax implications which would result from the realisation of the asset at the balance sheet date at the stated value.

Transitional arrangements
On the introduction of this standard the opening balance on deferred taxation account 40 should be calculated or recalculated on the basis set out in this standard and the necessary provision set up or the existing provision adjusted accordingly, as a prior year adjustment.

Date from which effective
The accounting practices set out in this statement should be adopted as soon as 41 possible and regarded as standard in respect of financial statements relating to accounting periods beginning on or after 1st January 1979.

Part 4 – Special considerations in applying
the standard to companies subject to taxation
in the Republic of Ireland

42   The general provisions of the standard will be applicable to companies in the Republic of Ireland with the exception of the requirements relating to advance corporation tax which may be ignored.

43   As regards stock appreciation relief the provisions of the standard should be applied having regard to the specified legislation under which relief is claimed.

44   Certain Irish companies and branches of foreign companies are totally relieved from corporation tax (or in some cases subject to tax at reduced rates) on profits arising from the export of manufactured goods and services (export sales relief and 'Shannon' relief). The effective rate of tax can vary as a result of the pattern of trading which gives rise to the relief. Where such companies have timing differences originating during the period of total relief or of reduced rates and it can be seen with reasonable probability that these differences will reverse after expiry of the relief period (or when the reduced rates no longer apply) then provision should be made for the taxation deferred. The amount of tax to be deferred in respect of such timing differences should be calculated by reference to the effective rate estimated to be applicable in the years of reversal or, where it is impractical to make such estimates because of the pattern of trading, by reference to the standard rate of corporation tax applicable when the provision is made.

45   With effect from 1st January 1977 a reduced rate of corporation tax may apply to the profits of a company carrying on a trade which consists wholly or almost wholly of the manufacture of goods provided that the company achieves certain specified increases of sales and employment. Reference should be made to the specific legislation under which relief is claimed. The relief is, under present legislation, for a limited period of three financial years from 1st January 1977. In calculating deferred taxation provisions where a reduction rate applies, similar considerations to those given in paragraph 44 should be taken into account.

16

Current cost accounting

Contents

Current cost accounting
(Issued March 1980)

The provisions of this Statement of Standard Accounting Practice should be read in conjunction with the Explanatory Foreword to Accounting Standards *and need not be applied to immaterial items.*

In particular, the following extract from the Explanatory Foreword is emphasised to assist those who prepare or use current cost accounts prepared in conformity with this standard:

Accounting standards are not intended to be a comprehensive code of rigid rules. It would be impracticable to establish a code sufficiently elaborate to cater for all business situations and circumstances and every exceptional or marginal case. Nor could any code of rules provide in advance for innovations in business and financial practice.

Moreover it must be recognised that there may be situations in which for justifiable reasons accounting standards are not strictly applicable because they are impracticable or, exceptionally, having regard to the circumstances, would be inappropriate or give a misleading view.

In such cases modified or alternative treatments must be adopted and, as noted, departure from standard disclosed and explained. In judging exceptional or borderline cases it will be important to have regard to the spirit of accounting standards as well as to their precise terms, and to bear in mind the overriding requirement to give a true and fair view.

Where accounting standards prescribe specific information to be contained in accounts, such disclosure requirements do not override exemptions from disclosure requirements given to and utilised by special classes of companies under Statute.

Part 1 – Explanatory note

Scope

1   This statement applies to most listed companies and other large entities* whose annual financial statements are intended to give a true and fair view of the financial position and profit or loss. It does not apply to:

   (a) unlisted entities unless they would be classified as large companies in the prospective UK/Irish legislation based on the EEC Fourth Directive on Company Law. (It is intended to adopt the precise definition of large companies used in the legislation when this is enacted and operative in the UK and the Republic of Ireland.);

   (b) most wholly owned subsidiaries; and

---

*In this standard the term 'entities' includes those companies and other enterprises which normally come within the scope of Statements of Standard Accounting Practice.

(c) a number of specific types of entity, on the grounds that the current cost accounting (CCA) system in this standard may not be wholly appropriate to them. Such entities are encouraged to implement any parts of the standard that are appropriate to their businesses, and generally to consider how the impact of price changes can best be reflected in their financial statements.

Introduction

In most systems of accounting, profit is determined after making charges against revenue to provide for the maintenance of capital. Since the definition of capital varies according to the accounting concept adopted, the method of determining profit also varies.

This standard provides for current cost information to be included in annual financial statements in addition to historical cost information. The CCA system is based upon a concept of capital which is represented by the net operating assets of a business. These net operating assets (fixed assets, stock and monetary working capital) are the same as those included in historical cost accounts, but in the current cost accounts the fixed assets and stock are normally expressed at current cost. The net operating assets can be said to represent, in accounting terms, the operating capability of the business and usually will have been financed both by shareholders' capital and borrowings.

A change in the input prices of goods and services used and financed by the business will affect the amount of funds required to maintain the operating capability of the net operating assets. In contrast to historical cost accounts, current cost accounts are designed to reflect this in the determination of profit and in the balance sheet.

The objective of CCA

The basic objective of current cost accounts is to provide more useful information than that available from historical cost accounts alone for the guidance of the management of the business, the shareholders and others on such matters as:

(a) the financial viability of the business;

(b) return on investment;

(c) pricing policy, cost control and distribution decisions; and

(d) gearing.

In determining current cost profits for an accounting period, the objective is achieved in two stages:

In the first stage, *the current cost operating profit* is determined. This is the surplus arising from the ordinary activities of the business in the period after allowing for the impact of price changes on the funds needed to continue the existing business and maintain its operating capability but without taking into account the way in which it is financed. It is calculated before interest on net borrowing and taxation.

In the second stage the *current cost profit attributable to shareholders* is determined. In arriving at this profit, account is taken of the way in which the business is financed. To the extent that the net operating assets of the business are financed by borrowing, the full allowance for the impact of price changes on operating

2

3

4

5

6

capability made in arriving at operating profit may not be required, because the repayment rights of lenders are fixed in monetary amount.

Current cost profit attributable to shareholders therefore reflects the surplus for the period after allowing for the impact of price changes on the funds needed to maintain the shareholders' proportion of the operating capability. It is shown after interest, taxation, the gearing adjustment and extraordinary items.

7   In the balance sheet the objective is met by including, where practicable, the assets at their value to the business* based on current price levels. This provides a realistic statement of the assets employed in the business and enables a relationship to be established between the current cost profit and the net assets employed.

Current cost operating profit

8   Three main adjustments to trading profit, calculated on the historical cost basis before interest, are required to arrive at current cost operating profit. These are called the depreciation, cost of sales and monetary working capital adjustments.

Depreciation adjustment

9   The depreciation adjustment allows for the impact of price changes when determining the charge against revenue for the part of fixed assets consumed in the period. It is the difference between the value to the business of the part of fixed assets consumed during the accounting period and the amount of depreciation charged on an historical cost basis. The resulting total depreciation charge thus represents the value to the business of the part of fixed assets consumed in earning the revenue of the period.

Cost of sales adjustment

10   The cost of sales adjustment (COSA) allows for the impact of price changes when determining the charge against revenue for stock consumed in the period. It is the difference between the value to the business of stock consumed and the cost of stock charged on an historical cost basis. The resulting total charge thus represents the value to the business of stock consumed in earning the revenue of the period.

Monetary working capital adjustment

11   Most businesses have other working capital besides stock involved in their day-to-day operating activities. For example, when sales are made on credit the business has funds tied up in debtors. Conversely, if the suppliers of goods and services allow a period of credit, the amount of funds needed to support working capital is reduced. This monetary working capital is an integral part of the net operating assets of the business. Thus, the standard provides for an adjustment in respect of monetary working capital* when determining current cost operating profit. This adjustment should represent the amount of additional (or reduced) finance needed for monetary working capital as a result of changes in the input prices of goods and services used and financed by the business.

12   In a business which holds stocks, the monetary working capital adjustment (MWCA) complements the COSA and together they allow for the impact of price changes on the total amount of working capital used by the business in its day-to-day operations. For

---

*As defined in the definitions section of the standard.

example, the relationship between the MWCA made in respect of trade debtors and trade creditors and the COSA is as follows:

(a) when sales are made on credit the business has to finance the changes in its input prices until the sales result in a receipt of cash. The part of the MWCA related to trade debtors, in effect, extends the COSA to allow for this: and

(b) conversely, when materials and services are purchased from suppliers who offer trade credit, price changes are financed by the supplier during the credit period. To this extent extra funds do not have to be found by the business and this reduces the need for a COSA and in some cases for a MWCA on debtors. The part of the MWCA related to trade creditors reflects this reduction.

A MWCA is equally necessary in a business which does not hold stocks.

There can be difficulties in practice in identifying, on an objective basis, those monetary assets and liabilities which are part of the net operating assets of the business. Nevertheless, a practical way of doing this has to be accepted if the operating profit is to be identified. Reasonable accuracy and objectivity may usually be achieved by including only trade debtors and trade creditors within monetary working capital, with an extension in the case of financial institutions. However, fluctuations in the volume of stock, debtors and creditors may lead to contrary fluctuations in cash or overdraft. It is necessary to include this element of cash or overdraft within monetary working capital if to do so has a material effect on current cost operating profit. Monetary working capital may also include cash floats required to support the business operations. The treatment adopted should be applied consistently. **13**

The standard allows for the COSA and MWCA to be combined in the current cost profit and loss account. **14**

Purchasing skills
The benefits of good buying (and the costs of errors) should be, as with the historical cost system, included in the operating profit at the time the asset is used or sold. As discussed in the Guidance Notes, this normally happens through the inter-relationship of the MWCA with the other adjustments. **15**

The current cost profit attributable to shareholders and the gearing adjustment
The net operating assets shown in the balance sheet have usually been financed partly by borrowing and the effect of this is reflected, by means of a gearing adjustment, in arriving at current cost profit attributable to shareholders. No gearing adjustment arises where a company is wholly financed by shareholders' capital. While repayment rights on borrowing are normally fixed in monetary amount, the proportion of net operating assets so financed increases or decreases in value to the business. Thus, when these assets have been realised, either by sale or use in the business, repayment of borrowing could be made so long as the proceeds are not less than the historical cost of those assets. **16**

No account has been taken of the existence of borrowing in arriving at current cost operating profit, in that the operating adjustments (referred to in paragraph 8) make provision for the impact of price changes on all the net operating assets, however **17** financed. The gearing adjustment therefore abates the operating adjustments in the gearing proportion in deriving the current cost profit attributable to shareholders.

18   The gearing adjustment, subject to interest on borrowing, indicates the benefit or cost to shareholders which is realised in the period, measured by the extent to which a proportion of the net operating assets are financed by borrowing. The current cost profit attributable to shareholders is the surplus after making allowance for the impact of price changes on the shareholders' interest in the net operating assets, having provided for the maintenance of lenders' capital in accordance with their repayment rights.

19   The gearing adjustment included in this standard is necessary to determine the profit defined in paragraph 41. The adjustment is retrospective in that it arises wholly because of the manner in which net operating assets are financed in the period and is not dependent on the ability of the company to refinance any part before it is included in profit. The adjustment is generally practicable and objective and since any credit in the profit and loss account only abates adjustments made when assets are consumed or sold, it conforms with the fundamental accounting concepts set out in SSAP 2 *Disclosure of accounting policies*.

20   It is recognised that there are a number of possible methods for calculating a gearing adjustment. For the reasons set out it is believed that the method defined in the standard is the most appropriate and, on the grounds of the need for comparability between company accounts, it has been made definitive. This does not prevent those who wish to show in addition the effect of a different method of calculating a gearing adjustment from doing so by way of a note to the accounts. It would help users if those adopting this course explained their reasons for so doing.

21   There are some types of financing structure, such as those which may be found in certain public bodies, co-operatives and wholly owned subsidiaries, where a gearing adjustment strictly in accordance with the normal formula in this standard may be inappropriate or give a misleading view of attributable profit. In such cases if an alternative adjustment is considered appropriate to the circumstances it should be made in the profit and loss account and the treatment adopted described in a note. In the interests of achieving consistency in the accounts of nationalised industries these bodies are dealt with specifically in the standard. The adjustment based on the formula in the standard should also be disclosed in the note unless this would not be practicable.

Assets surplus to operating requirements and in excess of borrowing

22   Where an entity owns monetary current assets in excess of those needed for working capital such assets are not part of the net operating assets for the purposes of this standard and any income from them should be dealt with below current cost operating profit. These assets should firstly be set against borrowing when calculating the gearing adjustment. Any excess of these assets over the borrowing is not covered by the current cost framework, being more in the nature of assets held for investment of the kind held by entities excluded from the standard under paragraph 46 (c). This situation raises complex issues which have not yet been subject to adequate public debate and no adjustment is therefore required in the standard. Entities are encouraged to include information on any changes in the value to the business of such excess assets and in

their effective purchasing power. This should be given and described in a note to the accounts.

Distributable profit

The amounts that can prudently be distributed depend not only on profitability, but also on the availability of funds. This is so with all systems of accounting. When determining distribution policy, consideration must be given to factors not reflected in profit, such as capital expenditure plans, changes in the volume of working capital, the effect on funding requirements of changes in production methods and efficiency, liquidity, and new financing arrangements. The current cost profit attributable to shareholders should not be assumed to measure the amount that can prudently be distributed. Although the impact of price changes on the shareholders' interest in the net operating assets has been allowed for, the other factors still need to be considered. Even if the effect of such factors is neutral, a full distribution of the current cost profit attributable to shareholders may make it necessary to arrange additional finance (equal to the gearing adjustment) to avoid an erosion of the operating capability of the business. However, an increase in the value to the business of the assets may provide increased cover for such financing.

23

The current cost reserve

The current cost balance sheet includes a reserve in addition to those included in historical cost accounts. The additional reserve may be referred to as the current cost reserve. The total reserves will include, where appropriate:

24

(a) unrealised revaluation surpluses on fixed assets, stock and investments; and

(b) realised amounts equal to the cumulative net total of the current cost adjustments, that is:

   (i) the depreciation adjustment (and any adjustments on the disposal of fixed assets);

   (ii) the two working capital adjustments; and

   (iii) the gearing adjustment.

Changes in the rates used to translate the assets and liabilities of subsidiaries whose accounts are denominated in foreign currencies lead to translation differences arising on consolidation. In most circumstances these differences are, in effect, price changes which do not affect the operating capability of the group and in these cases they are not included in current cost profits but are directly reflected in reserves.

25

Interpretation of the amounts on current cost reserve can be complex for they depend not only on the impact of price changes on the net operating assets, but also on the first period for which current cost accounts conforming with this standard are published, the policies adopted in preparing historical cost accounts and other factors. Accordingly, the only specific disclosure requirement is to show movements on the current cost reserve during the period, and these may be combined with equivalent movements on historical cost reserves. However, entities are encouraged to disclose the information set out in the Appendix subject to any modifications they regard as relevant and useful in their circumstances.

26

Annual financial statements and accounting policies

27   The standard sets out the current cost information which should be disclosed to provide the user with a clear view of the results for the period and the financial state of the business at the balance sheet date. This consists of a current cost profit and loss account and a current cost balance sheet together with appropriate notes. It is expected that once entities have published their first current cost accounts they will also, where appropriate, disclose current cost information in interim accounts, preliminary statements, prospectuses and other financial statements.

28   The standard requires entities to publish current cost accounts in addition to historical cost accounts or historical cost information. This enables entities to publish both current cost and full historical cost accounts, and to decide in such circumstances which accounts are to be the main accounts. If they decide that the historical cost accounts are the main accounts (and the great majority of companies will probably so decide), the current cost accounts required by this standard will be of a supplementary nature. Some entities may, however, wish to publish current cost accounts as their main or only accounts*, in which case it will be necessary to supplement them with full historical cost accounts or adequate historical cost information. The historical cost disclosure requirements will be clarified when the EEC Fourth Directive is enacted in UK/Irish law. Meanwhile, an entity preparing current cost accounts as its only accounts should provide at least sufficient information to enable the user to ascertain the profit of the period under existing historical cost conventions.

29   Since the CCA system set out in the standard is an adaptation of the historical cost system, the accounting policies adopted will be generally the same for both. In particular, the current cost accounts encompass only those assets which are dealt with in historical cost accounts.

30   Statements of Standard Accounting Practice issued for use with historical cost accounts also apply to current cost accounts except where a conflict exists due to the conceptual difference between the systems. In particular, the fundamental accounting concepts set out in SSAP2 apply, i.e. the 'going concern', 'accruals', 'consistency' and 'prudence' concepts. The 'going concern' concept is particularly appropriate to CCA which relates operating profit to the maintenance of operating capability. The information on accounting policies should cover the current cost accounts. SSAP10 requires that the annual financial statements should include a statement of source and application of funds. Such a statement should be compatible with the main accounts although entities may present an additional statement compatible with the current cost accounts even if these are not presented as the main accounts. Two examples are given in the Guidance Notes.

---

*In the Green Paper *Company Accounting and Disclosure* (Sept 1979 Cmnd 7654) the Department of Trade indicate that 'individual companies at present have discretion to adopt full Current Cost Accounts in their main accounts, not merely in additional statements'. Those companies wishing to do so should consider the legal implications, for example, in relation to contractual obligations. In the year of any changeover, an adequate link with comparative figures should be given.

Methods appropriate to the preparation of current cost accounts

The standard sets out the basic principles. At this stage the ASC does not believe that it 31
would be right to be prescriptive about the methods which should be adopted when preparing current cost accounts. Guidance Notes have been published which the ASC
hopes will be helpful, since they offer practical solutions to some common situations.
However, they do not form part of the Standard and accordingly are not mandatory.

Interpretation, uses and limitations

Current cost accounts allow for the impact of specific price changes on the net operat- 32
ing assets, and thus the operating capability, of the business. The same tools of analysis
as those applied to historical cost accounts are generally appropriate. The ratios
derived from current cost accounts for such items as gearing, asset cover, dividend
cover and return on capital employed will often differ substantially from those revealed
in historical cost accounts but should be more realistic indicators when assessing an
entity or making comparisons between entities.

As with historical cost accounting, CCA is not a substitute for forecasting when such 33
matters as a change in the size or nature of the business are under consideration. It
assists cash flow forecasts, but does not replace them. It does not measure the effect of
changes in the general value of money or translate the figures into currency of
purchasing power at a specific date. Because of this it is not a system of accounting
for general inflation. Further, it does not show changes in the value of the business as a
whole or the market value of the equity.

Additional voluntary disclosures

It may assist users, particularly initially, if current cost accounts are accompanied by 34
explanations of the operating and attributable profit and assets employed. These
explanations could be based on the definitions included in the standard.

Those who wish to give additional information reflecting a gearing adjustment on a 35
basis different from that provided for in the standard should do so by way of a note
(paragraph 20).

The standard does not deal with the maintenance of financial capital in general 36
purchasing power terms. It is recognised that some users may be interested in a statement of the change in the shareholders' equity interest after allowing for the change
in the general purchasing power of money. A statement may therefore be given to
reflect this, on the lines illustrated in the Guidance Notes. This statement may be
particularly helpful in situations where there are excess monetary assets (see paragraph
22) or where part of the group has activities exempt under paragraph 46 (c).

As with accounts prepared on the historical cost basis, the CCA figures for profit and 37
capital employed in different years are not comparable unless they are adjusted to a
common price basis. It is the intention of the ASC to develop an exposure draft as soon
as possible indicating how such adjustments should be made, both to comparative
figures and 5/10 year statements. Meanwhile, entities are encouraged to give, as
additional information, comparative figures adjusted to a common price basis with
the period's results and also adjust any 5/10 year statements similarly.

Part 2 – Definition of terms

38   *Net operating assets* comprise the fixed assets (including trade investments), stock and monetary working capital* dealt with in an historical cost balance sheet.

39   *The operating capability* of the business is the amount of goods and services which the business is able to supply with its existing resources in the relevant period. These resources are represented in accounting terms by the net operating assets* at current cost.

40   *Current cost operating profit* is the surplus arising from the ordinary activities of the business in the period after allowing for the impact of price changes on the funds needed to continue the existing business and maintain its operating capability*, whether financed by share capital or borrowing. It is calculated before interest on net borrowing* and taxation.

41   *Current cost profit attributable to shareholders* is the surplus for the period after allowing for the impact of price changes on the funds needed to maintain their proportion of the operating capability. It is calculated after interest, taxation and extraordinary items.

42   *Value to the business* is:

     (a) net current replacement cost;

       or, if a permanent diminution to below net current replacement cost has been recognised,

     (b) recoverable amount*.

43   *Recoverable amount* is the greater of the net realisable value of an asset and, where applicable, the amount recoverable from its further use.

44   *Monetary working capital* is the aggregate of:

     (a) trade debtors, prepayments and trade bills receivable, plus

     (b) stocks not subject to a cost of sales adjustment, less

     (c) trade creditors, accruals and trade bills payable,

in so far as they arise from the day-to-day operating activities of the business as distinct from transactions of a capital nature.

Bank balances or overdrafts may fluctuate with the volume of stock or the items in (a), (b) and (c) above. That part of bank balances or overdrafts arising from such fluctuations should be included in monetary working capital, together with any cash floats required to support day-to-day operations of the business, if to do so has a material effect on the current cost operating profit.

*As defined.

In the case of banks and other financial businesses this definition is extended to cover other assets and other liabilities in so far as they also arise from the day-to-day operating activities of the business as distinct from transactions of a capital nature.

Net borrowing is the excess of: 45

(a) the aggregate of all liabilities and provisions fixed in monetary terms (including convertible debentures and deferred tax but excluding proposed dividends) other than those included within monetary working capital and other than those which are, in substance, equity capital

over

(b) the aggregate of all current assets other than those subject to a cost of sales adjustment and those included within monetary working capital.

Part 3 – Standard accounting practice

Scope

This standard applies to all annual financial statements intended to give a true and fair view of the financial position and profit or loss other than those of entities falling within the categories listed below: 46

(a) entities which do not have any class of share or loan capital listed on The Stock Exchange and satisfy at least two of the following three criteria:

  (i) they have a turnover of less than £5,000,000 per annum;

  (ii) their balance sheet total* at the commencement of the relevant accounting period is less than £2,500,000 as shown in the historical cost accounts; and

  (iii) the average number of their employees in the United Kingdom (UK entities) or in the Republic of Ireland (Republic of Ireland entities) is less than 250;

(b) wholly owned subsidiaries of companies or other entities where the parent is registered in the UK or the Republic of Ireland. This exemption does not apply where the parent is exempted under (c) or (d) below;

(c) (i) authorised insurers;

  (ii) property investment and dealing entities, with the exception of such entities as hold the properties of another entity within the group to which this Standard does apply; and

---

*For the purposes of this paragraph, the balance sheet total is defined as the total of the following assets:

Fixed assets (net book value) other than investments
Investments
Current assets including prepayments and accrued income (before deduction of current liabilities).

(iii) investment trust companies, unit trusts and other similar long-term investment entities; and

(d) entities whose long-term primary financial objective is other than to achieve an operating profit (before interest on borrowing); such entities may include charities, building societies, friendly societies, trade unions and pension funds.

Where an entity exempted under (c) or (d) above has subsidiaries which are not themselves exempted under these sections and which collectively exceed the limit in (a) above, the group accounts should include consolidated current cost information in respect of such subsidiaries.

47   Annual financial statements of entities coming within the scope of the standard should include, in addition to historical cost accounts or historical cost information, current cost accounts prepared in accordance with this standard. The current cost accounts should contain a profit and loss account and balance sheet, together with explanatory notes, disclosing the information set out in paragraphs 55–59.

48   This requirement to include current cost accounts in addition to historical cost accounts or historical cost information can be complied with by:

(a) presenting historical cost accounts as the main accounts with supplementary current cost accounts which are prominently displayed; or

(b) presenting current cost accounts as the main accounts with supplementary historical cost accounts; or

(c) presenting current cost accounts as the only accounts accompanied by adequate historical cost information. The historical cost disclosure requirements will be clarified when the EEC Fourth Directive is enacted in UK/Irish law. Meanwhile, an entity preparing current cost accounts as its only accounts should provide at least sufficient information to enable the user to ascertain the historical cost profit of the period under existing conventions.

The current cost profit and loss account

49   The current cost operating profit* is derived by making the following main adjustments to the historical cost trading profit (before interest on net borrowing*) to allow for the impact of price changes on the funds needed to maintain the net operating assets*:

(a) in relation to fixed assets, a depreciation adjustment being the difference between the proportion of their value to the business* consumed in the period and the depreciation calculated on the historical cost basis;

(b) in relation to working capital:

(i) a cost of sales adjustment being the difference between the value to the business and the historical cost of stock consumed in the period; and

(ii) an adjustment based on monetary working capital*.

---

*As defined in the definitions section of the standard.

Where a proportion of the net operating assets is financed by net borrowing, a gearing 50
adjustment is required in arriving at the current cost profit attributable to the
shareholders*. This should be calculated by:

(a) expressing net borrowing as a proportion of the net operating assets using
average figures for the year from the current cost balance sheets; and

(b) multiplying the total of the charges or credits made to allow for the impact of the
price changes on the net operating assets of the business by the proportion determined at (a).

This adjustment, normally a credit, could be a debit if prices fall.

No gearing adjustment should be made in the profit and loss accounts of Nationalised 51
Industries in view of the special nature of their capital structure. Accordingly, in such
cases interest on their net borrowing should be shown after taxation and extraordinary
items.

The treatment within the current cost profit and loss account of gains and losses on 52
asset disposals, extraordinary and exceptional items, prior year items, income from
associates, group consolidation adjustments, minority interests and the translation of
foreign currencies should, where practicable, be consistent with the definitions of profit
set out in this standard. Where this is impracticable the treatment adopted should be
disclosed in a note to the current cost accounts.

The current cost balance sheet
Assets and liabilities should be included in the balance sheet, as far as practicable, on 53
the following bases:

(a) *Land and buildings, plant and machinery and stocks subject to a cost of sales
adjustment* – at their value to the business.

(b) *Investments in associated companies* – either at the applicable proportion of the
associated companies' net assets stated under this standard or, where such information is not readily available, at directors' best estimate thereof. Allowance for
premium or discount on acquisition should be made as stated under (e) below.

(c) *Other investments (excluding those treated as current assets)* – at directors'
valuation. Where the investment is listed and the directors' valuation is materially
different from mid-market value, the basis of valuation and the reasons for the
difference should be stated.

(d) *Intangible assets (excluding goodwill)* – at the best estimate of their value to the
business.

(e) *Goodwill (premium or discount) arising on consolidation* – on the basis set out in
SSAP14. Where goodwill is carried at an amount established before the introduction of SSAP14 it should be reduced to the extent that it represents revaluation
surpluses relating to assets held at the date of the acquisition.

*As defined in the definitions section of the standard.

(f) *Current assets, other than those subject to a cost of sales adjustment* – on the historical cost basis.

(g) *All liabilities* – on the historical cost basis.

54   Reserves in the current cost balance sheet should include revaluation surpluses or deficits and adjustments made to allow for the impact of price changes in arriving at current cost profit attributable to shareholders. Amounts to reduce assets from net current replacement cost to recoverable amount* should be charged to the profit and loss account.

Contents of accounts

Profit and loss account

55   The current cost profit and loss account should show (not necessarily in this order):

(a) the current cost operating profit or loss;

(b) interest/income relating to the net borrowing on which the gearing adjustment has been based;

(c) the gearing adjustment;

(d) taxation;

(e) extraordinary items; and

(f) current cost profit or loss (after tax) attributable to shareholders.

56   A reconciliation should be provided between the current cost operating profit and the profit or loss before charging interest and taxation calculated on the historical cost basis giving the respective amounts of the following:

(a) depreciation adjustment;

(b) cost of sales adjustment;

(c) monetary working capital adjustment and, where appropriate, interest relating to monetary working capital; and

(d) other material adjustments made to profits calculated on the historical cost basis when determining current cost operating profit.

The adjustments for cost of sales and monetary working capital may be combined.

Balance sheet

57   The current cost balance sheet (which may be in summarised form when a full historical cost balance sheet is disclosed) should show the assets and liabilities of the entity on the bases required by this standard. Notes to the balance sheet should disclose the totals of net operating assets and net borrowing and their main elements. The balance sheet should be supported by summaries of the fixed asset accounts and the movements on reserves.

---

*As defined in the definitions section of the standard.

Notes to the accounts
The notes attached to the current cost accounts should describe the bases and methods 58
adopted in preparing the accounts particularly in relation to:

(a) the value to the business of fixed assets and the depreciation thereon;

(b) the value to the business of stock and work in progress and the cost of sales adjustment;

(c) the monetary working capital adjustment;

(d) the gearing adjustment;

(e) the basis of translating foreign currencies and dealing with translation differences arising;

(f) other material adjustments to the historical cost information; and

(g) the corresponding amounts.

Earnings per share
Listed companies should show the current cost earnings per share based on the current 59
cost profit attributable to equity shareholders before extraordinary items.

Group accounts
A company which is the parent company of a group and which is required to produce 60
current cost group accounts should produce such group accounts in accordance with
the principles set out in this standard. It need not however produce current cost
accounts for itself as a single company where historical cost accounts are the main
accounts.

Corresponding amounts
In all accounts prepared in accordance with this standard corresponding amounts for 61
the preceding periods should be stated. However unless current cost accounts are the
main accounts corresponding amounts need only be included for the first period for
which current cost accounts are prepared if they are readily available.

Relationship with other standards
Existing standards issued for use with historical cost accounts apply to current cost 62
accounts except where a conflict exists caused by the conceptual difference between the
systems. The four fundamental accounting concepts in SSAP 2 should be observed and
information on accounting policies should be given. The source and application of
funds statement required by SSAP 10 should be compatible with the main accounts.

Date from which effective
The accounting practices set out in this standard should be adopted as soon as 63
possible. They should be regarded as standard for annual financial statements relating
to accounting periods starting on or after 1st January 1980.

Appendix

This Appendix does not form part of the Statement of Standard Accounting Practice. The methods of presentation used are illustrative of the accounts of a manufacturing company. They are in no way prescriptive and other methods of presentation may equally comply with the standard. The example assumes that historical cost accounts are published as the statutory accounts.

EXAMPLE OF PRESENTATION OF CURRENT COST ACCOUNTS

Y Limited and Subsidiaries

**Group current cost profit and loss account
for the year ended 31st December 1980**

1979 £000		1980 £000
18,000	Turnover	20,000
	Profit before interest and taxation on the historical	
2,420	cost basis	2,900
1,320	Less: Current cost operating adjustments (note 2) . .	1,510
1,100	*Current cost operating profit*	1,390
(170)	Gearing adjustment . . . . (166)	
180	Interest payable less receivable 200	
10		34
1,090	Current cost profit before taxation	1,356
610	Taxation	730
480	*Current cost profit attributable to shareholders* . .	626
400	Dividends	430
80	Retained current cost profit of the year	196
16.0p	Current cost earnings per share	20.9p
5.2%	Operating profit return on the average of the net operating assets	6.0%

£000	**Statement of retained profits/reserves**	£000
80	Retained current cost profit of the year	196
1,850	Movements on current cost reserve (Note 4) . . .	2,054
NIL	Movements on other reserves	NIL
1,930		2,250
14,150	Retained profits/reserves at the beginning of the year	16,080
16,080	Retained profits/reserves at the end of the year . .	18,330

Where applicable, minority interests and extraordinary items should be presented in a manner consistent with the historical cost accounts.

EXAMPLE OF ALTERNATIVE PRESENTATION OF
CURRENT COST PROFIT AND LOSS ACCOUNT

Y Limited and Subsidiaries

**Group current cost profit and loss account
for the year ended 31st December 1980**

1979 £000		1980 £000
18,000	Turnover	20,000
2,420	Profit before interest and taxation on the historical cost basis	2,900
1,320	Less: Current cost operating adjustments (Note 2)	1,510
1,100	*Current cost operating profit*	1,390
180	Interest payable less receivable	200
920		1,190
610	Taxation	730
310	Current cost profit after interest and taxation	460
170	Gearing adjustment	166
480	*Current cost profit attributable to shareholders*	626
400	Dividends	430
80	Retained current cost profit of the year	196
16.0p	Current cost earnings per share	20.9p
5.2%	Operating profit return on the average of the net operating assets	6.0%

Statement of retained profits/reserves

£000		£000
80	Retained current cost profit of the year	196
1,850	Movements on current cost reserve (Note 4)	2,054
NIL	Movements on other reserves	NIL
1,930		2,250
14,150	Retained profits/reserves at the beginning of the year	16,080
16,080	Retained profits/reserves at the end of the year	18,330

Y Limited and Subsidiaries

**Summarised group current cost balance sheet
as at 31st December 1980**

1979			*1980*	
£000	£000		£000	£000
		Assets employed:		
	18,130	Fixed assets (Note 3)		19,530
		Net current assets:		
3,200		Stock	4,000	
700		Monetary working capital . .	800	
3,900		Total working capital . . .	4,800	
(400)		Proposed dividends. . . .	(430)	
(600)		Other current liabilities (Net) .	(570)	
	2,900			3,800
	21,030			23,330
		Financed by:		
		Share capital and reserves:		
3,000		Share capital	3,000	
12,350		Current cost reserve (Note 4) .	14,404	
3,730		Other reserves and retained profit	3,926	
	19,080			21,330
	1,950	Loan capital		2,000
	21,030			23,330

252

Y Limited and Subsidiaries

**Notes to the current cost accounts
for the year ended 31st December 1980**

1. *Explanatory notes*
   (see paragraph 58 of the Standard and the example in the Guidance Notes)

2. *Adjustments made in deriving current cost operating profit*

1979		1980
£000		£000
400	Cost of sales	460
70	Monetary working capital	100
470	*Working capital*	560
850	Depreciation	950
1,320	*Current cost operating adjustments*	1,510

3. *Fixed assets*

	31st December 1980			1979
	Gross	*Depreciation*	*Net*	*Net*
	£000	£000	£000	£000
Land and buildings	3,780	680	3,100	3,070
Plant and machinery	25,780	9,350	16,430	15,060
	29,560	10,030	19,530	18,130

4. *Current cost reserve*

	£000	£000	£000
Balance at 1st January 1980			12,350
Revaluation surpluses reflecting price changes:			
Land and buildings	200		
Plant and machinery	1,430		
Stocks and work in progress	490		
		2,120	
Monetary working capital adjustment . . .		100	
Gearing adjustment		(166)	
			2,054
Balance at 31st December 1980			14,404
of which: realised *(see (iii) below)* . .			2,494
unrealised			11,910
			14,404

(i) Where applicable, surpluses or deficits arising on the following should be shown as movements on reserves:
  (a) the revaluation of investments (other than those included in current assets);
  (b) the restatement of investments in associated companies; and
  (c) consolidation differences arising on foreign currency translations.
(ii) Where relevant, movements should be shown net of minority interests.
(iii) The realised element represents the net cumulative total of the current cost adjustments which have been passed through the profit and loss account, including the gearing adjustment.

5.   *Financing of net operating assets*
The following is the value to the business (normally current replacement cost net of depreciation on fixed assets) of the net operating assets at the balance sheet date, together with the method by which they were financed:

1979 £000		*1980* £000
18,130	Fixed assets	19,530
3,900	Working capital	4,800
22,030	*Net operating assets*	24,330
19,080	Share capital and reserves	21,330
400	Proposed dividends	430
19,480	*Total shareholders' interest*	21,760
1,950	Loan capital	2,000
600	Other current liabilities	570
2,550	*Net borrowing*	2,570
22,030		24,330

Guidance Notes on SSAP 16: Current Cost Accounting

These notes are for guidance only and do not form part of the statement of standard accounting practice

Introduction

General

1 The Statement of Standard Accounting Practice on Current Cost Accounting (CCA) – SSAP 16 – sets out the objectives when preparing the accounts and the disclosure requirements in annual financial statements. The primary purpose of the Guidance Notes is to recommend practical methods which will assist entities to comply with SSAP 16. The Guidance Notes are not mandatory.

2 The aim in writing the Guidance Notes has been to cover the most common situations which will be met in practice. It is not possible to lay down methods which will cover all situations. In situations where the suggested methods do not produce acceptable results consistent with the principles of CCA, other methods need to be developed. The more difficult practical problems must be solved in the light of experience with the system.

3 In following the Guidance Notes materiality should be taken into account.

4 The definitions of terms given in SSAP 16 apply also to the Guidance Notes.

Part I — Fixed assets

Introduction

5 Part I deals with fixed assets and depreciation in the following sections:

	Paragraphs
A – General principles	7-14
B – Plant and machinery	15-31
C – Land and buildings	32-42
D – Wasting and intangible assets	43-46
E – Depreciation	47-57
F – Other matters	58-62

6 Part I does not deal with:
(a) assets which are fixed in monetary terms;
(b) goodwill – goodwill arising on consolidation is dealt with under Group accounts paragraphs 124-126;
(c) investments and associated companies, which are referred to in SSAP 16 (paragraphs 38, 52 and 53) and in Part IV of these Guidance Notes.

A – General principles

7 There are many variations in the detailed methods used under historical cost (HC) accounting for recording fixed assets and calculating depreciation. These methods have been developed over the years to meet the particular circumstances of different businesses and many of them will continue to be appropriate under CCA. The essential change is the substitution of current costs for historical costs.

8 CCA requires that the existing fixed assets which are included in the HC balance sheet should be restated for the purposes of the CCA balance sheet at their value to the business by reference to current costs. The operating results should be calculated after charging depreciation based on these costs with a view to the maintenance of the net operating assets and thus the operating capability of the business.

9 It is emphasised that CCA is an adaptation of the HC system to allow for the impact of price changes. It does not seek to extend the boundaries of accounting into other areas not covered by the HC accounts and so does not seek to establish current costs for expenditure which has not been capitalised in the HC balance sheet.

10 In the normal case of a fixed asset in use in a business, the value to the business of the existing asset is the net current cost of a replacement asset which has a similar useful* output or service capacity. This capacity is called the asset's service potential. (It is appreciated that frequently service potential cannot be directly quantified — for instance, a particular replacement machine may give benefits in quality as well as quantity of output.)

11   In dealing with changes in the net book values of fixed assets, it is helpful to make a distinction between changes in the book value due to changes in the service potential and changes due to price movements. In HC accounting this distinction is not necessary because the net book value is not adjusted for price movements. In CCA, however, any change in the book value results from two variables, changes in service potential and changes in price levels.

12   If the above distinction is made, a general rule emerges whereby changes in net book value arising from changes in service potential are taken to the profit and loss account and changes in net book value due to changes in price levels are taken to the current cost reserve.

13   A particular example of this arises where, as in HC accounts, the net book value of an asset should be written down to a lower value because there has been a permanent diminution in value which has been recognised by management. This lower value is known as the re-coverable amount : it is discussed further in paragraphs 28-31.

14   On the commencement of CCA, permanent excess capacity (which represents a prior loss of service potential) should be taken into account in arriving at the net current replacement cost and thus the net transfer to current cost reserve. Thereafter the normal CCA principles for dealing with depreciation and the use of the recoverable amount apply.

B — Plant and machinery

Scope
15   This section covers physical assets other than land and buildings.

Basis of valuation
16   The value to the business of plant and machinery is its net current replacement cost, or, if lower, its recoverable amount.

---

* In the sense that a positive cash flow or cash flow saving results.

257

Calculation of current replacement cost

17 The net current replacement cost of plant and machinery is normally derived from its gross current replacement cost by reference to the proportion of the total working life that remains and the depreciation policy. The most convenient method of calculating the gross current replacement cost is normally through the application of relevant indices to existing gross book values. The cost indices may be those prepared by Government agencies, such as the UK Government Statistical Service*, or be generally recognised privately produced indices. They may alternatively have been compiled by a company on the basis of its own purchasing experience, but the work involved in the preparation, continuing compilation and substantiation of such internally generated indices should be carefully considered.

18 Indices are averages and so can be used for blocks of similar assets. Also the current costs are linked by the index to the costs actually incurred when the assets were purchased so that, for example, the effect of good buying is carried through to the recalculated figures. However, where indices are applied to historical costs which were affected by special factors at the time of acquisition of the assets that are not expected to be repeated in current circumstances, allowance will need to be made for these special factors before applying the indices.

19 The use of indices also ensures that there is a consistency of approach and temporary fluctuations in the index at one date will be self-correcting subsequently. For this reason the same indices should normally be applied in succeeding periods. However, for each period the directors should satisfy themselves that the use of those particular indices does produce realistic current replacement costs.

20 It may be found that the use of indices is impracticable, either because details of the age or historical cost of the assets are not available, or because there is no suitable index covering the class of assets involved. Even if it would be practicable to use indices, the directors may not be satisfied that the use of the available indices does produce realistic current replacement costs for particular assets or groups of assets. This may happen:
(a) if there has been substantial technological change (this subject is discussed further in paragraphs 25-27 and in Appendix (i)) ; or

---

*There are two publications currently available from H M Stationery Office – *Price Index Numbers for Current Cost Accounting (PINCCA)* and *Current Cost Accounting – Guide to price indices for Overseas Countries.*

(b) when changes in the costs of specific assets are known to have been significantly different from the changes in the index appropriate to that group of assets; or

(c) when the historical purchase cost of the asset to which the index is to be applied was affected by special circumstances which are unlikely to be repeated and for which allowance cannot accurately be made.

In such circumstances, the gross current replacement cost of the existing asset should be based on expert opinion or other evidence of the current cost of assets, or groups of assets, having a similar service potential; in some cases, for example, when assets are purchased frequently, it may be found possible to use actual purchase prices.

21 The extensive use of comparative quotations from suppliers or the use of suppliers' price lists in calculating replacement cost is often likely to be impracticable because of the work involved and the difficulty of obtaining reliable and comparable prices from year to year. However, the use of this method is not excluded in circumstances where it is practicable.

22 Normally, insurance values will not be appropriate to use as a basis for calculating replacement cost because they are based on different criteria from those appropriate for current cost accounting. However, data collected when calculating insurable values may be helpful.

23 Secondhand market prices should only be used for determining gross current replacement costs when the existing asset was bought in that market; to do otherwise would be to take account of factors other than price changes.

24 When plant is acquired over a period, indexation should be effected from the dates by reference to which the expenditure is recorded in the books. In the case of plant acquired on hire purchase, the relevant date will be the date at which the asset is first recorded.

Technological change

25 Fixed assets are seldom replaced by identical assets. It is implicit in CCA that the allowance for price changes should take technological change into account. It would be unrealistic to base current costs and depreciation on the current cost of a similar or nearly similar asset when an equivalent modern asset incorporating technological change could do the same work and perhaps cost only half as much.

26 The use of broadly based indices allows for some of the effects on current costs of gradual technological change. Nevertheless, it may sometimes be necessary to derive the equivalent current cost of an existing fixed asset from the cost of a modern asset. An example of how this may be achieved is given in Appendix (i).

27 It may also be frequently the case that an asset can be maintained in physical use almost indefinitely subject only to the limiting factors of changes in technology or changes in the market which make the product obsolete. Thus, in assessing the future life, the effect of these changes should be considered (paragraph 47).

Calculation of the recoverable amount

28 Management, as under HC accounting, may recognise that a permanent diminution in value has taken place and that a provision should be made by writing the asset down against profits immediately. This may happen, for example, when plant or machinery has become surplus to requirements, or its use is to be discontinued before the end of its normal life. In such circumstances, the value to the business will be the recoverable amount being lower than the net current replacement cost. It is emphasised that this is similar to the procedure that would apply under the historical cost convention.

29 There are commonly two situations which may arise. First, the asset is put out of use immediately and is sold or scrapped. The recoverable amount is then the current realisable amount net of realisation expenses. Second, the asset continues in use for a period. Then, as in HC accounting, the recoverable amount is the total estimated amount which can be recovered from its use, normally calculated by reference to the estimated cash flows arising from its future use and its ultimate disposal. Such amounts should be calculated net of any realisation expenses and at price levels current at the date of the accounts, not at estimated future price levels. As in HC accounts it is not usual to discount the future cash flows. The difference between the recoverable amount and the net current replacement cost is taken to profit and loss account.

30 Subsequently, the recoverable amount is written off over the remaining period of use. If price levels change from those existing at the date of the original calculation, the remaining recoverable amount is adjusted by transfer to or from the current cost reserve. Changes for other reasons should be taken to the profit and loss account.

31 It is appropriate to raise asset values (and therefore depreciation) in line with rises in costs even if a company's business is declining or at present unprofitable. This is so until such time as a permanent diminution in value below current replacement cost is recognised so that assets have to be reduced to their recoverable amount. On the commencement of CCA such a reduction should be debited to the current cost reserve on the grounds that it accrued over previous periods of account and subsequently the normal rules mentioned above apply.

C – Land and buildings*

Specialised buildings

32 Certain types of buildings, specialised because of their location or arrangement, the form of their construction, or perhaps their size, are rarely sold except by way of sale of the business in which they are used. Typically, many industrial buildings on works sites come into this category. The current cost of such buildings should be evaluated on the same principles as plant and machinery as set out in Part B (paragraphs 15 to 31 above). The underlying land should be valued on the basis applying to non-specialised buildings unless it is immaterial in relation to the total assets of the business.

33 However, certain kinds of buildings, such as hotels, petrol filling stations, cinemas, public houses, are normally valued and recorded in the HC accounts on a basis which includes inherent trading potential** (also commonly referred to as 'goodwill which runs with the property'). They are commonly bought and sold as continuing businesses. Accordingly, they should be treated as non-specialised buildings because the written down replacement cost basis which is used for specialised buildings cannot be applied to the goodwill element.

Non-specialised buildings

34 Other buildings, such as the majority of offices, shops and general purpose industrial units, are commonly bought and sold together with the underlying land as one asset. The normal method of acquiring such properties is by purchase on the open market. Accordingly, the net current replacement cost of such properties will be the estimated cost of purchasing the existing property on the open market, rather than the cost of rebuilding on the same site plus the current cost of the

---

*Reference to the *Guidance Notes on the Valuation of Assets* prepared by the Royal Institution of Chartered Surveyors may be of assistance in valuing land and buildings.

**Reference to the *Background Paper No. 7* prepared by the Royal Institution of Chartered Surveyors may also be of assistance in the valuation of such properties.

land. Movements in market values of such properties vary widely according to their exact location and other characteristics, so that the use of indices to obtain current replacement costs is likely to be unsatisfactory. In these circumstances, their net current replacement cost can best be ascertained by individual valuation at their open market value for existing use. By adopting this basis, the land and buildings are valued together, although for the purpose of calculating depreciation on the buildings, an estimate will need to be made of the building element.

35 Accordingly, all owner-occupied land and non-specialised buildings should be valued at their open market value for the existing use (including incidental acquisition costs where material).

36 The categorisation of buildings between 'specialised' and 'non-specialised' is not exact. It should be decided by management according to the circumstances and once decided should not normally be changed.

37 The current replacement cost of land and buildings which are not owner-occupied and are let or held for letting at arm's length to third parties should be obtained by valuing them at their open market value. This amount should be increased by an estimate, at current price levels, of the acquisition costs where these are material and the original costs were capitalised.

38 Land and buildings which are surplus to the present and future requirements of the business should be valued at their open market value less costs of disposal, i.e. at their net realisable value.

Adaptation costs

39 Frequently, substantial additional expenditure is incurred and capitalised in order to make a property suitable for the particular requirements of the business. Although such adaptation costs may not necessarily add proportionately to the open market value of the property, they do form part of the business's net operating assets. In such a situation the basic property can be carried at market value and the adaptation costs treated separately like specialised buildings, i.e. using the same principles as for plant and machinery.

Frequency of valuations

40 The frequency of valuations should be decided having regard to such factors as the extent to which property values generally have changed since the last valuation. It is unlikely that valuations at intervals of more than five years will be sufficient to ensure that the values adopted in the accounts are not significantly different from current values. In the years between such valuations, the directors should consider whether the values should be updated in the light of the evidence available to them (which may include the views of their professional adviser).

Valuations

41 Valuations at open market value (whether for existing use or otherwise) should normally be carried out by persons holding a recognised professional qualification and having recent post qualification experience in the valuation of properties in the location and category of the properties concerned. Valuations may be carried out by external or internal valuers.

Buildings under construction

42 The current cost of specialised buildings under construction should be dealt with as for plant and machinery. Other buildings under construction should be restated at the lower of (a) their indexed cost and (b) the estimated completed open market value at current prices less the estimated cost at current prices to complete.

D – Wasting and intangible assets

Wasting assets

43 Wasting assets may be defined as fixed assets which, when consumed, cannot be renewed in the existing location. The most common example is mineral-bearing land or mineral rights. Under the historical cost convention, costs incurred in acquiring such rights or properties may or may not be treated as capital assets to be amortised over their estimated useful lives. Where acquisition costs have been capitalised, current replacement costs should, where possible, be based on the best evidence available as for other fixed assets. This will enable the current cost of the service potential consumed to be calculated and charged in arriving at the operating results. It is not intended that current capital costs should be established where it has not been the practice under the historical cost convention to capitalise such costs.

44 Exploration and development costs carried forward under the historical cost convention should be recalculated by reference to current costs.

Intangible assets

45 Intangible assets (such as patents and copyrights, but excluding goodwill) will often have service potential which is consumed by the business over their life in a similar way to physically identifiable fixed assets. They should in principle be restated at their value to the business to ensure that the current cost of the portion consumed is charged in the operating results and to present a realistic balance sheet. If it is impracticable to estimate the current replacement cost of such assets it is necessary to consider alternatives such as the application of a general index or the continuing use of the existing historical cost carrying values. As in the case of wasting assets, it is not intended that current capital costs should be established where it has not been the practice under the historical cost convention to capitalise such costs.

46 Intangible assets may include deferred revenue expenditure such as development expenditure. Such expenditure should be recalculated by reference to current costs.

E – Depreciation
General principles

47 Depreciation is a measure of the wearing out, consumption, or other loss of value of a fixed asset whether arising from use, effluxion of time or obsolescence through technology or market changes. Under the historical cost convention, this is measured by reference to the historical cost or where fixed assets have been revalued, the revalued amount. The charge is calculated by allocating the gross historical cost or revalued amount, less estimated residual values, of the assets as fairly as possible to the periods expected to benefit from their use. The only difference between HC accounting and CCA is that in the latter it is the current cost in the accounting period which forms the basis of the depreciation charge. The estimate of useful life should still take into account such factors as commercial and technological obsolescence. Accordingly, the charge for depreciation for a period should represent the estimated consumption of the value to the business during the period. The value to the business should, in principle, be that ruling at the date of consumption. However, in practice, either average or period end costs may suffice.

48 Changes in the net current replacement cost for reasons other than price changes represent changes in the estimated remaining service potential of the asset – for example, the normal depreciation charge represents a consumption of service potential. Similarly, changes in the basis of valuation from net current replacement cost to recoverable amount or vice-versa and profits or losses on disposal of assets, represent changes in service potential and as stated in paragraph 12 the effects are passed through the profit and loss account.

49 When assets such as land and buildings are valued at market value, this amount, i.e. the net current replacement cost, will be recorded in the accounting records. Subsequent depreciation charges are then deducted from the net current replacement cost. Any transfer to or from current cost reserve, when these assets are again revalued, will be calculated by reference to the net figure after depreciation.

Backlog depreciation

50 For assets other than land and buildings carried at open market value the restatement of the net current replacement cost due to price changes will be derived from a restatement of the gross current replacement cost. Consequently, the accumulated depreciation also requires to be restated. The difference arising on this restatement is known as backlog depreciation and is transferred to the current cost reserve. The transfer to or from current cost reserve is thus the net amount of the restatement of the gross current replacement cost and the restatement of the accumulated depreciation.

51 CCA measures the amount required to maintain the present operating capability of a business represented by the present net operating assets. In relation to fixed assets it does this by charging the value to the business at the time of consumption of the proportion of the asset which is consumed. Backlog depreciation does not form part of this consumption but represents the effect of current price changes on past consumption and so is not charged in arriving at the operating result.

52 Because backlog depreciation is not charged against revenue, the total of the current cost depreciation charges over the life of the asset will not equal the ultimate replacement cost of the actual asset being consumed. However, the depreciation charges create retained funds which are normally reinvested in other assets, fixed or current. These assets are then generally subject to adjustments to allow for price changes. In this way allowance for price changes is made on the funds retained in the entity as a result of past depreciation charges. As with HC, the provision of cash to replace individual assets in the future is a matter for financial management and remains outside the ambit of the accounting system.

Profits and losses on disposal of fixed assets

53 On the disposal of an asset, the value to the business included in the accounts should first be updated for changes in current cost between the beginning of the accounting period and the date of disposal and the difference taken to current cost reserve. Any further difference between the updated value to the business and the proceeds should be taken to profit and loss account in accordance with paragraph 48 being treated as an extraordinary item where appropriate.

54 The difference between the HC profit or loss on disposal and the equivalent current cost figure (which is equal to the difference between the net book values calculated on the HC and CCA basis at the date of disposal) is part of the reconciliation from the HC to the CCA profit and should be included as a current cost adjustment.

Asset lives and fully depreciated assets

55 It may happen that conservative asset lives or rates of depreciation have been used in the historical cost accounts, perhaps in order to make some allowance for inflation. This may result in there being a significant number of largely or fully depreciated assets still in use and, although the overall current cost depreciation charge may not be materially inaccurate if there have been subsequent additions, the asset values would be understated. On the introduction of CCA it is important that the existing asset lives and rates of depreciation should be reviewed in order to ensure that the CCA asset values and depreciation charges are realistic for all groups of assets*. Any resulting adjustment to the net current costs should be taken up in the initial transfer to current cost reserve.

56 In subsequent periods it is particularly important for the purpose of current cost accounting to make regular reviews of rates of depreciation and estimated remaining useful lives. Any effects in the current or future periods of such reviews should be taken through the profit and loss account as depreciation, being based on the current costs ruling at the time.

57 The accounting treatment adopted for dealing with changes in asset lives should be applied consistently and any material effects of changes in the treatment or in estimated lives should be disclosed.

---

*The existence of unrealistic asset values can have material effects on the CCA balance sheet and consequently on the calculation of the return on assets employed and on the gearing adjustment.

F – Other matters

Leased assets

58 The accounting treatment for leases in the context of historical cost accounting is currently being studied by The Accounting Standards Committee (ASC). ASC is considering whether assets, which are leased on terms which in substance transfer the full risks and rewards of ownership to the lessee, should be capitalised by the lessee on the grounds that the transaction is primarily a method of financing the business. It is not the intention in SSAP 16 to antici-pate any future recommendations of ASC with regard to leased assets. Nevertheless, many lessee companies will have paid prem-iums for leases which are treated as capital assets or will have capi-talised, to some degree or another, their interest in leased assets. In such cases, where the amounts which have been capitalised are significant, current replacement costs of these amounts will need to be ascertained as for other fixed assets. It is not recommended that current capital costs for leasehold interests should be established when it is not the practice under the historical cost convention to capitalise such costs. In these circumstances, the current rental paid is taken to represent the full current cost to the lessee for the use of the leased asset, and there is no need to take account of comparative market rates.

59 Leased assets which are accounted for as fixed assets in the accounts of the lessor companies should be restated at their current cost as for other fixed assets and additional depreciation should be charged thereon. If the rentals receivable are fixed in money terms, it may be necessary to pay particular attention to the recoverable amount. Alternatively, if the leased assets are treated as monetary assets, their book value being calculated by reference to the capitalised value of rental income, an adjustment similar to a monetary working capital adjustment should be made.

Capital based government grants

60 The accounting treatment of capital based Government grants is laid down in SSAP 4. SSAP 16 does not seek to change this. A capital based Government grant represents in CCA a reduction in the gross current cost and a change in grant represents a price change. Consequently, in principle, the current rates and availability of grants should be taken into account for CCA. This applies whether the grants have been deducted from the cost of the assets or accoun-ted for separately as deferred credits.

61 However, it may not always be practicable to establish the current applicable rates and availability of such grants because of changes in Government regulations or because the grant would be to some extent discretionary and subject to negotiation. There may also be difficulty in identifying grants which have been received in the past with the assets to which they relate. Similar difficulties may arise when grants have been accounted for on a deferred credit basis. It may, therefore, be necessary to adopt a more general approach when assessing current costs for assets still eligible for grants. The use of indices may ease the position. This is because the application of indices to historical figures, net of grant, will produce acceptable CC figures, provided the eligibility for grant and the rate of grant have not materially changed since acquisition.

62 Where such grants are a material factor in the accounts, the treatment adopted for CCA should be disclosed.

Part II — Working capital

Introduction

63 Working capital includes stock and work in progress (stock) and monetary working capital*. Part II of the Guidance Notes deals with the CCA treatment of working capital in the following sections:

	Paragraphs
A – General principles	64–67
B – Stock – General	68–72
C – Stock – Methods	73–75
D – Stock – Special situations	76–87
E – Monetary working capital	88–105

A – General principles

64 SSAP 16 states that the current cost operating profit* is derived by making three main adjustments to the historical cost trading profit, (before interest on net borrowing*) to allow for the impact of price changes on the funds needed to maintain the net operating assets. The first relates to fixed assets; the others relate to working capital and are:

(a) a cost of sales adjustment (COSA), which is the difference between the value to the business* and the historical cost of the stock consumed in the period; and

(b) a monetary working capital adjustment (MWCA) which is the amount of additional (or reduced) finance needed for monetary working capital (MWC) as a result of changes in the input prices of goods and services used and financed by the business.

65 It is in the nature of working capital that it regularly circulates in the course of trading. The constituent elements of working capital (e.g. stock, trade debtors, trade creditors, and in some cases bank balance or overdraft), although separately identifiable, are inter-dependent. Fluctuations in the level of one element will give rise to contrary fluctuations in another. Thus, if prices do not change over the accounting period, the combined net total of working capital may remain constant or change at a constant rate.

66 It follows that the COSA and MWCA are inter-related. Although they are described separately below, and will usually be calculated separately, there are some situations where stock should be treated, for calculation purposes, as if it were monetary working capital (see paragraph 72). As the two adjustments are complementary, it can

---

*As defined in the definitions section of SSAP 16.

269

happen that inaccuracies arising when each is calculated separately are eliminated when combining the two. It is primarily for these reasons that SSAP 16 does not require the COSA and MWCA necessarily to be disclosed separately. It is important that the methods, indices, and intervals used in calculating the adjustments are compatible.

67 In the current cost balance sheet, stock subject to a COSA should be included at its value to the business at the balance sheet date. Monetary working capital, including stock treated as such, should be included on the historical cost basis.

B – Stock – General

68 The value to the business of an item of stock is the lower of its current replacement cost and its recoverable amount (i.e. net realisable value).

69 The current replacement cost of an item of stock is the cost at which it could have been replaced in the normal course of business at the valuation date. The valuation date is the date when the stock is consumed or the date of the balance sheet as appropriate. In principle, the current replacement cost relates to items for delivery on the valuation date rather than the cost of orders on that date*. In the case of labour and overheads, current replacement cost is based on the costs ruling at the valuation date.

70 In principle, current replacement cost relates to an item which is identical to that consumed, purchased or produced in the same way, and this is so regardless of whether replacement with an identical item will actually take place or not. However, it may be difficult to ascertain current replacement cost if stock consumed is not replaced with identical stock. In these circumstances, if replacement is made with an item which is substantially similar to the stock consumed, the cost of the new item should be used as the current replacement cost. Alternatively, a price index relating to a class of goods which is similar to that consumed may be used whether the replacement is similar or not. Failing this, a general price index should be used.

71 Amounts written off the current replacement cost of stock to reduce it to recoverable amount should be charged to profit and loss account (see also Appendix (iii) paragraph 7).

---

*If using PINCCA indices to establish value to the business see also Appendix (ii) – paragraph 3(b).

Stock treated as monetary working capital

72 There are some situations where a COSA cannot be made and in these situations the relevant stock should be included within MWC and treated as described in paragraph 102. Such situations include dealing stock, certain types of contract work in progress and, in certain circumstances, seasonal purchases. These are covered in Section D, Special situations.

C – Stock – Methods

73 No single prescribed method of calculating the effect of price changes on the current replacement cost of stock can be capable of universal application. The method used should be appropriate to the type of stock, the nature of activities of the company, any seasonal trading pattern during the period and the system of bookkeeping in force. In selecting the method, account should also be taken of the cost of applying the method and the likely materiality of the adjustment arising from it.

74 Appendix (ii) describes some methods for calculating the effect of price movements on stock. Appendix (iii) explains the use of the averaging method which provides a practical means for calculating the COSA in many businesses. An example of the use of the averaging method is included in Appendix (vii).

75 The current cost reserve should include the COSA and any difference between the balance sheet amount at which stock is included in historical cost and current cost accounts. An example appears in Section D of Appendix (vii).

D – Stock – Special situations

Seasonal purchases

76 In certain cases (e.g. seasonal produce) there may be no relevant replacement cost at the date when the stock is consumed and it may be difficult or impossible to ascertain or estimate the future replacement cost. Furthermore, where buying and selling prices are volatile, the matching of this season's selling prices against next season's buying prices (even if they were known) might give an accounting result which would not reflect fairly the activities of the period. In these circumstances, where replacement with similar produce is intended, a COSA should be made, if possible, based on a price index which corresponds with the long-term trend in replacement costs. Some businesses, however, may not intend to replace with similar produce but will wish to choose, each season, from the range of opportunities open to them. This situation may be recognised by treating the stock as monetary working capital and a MWCA should then be made which will broadly maintain the ability of the business to continue to take advantage of such opportunities.

Commodities and metals

77 A processing or manufacturing business may use commodities or metals which are subject to volatile price changes. The combined COSA and MWCA should allow for the effect of price changes during the period on the funds needed to continue the business regardless of whether stock consumed is replaced immediately or not.

Dealing stock

78 In some cases (e.g. in certain commodity dealing activities) an identifiable part of a business activity involves the purchase of assets mainly with a view to gaining the benefit of an increase in their market value, e.g. by sale in the market in which they were purchased. Therefore, the current replacement cost at the time of sale would be equal or close to the selling price. It is characteristic of this type of business that prices fluctuate and that the business may, at certain times, hold cash instead of stock or sell short.

79 It would be inappropriate, in these circumstances, to make a COSA which, being based on current replacement cost, would effectively eliminate all or most of the profit or loss resulting from the transaction. Such a treatment would not reflect the nature of the activities of the business. Therefore :
(a) profits (or losses) on such stock should be included in the profit and loss account on the normal historical cost basis, and in consequence
(b) dealing stock should be treated for calculation purposes as if it were monetary working capital and an adjustment based on this included in the profit and loss account (paragraph 102).

Purchasing skills and special purchases

80 As mentioned in paragraph 15 of SSAP 16, the benefits of good buying (and the costs of errors) should be included in current cost operating profit. Concern has been expressed that, although such benefits are reflected in HC profits, it may not happen under CCA.

81 The exercise of purchasing skills can result in 'special purchases', that is stocks additional to normal requirements being obtained in anticipation of a price increase or in stocks being obtained at special prices (i.e. prices which would not be reflected in external indices). In the former case, the volume change in stock is offset by a compensating change in monetary working capital and this may need to be reflected in the MWCA to ensure that the proper result is obtained.

82 The way in which the effect of special purchases is reflected in accounts will depend on the method used to determine price changes and on whether the stock is sold in the same period as it is acquired. Some situations are discussed below; a beneficial purchase is assumed.

(a) Where the special purchase is sold in the same period as it is acquired, the full benefit will automatically be included in the current cost operating profit where the averaging method is used.

(b) Where the special purchase is in stock at the period end, the time at which the benefit is included in the profit and loss account depends on the method used to ascertain the price changes on which the working capital adjustments are based:

(i) where price changes are based on external indices, the benefit will broadly be included in operating profit, but not until it is reflected in HC profits;

(ii) where price changes are based on the actual purchasing experience of the company (or indices based on those prices which reflect the timing and weighting of purchases, including the special purchases), the special price will be taken into account in arriving at the current cost at the next valuation date* after the special purchase and thus the benefit will be reflected from that date.

Contract work in progress

83 Contracts may be divided, for CCA purposes, into two groups. The first group consists of contracts which are broadly repetitive in nature. The second group relates to unique contracts. Construction and civil engineering contracts may fall into either group.

84 Transactions in the first group will in character be similar to those in the case of normal manufactured goods and the current cost of sales should be calculated in the same way.

85 The second group will tend to raise problems that are more difficult in view of the fact that each contract is unique. A COSA should, if practicable, be calculated using indices appropriate to the business. However, in some circumstances, relevant replacement cost may be difficult or impossible to ascertain in which case the work in

---

*Defined in paragraph 69.

273

progress net of progress payments, may be treated as a monetary asset and be subject to a MWCA. Land held for development should also be treated as monetary working capital if a COSA is not practicable.

Progress payments receivable

86 A progress payment is an amount received or receivable in connection with the financing of stock prior to its sale. The burden of financing the stock covered by the progress payment is not subsequently borne by the business. In recognition of this, a progress payment should be deducted from the value of the stock to which it relates and only the net amount should be subject to adjustment.

87 Progress payments should be related to stock on a contract by contract basis. Any excess of the amount of a progress payment over the value of the stock to which it relates should be treated as a liability forming part of monetary working capital.

E – Monetary working capital

Introduction

88 The MWCA is made in the calculation of current cost operating profit and takes the form of a charge or credit to profit and loss account with the corresponding credit or charge to the current cost reserve. The objective of and reason for the MWCA is set out in the Explanatory Note to SSAP 16 and its interrelationship with the COSA is considered earlier in this section.

The items to be included in the adjustment

89 SSAP 16 requires that the MWC should include only items used in the day-to-day operating activities of the business. It includes trade debtors (including, for example, trade bills receivable, prepayments and VAT recoverable) and trade creditors (including, for example, trade bills payable, accruals, expense creditors and VAT payable). MWC should not include creditors or debtors relating to fixed assets bought or sold or under construction.

90 Bank balances or overdrafts may fluctuate with the level of stock, trade debtors or trade creditors. That part of bank balances or overdrafts arising from such fluctuations should be included in MWC together with cash floats required to support the day-to-day operations of the business if to do so has a material effect on current cost operating profit. (Paragraph 101)

91 Certain items of stock which have not been subject to a COSA are also to be included in MWC for the purposes of the adjustment. (Paragraph 102)

92 In the case of banks and other financial businesses, the definition of MWC is extended to cover other assets and liabilities in so far as they also arise from the day-to-day operating activities as distinct from transactions of a capital nature. (The MWC of banks is commonly described by them as their 'free capital'.)

The method of calculating the MWCA

93 Determine the items to be included as MWC* (described in the rest of this section as debtors and creditors).

94 Determine the interval or intervals over which the calculations will be made. (Paragraph 66)

95 Ascertain separately the relevant indices to be used in adjusting debtors and creditors.
(a) The index for debtors should reflect changes in the current cost of goods and services sold attributable to changes in input prices (including labour rates) over the period the debt is outstanding. Indices of selling prices may be used where these provide a fair approximation of the cost changes in amount and time.
(b) The index for creditors should reflect similar changes in the cost of the items which have been financed by those creditors over the period the credit is outstanding.
(c) Where the percentage changes in the indices to be used on debtors and creditors are similar, a single index can be used and the adjustment can be determined in one calculation as shown in Section B of Appendix (vii). In some businesses a sufficiently close approximation may be obtained by using the same index as for stock.

96 Apply the relevant index or indices to the debtors and creditors to determine the MWCA. In principle, in calculating the adjustment on debtors the profit element in debtors should be excluded. However, the total amount of debtors can be used where this gives a fair approximation.

97 An averaging method, compatible with the method used for the COSA, may be used to calculate the adjustment. This is discussed in Appendix (iii) and demonstrated in Appendix (vii).

---

*As defined in the definitions section of SSAP 16.

98 Where the MWC is a net liability greater than the value of stock, the excess is not funding working capital and so should be excluded when calculating the MWCA. The excess will in consequence be included in net borrowing for the purpose of calculating the gearing adjustment. (Paragraph 112).

Inclusion of cash or overdrafts within the calculation of the MWCA

99 As noted in paragraphs 65 and 90, there are circumstances where cash or overdrafts should be included in the MWC.

100 One such circumstance arises if the business uses material cash floats in the conduct of its normal day-to-day operations.

101 Another arises where, in the normal course of business, a company experiences significant fluctuations in its purchases or sales, because of a periodic or seasonal cycle inherent in the nature of the business, or for other reasons that create significant variations in the volume of its stock, debtors or creditors. Where such situations lead to material temporary changes in cash or overdraft balances at a time when suppliers' prices are changing, the MWC should include this element of cash or overdraft over the interval in question.

Stock not subject to a cost of sales adjustment

102 There are some situations where a COSA is not appropriate for certain categories of stock. This may apply to :
(a) stock related to long-term contracts, net of progress payments ;
(b) seasonal agricultural produce ;
(c) stock held for dealing purposes ; or
(d) land held for development.

Where this applies, the items concerned should be subject to an MWCA. This should be made by applying, on a consistent basis from year to year, an index of price change most appropriate to the stock in question and the general nature of the business, having regard to the objective of the adjustment. In the absence of a more appropriate index a general index should be used as in the case of a financial business (paragraph 104 below), and the basis adopted should be explained.

MWCA : Banks and other financial businesses

103 Where the items that comprise working capital are wholly of a financial nature, as in a banking or similar business, the provision for maintenance of operating capability – the output of financial services – should, in principle, be calculated by reference to changes in the prices of the assets of undertakings for which the business provides finance.

104 For example, in a general banking business the most suitable measure would be the implied change in the average price level of the gross domestic product in the country in which it operates. As the latter is not available on a monthly basis, and is subject to recalculation, the best available proxy measure should be used. At present in the UK this is the general index of retail prices. The MWCA is obtained by calculating the change in MWC due to price changes in the relevant accounting period, as shown in Appendix (vii).

MWCA : Non-financial service industries

105 In non-financial industries where the operating capability is related to the output of services and where stocks may be relatively small, the MWCA should be calculated by selecting and adhering to an index which is considered most appropriate having regard to the general objective of the adjustment as outlined in the Explanatory Note to SSAP 16.

Part III — The gearing adjustment

General

106 The fixed assets and the working capital commonly will have been financed in part by borrowing. Where such borrowing is fixed in monetary amount, any liability to repay remains unaltered, even when price changes affect the operating assets of the business financed by it. If prices rise, the value to the business of assets exceeds the borrowing that has financed them. The excess (less interest payable on the borrowing) in effect accrues to the shareholders, and is realised as the assets are used or sold in the ordinary course of business. The existence of borrowing during a period of rising prices thus provides a benefit to shareholders which offsets, to a greater or lesser extent, the cost of servicing the borrowing and conversely when prices decline.

107 No account has been taken of the existence of borrowing in arriving at current cost operating profit. In these circumstances the profit attributable to shareholders would be under-stated (or where prices fall, over-stated) if the whole of the additional depreciation, the COSA and the MWCA were charged (or where appropriate, credited) in the profit and loss account. The total amount of these adjustments should therefore be abated by a further adjustment, the 'gearing adjustment', in the proportion that finance by borrowing bears to the sum of this plus the shareholders' interest. In calculating the gearing proportion the borrowing should be reduced to a net figure (the 'net borrowing') by the amount of any cash or other monetary current asset that is not included in monetary working capital.

108 The current cost profit attributable to shareholders will thus reflect the result of adjustments to the historical cost trading profit which, taken together, allow for the impact of price changes on that proportion of the net operating assets which is related to the shareholders' interest.

109 In some circumstances, because of particular features of the capital structure, a gearing adjustment calculated as specified in paragraph 107 is inappropriate or misleading. This may apply to :
(a) wholly owned subsidiaries, e.g. of overseas companies, where certain loans advanced from other group companies are equity capital in substance. Such loans should be treated as equity capital when calculating a gearing adjustment (SSAP 16, para. 45) ; and

(b) entities such as co-operatives where shares are redeemable at par at the call of individual shareholders so long as the entity is a going concern.

110 In such cases it is appropriate that:
(a) interest on borrowing should be treated as stated in paragraph 120; and
(b) the notes to the current cost accounts should include an explanation of the treatment adopted and, where practicable, state what the gearing adjustment would have been had all borrowing been strictly treated as such, and not as if it were in substance equity.

The calculation of the gearing adjustment

111 The gearing proportion is the ratio of net borrowing* to the average net operating assets over the year, taken at their current cost values. The amount of the net operating assets is the sum of:
(a) fixed assets, including trade investments. i.e. investments that are not classified as current; and
(b) stock and monetary working capital*.

The total of (a) and (b) can alternatively be arrived at as the sum of:
(c) net borrowing; and
(d) shareholders' interest (defined to include proposed dividends) taken from the current cost balance sheet.

112 The gearing proportion can thus be calculated as follows:
(a) ascertain the average net borrowing during the period. If net borrowing is negative, because monetary assets included exceed monetary liabilities included, no adjustment is needed as the excess is not part of the net operating assets. (See paragraphs 22 and 36 of SSAP 16.) However, more usually the liabilities will exceed the assets. The average may be taken to be the simple average of the opening and closing balance sheets unless there have been substantial changes in borrowings during the period, or other events** such that a weighted average would give a more appropriate indication. Let the average net borrowing be L;

---

*As defined in the definitions section of SSAP 16. Where debentures are convertible into shares but are not yet converted, they should be included in borrowing, as that is the actual position in the year under review. A deferred credit which is created when capital based Government grants are not deducted from the cost of an asset, should be treated as a deduction from fixed assets and not as part of net borrowing.

**When seasonality or other situations introduce a considerable fluctuation in the level of MWC, and the MWCA is calculated over a different interval from the gearing adjustment, the calculation of the gearing adjustment should ensure that material amounts of cash or overdraft are not excluded from, or included in, both adjustments.

(b)   ascertain the average shareholders' interest during the period as the average of share capital, reserves and proposed dividends (and including preference shares* and minority interests where applicable) as shown in the opening and closing current cost balance sheets. Let the average shareholders' interest be S ;

(c)   the gearing proportion is the ratio of the average net borrowing to the sum of this and the average shareholders' interest; that is

$$\frac{L}{L+S}$$

113 Ascertain the current cost adjustments made to allow for the impact of price changes on the net operating assets of the business (see paragraph 49 of SSAP 16). Let the sum of these be A.

114 The gearing adjustment is calculated by multiplying the sum of the adjustments (paragraph 113) by the gearing proportion (paragraph 112) so that the adjustment equals

$$\frac{L}{L+S}\times A.$$

A simple example appears in Appendix (vii).

115 Some companies have introduced a modification of the pure HC system by incorporating revaluations of their depreciating fixed assets into their HC balance sheet which will then increase the depreciation charged in HC accounts. The CC operating profit will not be affected, but the depreciation adjustment will be reduced, and in consequence the gearing proportion would be applied to a figure that is too low. Where the distortion thus introduced into the gearing adjustment would be material, the latter should be calculated by estimating the depreciation adjustment as it would have been if the historical cost accounts had not incorporated the revaluations. If this is not practicable the matter should be noted in the accounts.

116 If, temporarily, different asset lives are used in the calculation of the historical and current cost depreciation the HC depreciation ought, in principle, to be recalculated using the CCA lives. This is to isolate the additional depreciation on which the gearing adjustment should be based.

---

*SSAP 16 requires preference shares to be included within the shareholders' interest. The profit is therefore attributable to all shareholders, ordinary and preference, as required by the Companies Acts. Where a company has a material amount of preference shares with fixed repayment rights, it may wish to show in a note the effect of including preference share capital in net borrowing.

117 When fixed assets (including non-current investments) are disposed of, the adjustments converting historical cost profit to current cost profit must include any differences between (a) historical cost net book value and (b) current cost, net of any depreciation to date (refer also to paras. 53 and 54). This ensures that any profit or loss shown on disposal is calculated by reference to the current cost of the asset. The difference should be added to the other current cost adjustments for the purpose of calculating the gearing adjustment, i.e. it should be included in the amount ascertained under paragraph 113. Thus, if an asset has a written down historical cost of £100,000, a net current cost of £190,000 and is sold for £200,000, the gain of £10,000 will be included in the current cost operating profit: £90,000 will be included in the current cost operating adjustments and this portion is subject to a gearing adjustment. Appendices (v) and (vii) contain an example of this.

118 Where the current cost accounts are consolidated accounts the gearing adjustment should normally be calculated on a group basis. This, together with the appropriate treatment where there are associates and minorities, is discussed in Part IV, Group accounts.

Treatment of interest in the profit and loss account

119 Where MWC is made up of trade debtors and trade creditors, interest will not normally arise in the calculation of operating profit. Where cash, overdraft or bills are included in MWC the related interest should, where material, be included in arriving at operating profit. Similarly, where the nature of the business is such (e.g. in a banking business) that MWC contains items giving rise to material payments or receipts of interest, it is appropriate to include these before arriving at operating profit. Interest that does not enter into the calculation of operating profit is shown in arriving at profit attributable to shareholders.

120 Interest on borrowing that is not reflected in a monetary working capital or the gearing adjustment, perhaps because the borrowing was dealt with as if it were in substance equity capital, should be disclosed separately from interest on borrowing that has been reflected in such adjustments. Where practicable, the former kind of interest should be included in the profit and loss account after taxation and extraordinary items.

Part IV — Group accounts

Introduction

121 SSAP 16 requires that a company which is the parent company of a group and which is required to produce group accounts should produce current cost group accounts in accordance with the principles outlined therein. The objective remains the same: to give a true and fair view of financial position and profit or loss of the group as a whole. Accordingly, the methods of preparing such accounts are basically no different from those normally used for historical cost group accounts. However, there are certain aspects, mainly of a practical nature, which require special mention and these are discussed under the following headings:

	Paragraphs
A – Goodwill	124–126
B – The elimination of intra-group profits	127–129
C – Associated companies	130–134
D – Translation of foreign currencies	135–139
E – Monetary working capital and gearing adjustments	140–142
F – Minority interests	143–144

122 It is recognised that it may not be possible or practical for all foreign subsidiaries to prepare accounts using CCA principles and in such circumstances the directors of the parent company should make the best possible estimates of the figures required for the group accounts stating, where material, the bases adopted.

123 SSAP 16 (paragraph 46) excludes certain entities due to the nature of their business. This could cause two practical difficulties when producing current cost group accounts, namely:

(a) what should be done when a company has a subsidiary which is excluded from SSAP 16 and for which current cost accounts have not been prepared? For example, this may apply to an insurance or property company which is a subsidiary of a manufacturing company. In this case, if material, the profits and net assets of the subsidiary should be included on the same basis as in the historical cost accounts and separately distinguished;

(b) what should be done when a company is excluded but has a material subsidiary which falls within the scope of SSAP 16 (as a result of the final section of paragraph 46), for example, a property company having manufacturing companies as subsidiaries? In this case, consolidated current cost accounts in respect of such subsidiaries should be included as supplementary information in the group accounts if, by virtue of their collective size, they fall within the scope of SSAP 16.

A – Goodwill

124 This section of the Guidance Notes is confined to the accounting adjustments to goodwill arising on the acquisition of subsidiaries and which has not been written off in the historical cost accounts.

125 It has been common practice prior to the implementation of SSAP 14 on group accounts for companies to calculate the value of goodwill arising on the acquisition of a company by reference to the subsidiary's book value of the net assets acquired. On producing current cost accounts, such goodwill retained in the historical cost consolidated accounts should be offset against revaluation surpluses resulting from the current cost revaluation of the relevant assets to the extent that such surpluses existed at the time of acquisition. Thus, the value of such goodwill in the current cost accounts should be the difference between the purchase price and the value to the (acquiring) business of the net assets acquired at the date of acquisition, less any amounts written off. If this is not done there is a danger of double counting through the inclusion of surpluses both in the revaluation of fixed assets and in the value of goodwill. Where the acquisition took place some time ago it may be impracticable to estimate the then current value to the business of the assets acquired; in these circumstances, in order to avoid the risk of double counting, goodwill arising on the acquisition should be offset against the current cost reserve.

126 SSAP 14, paragraph 29, states:
'When subsidiaries are purchased, the purchase consideration should be allocated between the underlying net tangible and intangible assets other than goodwill on the basis of the fair value to the acquiring company.'

Accordingly, the problem outlined in paragraph 125 should not arise in respect of future acquisitions if a 'fair value' is taken to be the value to the business.

B – The elimination of intra-group profits

127 In preparing historical cost group accounts it is necessary to eliminate from the group profit any material profit which has arisen from the sale of stock (or fixed assets) from one group company to another to the extent that the purchasing company still holds the asset at the end of the accounting period.

128 If the effect of intra-group profits is not considered sufficiently material to make the necessary adjustments in the historical cost accounts then it is also unlikely to be sufficiently material to necessitate any adjustments in the current cost accounts.

283

129 When intra-group profits are eliminated in the HC group accounts, corresponding adjustments on a current cost basis should be made in the current cost group accounts taking the following points into consideration:

(a) the amount to be eliminated in the preparation of the group accounts should in principle be the current cost operating profit realised by the first member of the group but unrealised as regards the group as a whole. It should be noted that if replacement costs have moved since the date of the inter-company sale the change in balance sheet stock value to the new replacement cost will not equal the amount to be eliminated from the operating profit of the group;

(b) so far as practicable the total group current cost operating profit and COSA should be calculated by reference to the replacement cost to the group at the date of final sale.

Appendix (iv) gives examples which illustrate the principles involved.

C – Associated companies

130 The definition of an associated company and its accounting treatment are set out in SSAP 1.

131 The treatment of income of associated companies within the current cost profit and loss account should, where practicable, be consistent with the principles of CCA as set out in SSAP 16. The investing company's current cost profit and loss account should therefore include its share of the current cost profit less losses of the associated companies.

132 An investing company or group has an equity interest in associated companies and this investment normally forms part of the investing company's or group's net operating assets. Therefore the attributable proportion of any profit of the associated companies, after interest on their net borrowing and their individual gearing adjustments but before taxation and extraordinary items, should normally be included within the current cost operating profit of the group. The relevant proportion of any tax charges or extraordinary items of associates should be dealt with as required in SSAP 1.

133 The amount at which the investing company's or group's interest in the associated company should be shown in the group current cost balance sheet is:

(a) the applicable proportion of the associated company's net assets stated under SSAP 16 together with,

(b) any goodwill, that is the difference between the cost of acquisition and the value to the business of the net assets at the date
of acquisition less any amounts written off.

134 Where the associated company does not produce current cost
figures, the directors should make their best estimate of them. Where
the amounts involved are material to the investing company's result,
the bases and methods adopted by the directors in arriving at the
current cost figures should be disclosed.

D – Translation of foreign currencies

135 The accounts of overseas subsidiaries and associated companies
should normally be prepared on a CCA basis in the foreign currencies
concerned and then translated into sterling. Where estimated figures
are used (paragraph 122) the same procedures should be adopted.

136 In preparing their historical cost group accounts most companies
translate assets and liabilities which are recorded in foreign currencies
using either the exchange rate ruling at the balance sheet date (the
'closing rate' method) or the rates ruling at the date on which the
amount recorded in the accounts was established (the 'temporal'
method). In preparing a current cost balance sheet, foreign currency
assets and liabilities are stated at value to the business – i.e. the date
on which the amount is established in the accounts is the balance
sheet date. The 'temporal' method thus gives the same answer as the
'closing rate' method.

137 Profit and loss items may be translated at the closing rate of
exchange or the average rate.

138 In most circumstances translation differences arising on consolidation are price changes. As such they should be credited (or
debited) to reserves since they do not affect the operating capability
of the group (SSAP 16, paragraph 25).

139 SSAP 16 requires that the methods adopted should be stated
in the notes to the current cost accounts.

E – Monetary working capital and gearing adjustments

140 The appropriate method of computing these adjustments will depend on the circumstances of each individual group and the companies within that group, but it is believed that the methods set out below will be suitable in most cases.

141 The MWCA should, where practicable, be calculated on an individual company-by-company basis and then aggregated to produce the consolidated adjustment. When inter-company dèbt is included as a component of the working capital of one group company it should be correspondingly treated in the other group company and care should be taken that no material distortion arises in group terms due to the use of different indices.

142 The gearing adjustment should normally be calculated on a group basis in order to avoid anomalies which could occur where the pattern of inter-company financing does not mirror the external group financing arrangements.

F – Minority interests

143 Where there are substantial minority interests in a group the proportion of current cost adjustments (including the gearing adjustment) applicable to minorities should be calculated by reference to their holding in each individual company.

144 The gearing adjustment needs special mention. The total group gearing adjustment should firstly be calculated on a group basis before making any allowance for minorities, and with minority interests included as part of shareholders' interest. This total adjustment should then be apportioned between the minority shareholders and the shareholders of the parent company. Where minority interests are substantial, or where the gearing of the individual companies or their rate of price change is not close to the group average, the gearing adjustment relating to minorities should be calculated by reference to the accounts of the relevant subsidiaries, and the proportionate share of the minority interest. This gearing adjustment relating to minorities is then deducted from the total group adjustment leaving the adjustment relating to the shareholders of the parent company. In some cases the total group gearing adjustment may be apportioned using the simplified method illustrated overleaf.

Average amounts calculated from the current cost balance sheet:

Share capital and reserves	£70
Minority interests	5
Net borrowings	25
	£100

If the current cost operating adjustments (including those relating to minorities) in the current cost group profit and loss account amount to £200 the gearing adjustment will amount to £50 $\left(\text{i.e. } \frac{25}{100} \times 200 \right)$ of which £46.7 $\left(\text{i.e. } \frac{70}{70+5} \times 50 \right)$ is attributable to the shareholders of the parent company and £3.3 $\left(\text{i.e. } \frac{5}{70+5} \times 50 \right)$ to the minority shareholders. The latter amount will be taken into account in arriving at the profit or loss attributable to minority shareholders in the current cost profit and loss account.

Modern equivalent asset

1 In determining the gross current replacement cost of fixed assets, the objective is to make a realistic estimate of what it would now cost to acquire an asset which has the same service potential as that of the existing asset when acquired. If the design of the particular assets has not changed significantly, there is no problem, and an index or other estimate of the current cost of those same assets can be used. Even if there have been changes, either in the methods of manufacture or in the detailed design, it will commonly be found that application of an index for the industry or for the class of assets involved will give a result of acceptable accuracy.

2 However, it may happen that the technology has changed significantly, so that a modern substitute for the existing asset would be markedly different in its:

  (a) initial capital cost;
  (b) operating costs;
  (c) life; or
  (d) output.

3 The effect of (b), (c) and (d) is that the modern asset will probably have a different service potential from the existing asset. However, these differences may also have an effect on the capital cost of the modern substitute. In these situations it would be unrealistic to take the cost of the modern asset and use it without adjustment as the current cost of the existing asset. For example, the modern asset may have a higher capital cost (e.g. it may incorporate computer control) but lower operating costs per unit of output. If the higher capital cost were adopted, the operating profit would have to bear a higher depreciation charge as well as the existing higher operating costs. The true position is that the capital cost of the modern substitute includes the cost of the improvements so that like is not being compared with like.

4 There are two ways of approaching the problem, either of which should give a reasonable approximation. The simpler way is to use a broadly based or general price index, which, because of its wider base, may reflect a gradual change in technology in the industries concerned. Alternatively, if the modern asset were included in a different index from the existing asset then changes in that index could be used as being more relevant to the current technology.

5 However, in extreme cases and where major assets are involved, it may be necessary to check the results against calculations which make allowances for the difference in service potential. This is achieved by eliminating that part of the current capital cost of the modern asset which gives rise to improvement in output (by quantity or quality), operating costs or life. The aim is to ensure that there is no double counting as mentioned in paragraph 3 above. The calculation may sometimes be made by direct apportionment of the current capital cost by reference to comparative outputs or life. Quantifying the capital cost of an operating cost saving is more difficult. However, recourse to the discounting back of operating cost saving is only needed where the potential savings are likely to be substantial and there is no other way of estimating that part of the capital cost in the modern asset attributable to the difference in operating costs. A simple example relating only to output, is given below.

Original cost of each existing asset	£100,000
Price index for class of assets:	
(a) when existing asset acquired	120
(b) at the accounting date	180

Indexing original cost £100,000 $\times \dfrac{180}{120} =$ £150,000

Current cost of a modern asset	£220,000
Output of each existing asset	20,000 units p.a.
Output of a modern asset	40,000 units p.a.
Operating costs per unit and asset lives identical	
Current cost of existing service potential:	

$$£220,000 \times \frac{20,000}{40,000} = \qquad £110,000$$

6 The existing asset would be overvalued if either the indexed cost (£150,000) or the unadjusted cost of a modern asset (£220,000) were used. The current cost of replacing the service potential of each existing asset is £110,000, and this is the appropriate figure.

7 This reduction to the cost of a modern equivalent asset is effectively a reduction in the price of the service potential and does not represent a change in the volume of service potential remaining. Consequently, as for other price changes, the resulting change in the net current replacement cost is debited against current cost reserve. The amount of the debit may be small if depreciation has previously been based on estimates of asset life which have allowed for likely changes in technology.

8 It is emphasised that it is the current cost relating to the existing asset which is being estimated, and the cost of a modern equivalent asset is merely a guide to this objective. Even if the existing asset will not be replaced, it is necessary to attribute a current cost to its remaining service potential. Furthermore, it is current proven technology which should be considered, not future possible developments because the latter do not represent current costs. The current amount to be adopted should not exceed the current replacement cost of the actual existing asset.

Some methods for calculating the effect of price changes on stock

General

1 Various detailed methods are used under historical cost accounting for the valuation of stock and many will continue to be appropriate in CCA subject to the substitution of current for historical costs.

Methods

2 The following are some methods which may be appropriate in varying circumstances for calculating the current cost of sales and/or the balance sheet value.

(a) Where it is not intended to trace the movement of individual items:

  (i) the use of an index or indices obtained (see paragraph 3 below) or prepared by the business, which reflect the changes in the prices of goods and services used by the business during the period, in conjunction with the averaging method described in Appendix (iii) ; or

  (ii) the use of standard costs (updated where necessary by the appropriate allocation of price variances) applicable at the valuation date.

(b) Where it is intended to trace the movement of individual items:

  (i) the use of costs actually being incurred by the business at the valuation date for some or all of the various cost elements, i.e. purchased materials or services, labour and overheads ;

  (ii) for purchased items where no relevant materials or services have been purchased at or near the date of sale, the use of suppliers' official price lists, catalogues, etc., with appropriate deductions for trade discounts ; or

  (iii) the application of appropriate price indices to the cost of individual items of stock.

It may be necessary for some businesses to use different methods of calculating the effect of price changes for different sections of the business or for different cost elements of the stock.

The 'last in first out' (LIFO) method may be appropriate for calculating the COSA in certain limited circumstances where stock volumes do not fluctuate substantially and the replacement of stock is frequent and recent. However, in a period of increasing cost levels the use of LIFO produces a balance sheet figure for stock which becomes progressively further removed from value to the business and which must therefore be restated at its value to the business.

Indices

3 (a) A relevant price index is a price index prepared by government agencies, such as the UK Government Statistical Service, or a generally recognised privately produced index or an index compiled by the business on the basis of its own experience. The same indices should normally be applied in succeeding periods.

(b) Most government indices are based on order prices (so far as the firms supplying the quotation can provide them) rather than delivery prices in the month stated, although the latter is more appropriate for CCA (see paragraph 69). Where such indices are used for calculating the effect of price changes, it may be adequate for businesses to ignore time lags between order and delivery and to use the index number given for the month, even though it might reflect a price for delivery at some time in the future. However, when the rate of price change substantially alters it will be necessary to take account of material time lags when selecting index numbers. This might be done by using indices from the month in which stock would be ordered to obtain delivery on the valuation date.

The use of the averaging method

This appendix describes the use of the averaging method to calculate the cost of sales adjustment (COSA) and the monetary working capital adjustment (MWCA). An example of the calculation of these and of the gearing adjustment is given in Appendix (vii).

Cost of sales adjustment

1 In the absence of major distorting factors, the averaging method enables the cost of sales in the historical cost accounts to be adjusted to the current cost of sales at the date of consumption. This is achieved as follows:

— The historical cost of opening stock is converted to average current cost during the period;
— the total of purchases and other costs incurred during the period is left unaltered; and
— the historical cost of closing stock is converted to average current cost during the period.

The COSA is the difference between the historical and current cost of sales.

2 The averaging method enables the COSA to be calculated reasonably accurately where stock volumes have been constant throughout the period or have been increasing (or decreasing) at a constant rate. In these circumstances, the average current cost during the period may be calculated by using a simple average of the period's prices selected at regular intervals.

3 The averaging method may also be used where the stock volume has not been constant or changing at a constant rate. The COSA should then be calculated at the most frequent intervals practicable (e.g. monthly), since the inaccuracies which may result in these circumstances will thereby be minimised. However, any related MWCA should also be calculated at the same intervals.

4 Where stock volumes fluctuate, however, the effect thereof may be broadly offset by similar but opposite fluctuations in the related net monetary working capital. Over the whole accounting period, therefore, the combined total of stock and related monetary working capital may remain constant or may change at a constant rate. In such a situation, it may not be necessary, for the purposes of the published accounts alone, to calculate the COSA and MWCA more frequently than at the intervals at which the information is published, provided that the same method (e.g. the averaging method) and the same indices or prices are used for both calculations. Whilst both adjustments, calculated in this way may separately contain inaccuracies, these will tend to offset each other.

5 Where the average current cost of the opening and closing stocks can be determined from the accounting system, the figure so determined should be used, but where this cannot be done, the average current cost should be determined by reference to a relevant price index (see paragraph 3(a) of Appendix (ii)), provided that the historical cost of stock has been calculated using the "first in first out" method. Where the prices of identifiable elements (e.g. materials, labour and overheads) of stock have changed at materially different rates during the period the calculation should, where possible, be made separately for each element.

6 It will normally be necessary to ascertain the average age of the opening and closing stocks so that the price index numbers appropriate to those dates may be applied. However, where ageing will not give a significantly different answer, the index numbers at the balance sheet dates may be used for the COSA and no adjustment will be necessary for the balance sheet valuations.

7 Where stocks have been reduced to recoverable amount by provisions or write downs, the amount written-off will have been retained and reinvested in assets which, in turn, give rise to CC adjustments. Thus, in these circumstances, the averaging calculation should be based on the recoverable amount. In principle, the stock should be aged to ascertain the index relevant for the adjustment and the increase in carrying values, arising when input prices increase whilst the stock remains unsold, should be reviewed to ensure that the resulting balance sheet value does not exceed the current recoverable amount. In practice it may be adequate to treat such stock as if it were monetary working capital.

Monetary working capital adjustment

8 A similar method may be used for calculating the MWCA. This method is set out in the example which follows in Appendix (vii). The proviso set out in paragraph 3 above also applies to the calculation of the MWCA.

293

Illustration of elimination of intra-group profits

The example below deals with (i) the transfer within a group and (ii) the subsequent external sale of one item of stock.

(i)	Historical cost to A	£100
	Transfer price to B	£150
	Current replacement cost to A at time of transfer	£120
	Current replacement cost to A at balance sheet date	£130

In subsidiary A, current cost operating profit will be £30 and credit to current cost reserve will be £20.

On consolidation the stock in the balance sheet should be reduced from £150 to £130 (i.e. by £20), but the current cost operating profit to be eliminated is £30. The difference of £10 should be credited to current cost reserve as it represents an increase in the current replacement cost to the group whilst the stock was held by B.

(ii) In this part of the example it is assumed that the same item of stock is sold outside the group by B for £200 and at the date of sale the current replacement cost of the item of stock to A had increased to £140, but the transfer price from A to B (i.e. current replacement cost to B) was still £150.

	A	B	Sub-Total	Consolidation Adjustment	Group Total
Current cost operating profit	30	50	80	20−	60
Current cost reserve (COSA)	20	—	20	20+	40
Total Reserves	50	50	100	—	£100

The consolidation adjustment is necessary as there has been an increase in current replacement cost so far as the group is concerned (which should be credited as an additional COSA to the current cost reserve) although it has been treated as operating profit so far as B is concerned.

A format for supplementary current cost accounts

This Appendix illustrates a set of current cost accounts. The numbers are based on calculations shown in the workings in Appendix (vii) (references are to that Appendix). The format complies with SSAP 16 although certain additional interpretative data has been added.

These accounts do not contain all the information required in statutory accounts.

Z LIMITED
Current cost profit and loss account
for the year to 31 December 1979

Reference to workings in Appendix (vii)	1978 £'000		1979 £'000
xx		Turnover	64,000
		Historical cost trading profit before interest	5,200
A/B		*Less:* Current cost operating adjustments (Note 2)	3,120
		Current cost operating profit	2,080
C		Gearing adjustment	(910)
		Interest on net borrowing	1,000
			90
		Current cost profit before taxation	1,990
		Taxation	700
		Current cost profit attributable to shareholders	1,290
		Dividends	300
		Retained current cost profit of the year	990

Statement of retained profits/reserves

Retained current cost profit of the year	990
Movements on current cost reserve	1,998
	2,988
Reserves at the beginning of the year	12,540
Reserves at the end of the year	15,528
Operating profit : Return on average net operating assets	6.9%
Earnings per share	19.8p
Asset value to the business per share (year end)	340p
Dividend cover, based on CC attributable profit	4.30

The notes on pages 48 to 51 form part of these accounts.

Example of alternative presentation of current cost profit and loss account

Z LIMITED
Current cost profit and loss account
for the year to 31 December 1979

Reference to workings in Appendix (vii)	1978 £'000		1979 £'000
xx		Turnover	64,000
		Historical cost trading profit before interest	5,200
A/B		Less: Current cost operating adjustments (Note 2)	3,120
		Current cost operating profit	2,080
		Interest on net borrowing	1,000
			1,080
		Taxation	700
		Current cost profit after interest and taxation	380
C		Gearing adjustment	910
		Current cost profit attributable to shareholders	1,290
		Dividends	300
		Retained current cost profit of the year	990

Statement of retained profits/reserves

Retained current cost profit of the year	990
Movements on current cost reserve	1,998
	2,988
Reserves at the beginning of the year	12,540
Reserves at the end of the year	15,528
Operating profit : Return on average net operating assets	6.9%
Earnings per share	19.8p
Asset value to the business per share (year end)	340p
Dividend cover, based on CC attributable profit	4.30

The notes on pages 48 to 51 form part of these accounts.

Z LIMITED
Summarised current cost balance sheet
at 31 December 1979

Reference to workings in Appendix (vii)	1978 £'000	1978 £'000		1979 £'000	1979 £'000
			Assets employed:		
A.9		18,440	Fixed assets (Note 4)		18,808
			Net current assets:		
B.3	6,100		Stock	8,220	
			Monetary working capital		
B.4	4,000		(net)	4,500	
	10,100		Total working capital	12,720	
	(250)		Proposed dividends	(300)	
			Other current liabilities		
	(2,750)		(net)	(700)	
		7,100			11,720
		25,540			30,528
			Financed by:		
			Share capital and reserves:		
	6,000		Share capital	7,000	
	—		Share premium	1,000	
D			Current cost reserve		
	7,038		(Note 5)	9,036	
			Other reserves and		
	5,502		retained profit	6,492	
	12,540			15,528	
		18,540			23,528
		6,000	Convertible debentures		6,000
		1,000	Deferred tax		1,000
		25,540			30,528

The notes on pages 48 to 51 form part of these accounts.

Notes to current cost accounts*

Note 1

A. General description of current cost accounts

The current cost accounts on pages 45 to 51 have been prepared in compliance with SSAP 16. The current cost system, whilst not a system of accounting for general inflation, allows for price changes specific to the business when reporting assets employed and profits thereon.

The *current cost operating profit* is the surplus (before interest and taxation) arising from the ordinary activities of the business in the period. It is determined after allowing for the impact of price changes on the funds needed to maintain the productive assets of the business (the net operating assets) but does not take into account the way in which these assets are financed.

This result is achieved by making adjustments to trading profit before interest calculated on the historical cost basis. These adjustments are described in sections B and C below and are set out in Note 2.

The *current cost profit attributable* to shareholders is the surplus after allowing for the impact of price changes on the funds needed to maintain only their proportion of the net operating assets. It is shown after interest, taxation and the gearing adjustment described in Section D below.

In the *balance sheet* fixed assets and stocks are included at their current cost (net of depreciation on fixed assets).

Corresponding amounts for the previous period are shown in values relating to last year, without further adjustment. This is the first year for which the company has prepared current cost accounts and corresponding figures are not shown in the profit and loss account since they are not readily available.

B. Fixed assets and depreciation

The gross current cost of fixed assets has been derived as follows:
Plant and specialised buildings have been restated using appropriate Government indices applied to the historical costs.

The current cost of land has been estimated by the directors.

Asset lives have been reviewed upon the introduction of current cost accounting and the existing asset lives were found to be adequate.

Total depreciation charged in the CC profit and loss account represents the average current cost of the proportion of fixed assets consumed in the period. The depreciation adjustment of £850,000 is the difference between the depreciation charge in the HC and CC accounts.

The adjustment of £900,000 on the disposal of fixed assets represents the difference between the historical and current cost net book values of the assets in question at the date of disposal.

---

*These notes incorporate the explanations referred to in paragraph 34 of SSAP 16.

C. Working capital
This includes stocks (including work in progress) and trade debtors less trade creditors.

In order to allow for the impact of price changes on working capital, two adjustments are made to the operating costs calculated on the historical cost basis, one on stock and the other on monetary working capital. The adjustments are based on movements in price indices issued by the Government Statistical Service. These indices reflect closely the changes in input prices experienced by the company.

D. The gearing adjustment
A proportion, called the gearing proportion, of the net operating assets of the business is financed by borrowing. As the obligation to repay borrowing is fixed in monetary amount, irrespective of price changes on the proportion of assets so financed, it is unnecessary to provide for the impact of price changes on these assets when determining the current cost profit attributable to shareholders. Thus, the gearing adjustment has been applied which abates the current cost operating adjustments by the average gearing proportion in the year.

E. Other accounting policies
Except as set out above the policies used in the current cost accounts are the same as those used in the historical cost accounts.

Note 2: Current cost adjustments made in deriving operating profit

Reference to workings in Appendix (vii)			1979 £'000
B.2	Cost of sales		810
B.4	Monetary working capital		560
	Working capital		1,370
A.7	Depreciation	850	
A.11	Fixed asset disposals	900	
	Fixed assets		1,750
	Current cost operating adjustments		3,120

Note 3: **Financing of the net operating assets**

The following is the net current replacement cost of the net operating assets at the balance sheet dates, together with the method by which they were financed:

1978 £'000		1979 £'000
18,440	Fixed assets	18,808
10,100	Working capital	12,720
28,540	*Net operating assets*	31,528
18,540	Share capital and reserves	23,528
250	Proposed dividends	300
18,790	*Total shareholders' interest*	23,828
6,000	Convertible debentures	6,000
1,000	Deferred tax	1,000
2,750	Other current liabilities (net)	700
9,750	*Net borrowing*	7,700
28,540		31,528

A.9   ## Note 4: **Fixed assets**

	31 December 1979			1978
	Gross CRC*	Dep'n	Net CRC*	Net CRC*
	£'000	£'000	£'000	£'000
Land	4,610	—	4,610	3,310
Plant and machinery	26,910	12,712	14,198	15,130
TOTAL	31,520	12,712	18,808	18,440

---

*Current replacement cost.

D   *Note 5:* **Current cost reserve**

		£'000	£'000	£'000
	Balance at 1 January 1979			7,038
	Revaluation surpluses reflecting price changes :			
A.8/9/10	Land	300		
A.8/9/10	Plant and machinery	1,118		
B.3	Stocks and work in progress	930		
			2,348	
B.4	Monetary working capital adjustment		560	
C	Gearing adjustment		(910)	
				1,998
	Balance at 31 December 1979			9,036
	of which : realised			2,210
	unrealised			6,826
				9,036

The realised element represents the net cumulative total of the current cost adjustments which have been passed through the profit and loss account. Thus, it represents the difference between historical and current cost profits since current cost accounts were first prepared, in this case since 1 January 1979.

Additional voluntary disclosures

I – Statement of source and application of funds
II – Statement of change in shareholders' equity interest

I   In current cost accounts the flows of funds imposed on the business by changes in its input prices are isolated leaving the remainder as the result of other factors. Changes in the volume at constant prices of the total net operating assets and of their constituent elements can thus be shown.

A number of possible formats exist for a statement of source and application of funds. Two suggestions follow, both starting with the current cost operating profit. Either format would comply with SSAP 10, *Statements of source and application of funds,* and may be used even if the current cost accounts are not regarded as the main accounts.

The second format closely follows example 1 in SSAP 10. The first illustrates a different approach.

Neither format shows the gearing adjustment on the face of the statement although it is possible to modify either statement to include it.

II   CCA does not deal with the maintenance of financial capital in general purchasing power terms. Some users may be interested in a statement of the change in shareholders' equity interest after allowing for the change in the general purchasing power of money. Such a statement may be particularly helpful in situations where there are excess monetary assets or where part of the group has activities exempt under SSAP 16 (paragraph 46(c)). A possible format is given on page 56.

Statement of source and application of funds
for the year to 31 December 1979
(based on current cost accounts)

Reference to workings in Appendix (vii)	1978 £'000		1979 £'000
	xx	Generated from operations	
		Current cost operating profit	2,080
		Less profit and loss items associated with the movement of funds :	
		Interest	(1,000)
		Current taxation : paid	(750)
		change in provision	50
		charge for year	(700)
		Dividend : paid	(250)
		change in provision	(50)
		proposed for year	(300)
			(2,000)
		Retained earnings of the period, excluding gearing credit	**80**
		Application of funds	
		Fixed assets :	
A.3		Purchases	(2,700)
A.11		Proceeds on disposals	2,000
A.11		Current cost profit on disposal	(100)
			1,900
A.7		Depreciation (CC)	1,850
		'Volume' decrease	1,050
		Working capital :	
		Increase in stock	(2,120)
		Increase in MWC	(500)
			(2,620)
		Current cost working capital adjustments	1,370
B.3		Change in revaluation surplus on stock	120
			1,490
		'Volume' increase	(1,130)
		Increase in net operating assets during the period	**(80)**
		*Change in net operating assets at constant prices, giving rise to external funding requirements**	Nil
		Proceeds from issue of new shares	2,000
		Decrease in net short term liabilities	(1,700)
		Decrease in HP creditors	(300)
		Decrease in provision for taxation	(50)
		Increase in provision for dividend	50
			Nil

*A measure of the extent to which the business was self sustaining in the period. It is a coincidence that the value is Nil.

Statement of source and application of funds
for the year to 31 December 1979
(based on current cost accounts)

Reference to workings in Appendix	1978 £'000			1979 £'000
(vii)	xx	*Generated from operations* Current cost operating profit		2,080
		Less profit and loss items associated with the movement of funds :		
		Interest	(1,000)	
		Current taxation : paid	(750)	
		change in provision	50	
		charge for year	(700)	
		Dividend : paid	(250)	
		change in provision	(50)	
		proposed for year	(300)	
			————	(2,000)
		Retained earnings of the period, excluding gearing credit		80
		Application of funds		————
		Fixed assets :		
A.3		Purchases	(2,700)	
A.11		Proceeds on disposals	2,000	
A.11		Current cost profit on disposal	(100)	
			1,900	
A.7		Depreciation (CC)	1,850	
			————	
		'Volume' decrease		1,050
		Working capital :		
		Increase in stock	(2,120)	
		Increase in MWC	(500)	
			(2,620)	
		Current cost working capital adjustments	1,370	
B.3		Change in revaluation surplus on stock	120	
			1,490	
		'Volume' increase	————	(1,130)
		Increase in net operating assets during the period		(80)
				————
		Change in net operating assets at constant prices, giving rise to external funding requirements *		Nil
				════
		Proceeds from issue of new shares		2,000
		Decrease in net short term liabilities		(1,700)
		Decrease in HP creditors		(300)
		Decrease in provision for taxation		(50)
		Increase in provision for dividend		50
				————
				Nil
				════

*A measure of the extent to which the business was self sustaining in the period. It is a coincidence that the value is Nil.

		1978 £'000			1979 £'000
(1)		*Movements in fixed assets*			
		Purchases			(2,700)
		Proceeds on disposal	2,000		
		CC profit on disposal	(100)		
			———		1,900
		Depreciation			1,850
		'Volume' decrease (Note 2)			1,050
(2)		*Volume change in net operating assets during* *the period at constant prices*			
		Retained earnings in the period	990		
		Exclude gearing credit	910		
			———		80
		Invested as follows:			
		in fixed assets (decrease)	1,050		
		in working capital (increase)	(1,130)		
			———		(80)

Statement of change in shareholders' equity interest after allowing for change in the general purchasing power of money for the year ended 31 December 1979

	£'000
Equity interest at the beginning of the year as shown in the current cost accounts	18,540
Share capital issued during the year (30 June)	2,000
	20,540
Amount required to compensate for the change in the general purchasing power of money during the year (see Note)	1,626
	22,166
Equity interest before dividends at the end of the year as shown in the current cost accounts	23,828
Excess	1,662

This indicates that reserves before dividends (£300,000) as measured by the current cost accounts have increased during the year by £1,662,000 more than that required to compensate the funds invested by the shareholders for the fall in the UK in the general purchasing power of money during the year.

The excess can be analysed as follows:

	£'000
Current cost profit attributable to shareholders	1,290
Effect on equity interest of price changes experienced by the company being greater than the general rate of UK inflation	372
	1,662

Note
The price index used to calculate the £1,626,000 in the above calculation is the general index of changes in retail price, as follows:

31 December 1978	188.4
30 June 1979	197.2
31 December 1979	204.2
Percentage change in the year —	8.39%

(The use of the retail price index is preferred but other general indices could be used. The index used should be disclosed.)

The workings leading to the current cost accounts presented in appendices (v) and (vi)

The example builds up the figures for the annual financial statements which are shown in Appendices (v) and (vi). This Appendix sets out the historical cost accounts which are subject to adjustment and the workings in the following sections:

Section A – Fixed assets and depreciation
B – Stock and monetary working capital
C – The gearing adjustment
D – The current cost reserve

The basic data from which the current cost accounts are prepared is the following set of historical cost accounts, together with the additional information shown on pages 59 to 69.

Z LIMITED
Historical cost profit and loss account
for the year ended 31 December 1979

1978 £'000		1979 £'000
xx	Turnover	64,000
	Trading profit (including HC profit on fixed asset disposal − £1,000,000)	5,200
	Less net interest payable	1,000
		4,200
	Corporation tax	700
	Profit attributable to shareholders	3,500
	Proposed dividends	300
	Retained profit of the year	3,200

Statement of retained profits/revenue reserves

Retained profit of the year	3,200
Revenue reserves at the beginning of the year	5,502
Revenue reserves at the end of the year	8,702

Z LIMITED
Historical cost balance sheet at 31 December 1979

	1978			1979	
£'000	£'000			£'000	£'000
	11,502	Fixed assets			12,202
		Current assets:			
2,000		Cash		3,000	
6,000		Stock		8,000	
9,000		Trade debtors		10,500	
17,000				21,500	
		Current liabilities:			
5,000		Trade creditors		6,000	
1,000		HP creditors		700	
3,000		Overdraft		2,300	
750		Taxation		700	
250		Proposed dividend		300	
10,000				10,000	
	7,000	Net current assets			11,500
	18,502				23,702
	6,000	Share capital			7,000
		Reserves:			
	—	Share premium			1,000
	5,502	Revenue			8,702
	11,502	Shareholders' capital and reserves			16,702
	6,000	Convertible debentures			6,000
	1,000	Deferred tax			1,000
	18,502				23,702

Supporting data, calculations and workings for the production of current cost accounts

Section A – Fixed assets and depreciation

HISTORICAL COST

Plant and machinery

(1) Plant and machinery has in the past been depreciated on a straight line basis over 14 years. Upon the introduction of CCA it is necessary to review the asset lives used for depreciation purposes. As a result of this review it was decided that a life of 14 years was appropriate and thus should be adopted for CCA purposes. On 1 January 1979, the plant and machinery in the historical cost records included the following:

Year of purchase	Historical cost £'000	Accumulated depreciation £'000
1966	600	557
67	400	343
68	400	314
69	800	571
70	—	—
71	—	—
72	800	400
73	2,100	900
74	700	250
75	1,000	285
76	400	86
77	4,100	585
78	2,900	207
Total assets being depreciated	14,200	4,498

	£'000
(2) The HC depreciation charge for the year is based on cost as follows:	
Gross HC of assets at 1 January 1979, still being depreciated	14,200
Disposals*	(1,600)
Additions	1,700
	14,300
The year's charge is (one-fourteenth) (say)	1,000

---

*Proper records of disposals have been kept and thus all assets with a cost attributable to them exist and are still in use. In practice it is necessary to relate disposals and accumulated depreciation to the year of acquisition; these would then be included in the table in Note 1. This detail is not shown throughout this example in order to reduce the size of the tables and detail shown. For the purposes of this example the gross current cost (GCC) of these disposals at 1 January 1979 is £3,000,000 with related accumulated depreciation of £1,100,000.

(3) Summary of HC movements in fixed assets:

	Freehold land	Plant and machinery			Total
	Historical cost	Historical cost	Depre- ciation	Net	
	£'000	£'000	£'000	£'000	£'000
At 1 January 1979	1,800	14,200	(4,498)	9,702	11,502
Disposals	—	(1,600)	600	(1,000)	(1,000)
Additions	1,000	1,700	—	1,700	2,700
Depreciation	—	—	(1,000)	(1,000)	(1,000)
At 31 December 1979	2,800	14,300	(4,898)	9,402	12,202

CURRENT COST
Plant and machinery
(4) On 1 January 1979, the current cost and accumulated depreciation of the plant and machinery comprised:

Year of purchase	PINCCA index ref xx (Mid Year)	Gross current cost at 1 January, 1979 £'000	Accumulated depreciation £'000
1966	41.7	2,050*	1,900
67	43.3	1,310	1,120
68	43.6	1,310	1,030
69	45.5	2,500	1,780
70	46.8	—	—
71	51.5	—	—
72	57.4	1,990	990
73	61.4	4,870	2,090
74	65.5	1,520	540
75	77.4	1,840	530
76	100.0	570	120
77	113.8	5,130	730
78	133.7	3,090	220
		26,180	11,050

(5) Index at 31 December 1978 — 142.5
Index at 30 June 1979   — 149.2
Index at 31 December 1979 — 154.6

Example of calculation of GCC at 1 January 1979 of asset bought in 1966:
$$600 \text{ (HC)} \times \frac{142.5}{41.7} = 2,050$$

---

*See note (5)

311

(6) For simplicity, it is assumed that all plant and machinery is covered by one index and has one life measurement for depreciation purposes. In practice, a number of indices and lives may be applicable in which case tables such as those in Notes (A.1) and (A.4) would be necessary for each combination of index/life. If the information to arrange costs in this way is not available then the indexation route to the ascertainment of current cost may not be available.

(7) The depreciation charge for the year is based on average current cost, as follows:

	£'000
All assets at gross current cost on 1 January 1979 (A.4)	26,180
Less disposals at gross current cost on 1 January 1979 (A.2 footnote)	3,000
	23,180

Adjusted to the average current cost for the year

$$\left(£23,180,000 \times \frac{149.2}{142.5} \right) \qquad 24,270$$

Additions during the year (which are assumed to be at average cost) – (A.3)   1,700

           25,970

The year's current cost depreciation charge of one fourteenth of £25,970,000 is £1,855,000 (say)   1,850
Less depreciation already charged in the HC accounts (A.2)   1,000

Depreciation adjustment   850

Current cost reserve

(8) The transfer to current cost reserve, in respect of price changes during the year on fixed assets, is arrived at as follows:

	Current cost	Accumulated depreciation
	£'000	£'000
Plant and machinery		
At 1 January 1979 (A.4)	26,180	11,050
Disposals (A.2)	(3,000)	(1,100)
Call this sum – A	23,180	9,950
Effect of price change thereon during year based on $\left(\dfrac{154.6-142.5}{142.5}\right) \times A$	1,968	845
Additions and depreciation charge in year – call this B ·	1,700	1,850
Effect of price change from mid to end of year $\left(\dfrac{154.6-149.2}{149.2}\right) \times B$	62	67
Transfer to CCR – gross and 'backlog' (net £1,118,000)	2,030	912
Total at 31 December 1979	26,910	12,712
Freehold land		
The directors' revaluation gave an uplift of:	300	—

(9) Summary of CC movements in fixed assets:

	Freehold land	Plant and machinery			Total
	Current cost	Current cost	Depreciation	Net	
	£'000	£'000	£'000	£'000	£'000
At 1 January 1979	3,310	26,180	(11,050)	15,130	18,440
Disposals (A.2)	—	(3,000)	1,100	(1,900)	(1,900)
Additions	1,000	1,700	—	1,700	2,700
Depreciation	—	—	(1,850)	(1,850)	(1,850)
Transfer to CCR (A.8/Section D)	300	2,030	(912)	1,118	1,418
At 31 December 1979	4,610	26,910	(12,712)	14,198	18,808

(10) Reconciliation of unrealised revaluation surpluses (URS) on fixed assets :

	HC	CC	URS	
Freehold land	£'000	£'000	£'000	
1 January 1979	1,800	3,310		1,510
Additions	1,000	1,000		—
Uplift	—	300	300	300
31 December 1979	2,800	4,610		1,810
Plant and machinery				
1 January 1979 (NBV)	9,702	15,130		5,428
Disposals (NBV) (A.11)	(1,000)	(1,900)	(900)	
Additions	1,700	1,700		—
Uplift (A.9) : gross	—	2,030		
backlog depreciation	—	(912) 1,118	1,118	
Depreciation charge	(1,000)	(1,850)	(850)	(632)
31 December 1979 (NBV)	9,402	14,198		4,796

(Note – there are no unrealised revaluation surpluses in the HC accounts.)

Fixed asset disposals

(11) Proceeds on disposal of fixed assets were £2,000,000. This gives rise to the following calculations of surplus on disposal :

	HC	CC	Difference
	£'000	£'000	£'000
Proceeds	2,000	2,000	—
NBV of asset disposals – HC (A.3)	1,000		
– CC (A.9)		1,900	900
Surplus on disposal – P &L	1,000	100	
Current cost operating adjustment on FA disposal – dr, P & L ;			
cr, asset account			900

314

SECTION B – Stock and monetary working capital

(1) It is assumed in the example that the change in stock levels occurred fairly evenly during the period and that the historical cost of the stock has been calculated on a 'first in first out' basis.

Appropriate index numbers for the COSA and MWCA are selected from the following table:

1978	October	173.3	
	November	175.4	(a)
	December	177.4	(b) (c)
1979	January	179.6	
	February	181.0	
	March	183.3	
	April	185.8	
	May	187.7	
	June	189.9	
	July	191.9	
	August	193.6	
	September	195.6	
	October	197.9	(d)
	November	200.1	
	December	202.4	(e) (f)
1980	January	204.4	

Note: Each index is applicable at the middle of the month concerned. The index series published by the Government Statistical Service in the booklet 'Price Index Numbers for Current Cost Accounting' (PINCCA) can be taken to be appropriate to the middle of the months concerned. Index reference XX has been used.

Index numbers used in this example

(a)	Mid November 1978	–		–	175.4
(b)	30 November 1978	–	(average of Nov/Dec)	–	176.4
(c)	31 December 1978	–	(average of Dec/Jan)	–	178.5
(d)	Mid October 1979	–		–	197.9
(e)	30 November 1979	–	(average of Nov/Dec)	–	201.3
(f)	31 December 1979	–	(average of Dec/Jan)	–	203.4
(g)	Simple monthly average based on twelve months to 31 December 1979			–	190.7

(2) *Calculation 1 – The cost of sales adjustment (COSA)*
In this example the opening stock represents three months' purchases and the closing stock represents five months' purchases.

COSA
Using the averaging method, the COSA is calculated as follows:
(i) Ascertain relevant index numbers:
    (a) Opening stock (mid November 1978)   –   175.4
    (d) Closing stock (mid October 1979)   –   197.9
    (g) Average for year to 31 December 1979   –   190.7
(ii) From the historical cost of the closing stock deduct the historical cost of the opening stock:
$$£8,000,000 - £6,000,000 = £2,000,000$$
(iii) Isolate the effect of the volume change: from the average current cost of the closing stock deduct the average current cost of the opening stock:

$$\left(\frac{\text{HC closing stock}}{\text{Closing index number}} \times \text{Average index number} \right)$$

$$\text{minus} \left(\frac{\text{HC opening stock}}{\text{Opening index number}} \times \text{Average index number} \right)$$

$$= \left(\frac{£8,000,000}{197.9} \times 190.7 \right) - \left(\frac{£6,000,000}{175.4} \times 190.7 \right) \qquad = £1,185,570$$

(iv) From the result in (ii) (the total increase) deduct the result in (iii) (the 'volume' increase) to give the COSA (the 'price' increase):

$$£2,000,000 - £1,185,570 = £814,430 \qquad \text{(say)} \qquad \mathbf{£810,000}$$

The above method is represented by the following formula:

$$\text{COSA} = (C - O) - Ia \left(\frac{C}{Ic} - \frac{O}{Io} \right)$$

Where   O =   Historical cost of opening stock
             C =   Historical cost of closing stock
             Ia =   Average index number for the period
             Io =   Index number appropriate to opening stock
             Ic =   Index number appropriate to closing stock

(3) *Balance sheet value of stock at current cost*

Stock should be stated in the balance sheet at value to the business. In order to ascertain its current cost, a separate calculation from the COSA must be made.

(i) Ascertain relevant index numbers:

    (c) At 31 December 1978   178.5

    (f) At 31 December 1979   203.4

(ii) Calculate current cost:

£'000

Opening stock (as at 31 Dec 1978) $6{,}000 \times \dfrac{178.5}{175.4} = 6{,}100$

unrealised revaluation surplus $(6{,}100-6{,}000)$ 100

Closing stock (as at 31 Dec 1979) $8{,}000 \times \dfrac{203.4}{197.9} = 8{,}220$

unrealised revaluation surplus $(8{,}220-8{,}000)$ 220

increase in unrealised revaluation surpluses   +120

The increase in unrealised revaluation surpluses (£120,000) is reflected in the current cost reserve, together with the COSA (£810,000).

(4) *Calculation 2 – The monetary working capital adjustment (MWCA)*

As the COSA is calculated using the averaging method, the MWCA should be calculated on a similar basis. The MWCA represents that part of the change in the amount of the MWC resulting from changes in price and excludes changes arising from volume.

In this example it is assumed MWC consists only of trade debtors and trade creditors. At both dates debtors exceed creditors. It is also assumed that the average age of the opening and closing MWC is one month.

£'000

The opening MWC is $(9{,}000-5{,}000)$ 4,000

The closing MWC is $(10{,}500-6{,}000)$ 4,500

The same index table is used as for the COSA and the index numbers for the opening and closing MWC reflect the average age of debtors and creditors*.

---

*Although it is, in principle, appropriate and consistent with the COSA calculation to base the index numbers on the average of the transaction dates which give rise to the debtors and creditors respectively, in practice, using end year dates for both COSA and MWCA may give a sufficiently accurate approximation if the rates of price change are not volatile. In this example, the profit element has, for the sake of simplicity, not been eliminated from debtors (paragraph 96).

The MWCA is calculated as follows:
(i) Ascertain relevant index numbers:
   (b) Opening MWC (30 November 1978)   —   176.4
   (e) Closing MWC (30 November 1979)   —   201.3
   (g) Average for year to 31 December 1979   —   190.7
(ii) From the balance sheet value of the closing MWC deduct the balance sheet value of the opening MWC:

$$£4,500,000 - £4,000,000 = £500,000$$

(iii) Isolate the effect of the volume change: From the value of the closing MWC deduct the value of the opening MWC (adjusting both values to the average price for the period):

$$\left(\frac{\text{Balance sheet value of closing MWC}}{\text{Closing index number}} \times \text{Average index number} \right)$$

$$\text{minus} \left(\frac{\text{Balance sheet value of opening MWC}}{\text{Opening index number}} \times \text{Average index number} \right)$$

$$= \left(\frac{£4,500,000}{201.3} \times 190.7 \right) - \left(\frac{£4,000,000}{176.4} \times 190.7 \right) = -£61,220$$

(iv) From the result in (ii) (the total increase) deduct the result in (iii) (the 'volume' increase) to give the MWCA (the 'price' increase):

$$£500,000 - (-£61,220) = £561,220 \quad \text{(say)} \quad \mathbf{£560,000}$$

In this case debtors exceed creditors and thus the adjustment is a charge against profits. Where creditors exceed debtors and prices are rising the adjustment will be a credit to profit (although note paragraph 98).

(v) The above method (which is identical to that used for the COSA) is represented by the following formula:

$$MWCA = (C - O) - Ia \left(\frac{C}{Ic} - \frac{O}{Io} \right)$$

Where   O =   Opening MWC
           C =   Closing MWC
          Ia =   Average index number for the period
          Io =   Index number appropriate to opening MWC
          Ic =   Index number appropriate to closing MWC

Section C – The gearing adjustment

	Opening £'000	Closing £'000
The net borrowing is as follows :		
Convertible debentures and deferred taxation	7,000	7,000
HP creditors	1,000	700
Bank overdraft	3,000	2,300
Taxation	750	700
Cash	(2,000)	(3,000)
Total net borrowings – the average of which equals L	9,750*	7,700*
Share capital plus reserves from the current cost balance sheet**	18,540	23,528
Proposed dividends	250	300
Total shareholders' interest – the average of which equals S	18,790*	23,828*
Total – the average of which equals L+S	28,540*	31,528*

The average gearing proportion is derived from the formula in paragraph 114 of the Guidance Notes.

$$\frac{L}{L+S} \text{ equals } \frac{9,750+7,700}{28,540+31,528} = 29.1\%$$

The gearing adjustment is calculated by applying this percentage to the full adjustments made to allow for the impact of price changes as the net operating assets are used or sold.

Current cost adjustments :

		£'000
Depreciation	(A.7)	850
Fixed asset disposal	(A.11)	900
COSA	(B.2)	810
MWCA	(B.4)	560
	3,120 × 29.1% = 907,920 (say)	£910,000

---

*These totals are shown in Note 3 to the Accounts in Appendix (v).
**Although the balance sheet in Appendix (v), from which these numbers are taken, is fully analysed, the split between the current cost and revenue reserves will not be available at the stage when the gearing adjustment is being calculated. Additional shares were issued at a premium halfway through the year. If this additional finance had been raised earlier or later in the year a weighted average of the shareholders' interest would be used in the calculation of the gearing adjustment.

Section D – The current cost reserve

Reference to workings		1 Jan 1979	Revaluation adjustments during year	Profit and loss account[1]	31 Dec 1979
	UNREALISED revaluation surpluses arising on :	£'000	£'000	£'000	£'000
A8/A10	Land	[2]1,510	300		[2]1,810
A8/A10	Plant and machinery :		[3]2,030 [4](912)	[5](850) [6](900)	
	Balance	[2]5,428	1,118	(1,750)	[2]4,796
B3	Stocks	100	[8]930	[7](810)	220
	Consolidation of assets and liabilities denominated in foreign currencies	Nil	—	—	Nil
*	Total unrealised	7,038	2,348	(2,560)	6,826
P & L	REALISED in respect of adjustments on :				
	Fixed assets			1,750	1,750
	Cost of sales			810	810
	MWC			560	560
	Gearing			(910)	(910)
*	Total realised	Nil	—	2,210	[9]2,210
*	TOTAL	7,038	2,348	(350)	9,036

Note of explanation on CCR

[1] The unrealised revaluation surpluses on fixed assets and stock become realised by virtue of equivalent entries being passed through the profit and loss account in the form of current cost adjustments. At this time there is a transfer from the UNREALISED to the REALISED section of the CCR.

[2] These figures represent the difference between the historical cost and the value to the business of the assets concerned as shown in A.10 in the workings on fixed assets (page 63).

[3] Gross revaluation surplus ; less

[4] Backlog depreciation.

[5] Depreciation adjustment.

[6] Adjustment on disposal of fixed assets.

[7] COSA.

[8] In this example this is the derived figure, calculated from the other three. It is the net change in unrealised revaluation surpluses on stocks plus the COSA.

[9] This is the cumulative total of the CC P & L adjustments since current cost accounts were first prepared. It thus represents the cumulative difference between the HC and CC profits and thereby enables the reconstruction of cumulative HC revenue reserves, which may be of interest for legal purposes.

---

*See note 5 to current cost accounts (Appendix (v)).

Index to Statements of Standard Accounting Practice Nos. 1-6, 8-10 and 12-16

Indexing is by Statement and Statement number (Bold Type) and by paragraph number (italic type). Where Appendices have no paragraph numbers, references are to Appendix number, if any, or to example number.

ef = explanatory foreword
ex = example
n = footnote
p = preamble